Finding Froebel

Also available from Bloomsbury

Finding Froebel

The Man Who Invented Kindergarten

Helge Wasmuth, Ulf Sauerbrey, and Michael Winkler

BLOOMSBURY ACADEMIC

LONDON • NEW YORK • OXFORD • NEW DELHI • SYDNEY

BLOOMSBURY ACADEMIC
Bloomsbury Publishing Plc
50 Bedford Square, London, WC1B 3DP, UK
1385 Broadway, New York, NY 10018, USA
29 Earlsfort Terrace, Dublin 2, Ireland

BLOOMSBURY, BLOOMSBURY ACADEMIC and the Diana logo are trademarks of
Bloomsbury Publishing Plc

First published in Great Britain 2024

Cover design by Grace Ridge
Cover image © Bildarchiv Friedrich-Fröbel-Museum Bad Blankenburg (Picture Library
Friedrich-Fröbel-Museum Bad Blankenburg)

A catalogue record for this book is available from the British Library.

A catalog record for this book is available from the Library of Congress.

ISBN: HB: 978-1-3502-6924-8
PB: 978-1-3502-6923-1
ePDF: 978-1-3502-6925-5
eBook: 978-1-3502-6926-2

Typeset by Newgen KnowledgeWorks Pvt. Ltd., Chennai, India
Printed and bound in Great Britain

To find out more about our authors and books visit www.bloomsbury.com
and sign up for our newsletters.

Contents

Figures

Acknowledgements

Finding Froebel isn't the book we initially wanted to write. When we first discussed the idea of writing a book on Froebel together, we envisioned one on Froebel's educational theory and pedagogy of kindergarten and play, similar to our previous research. However, we soon realized that a different book was missing: a new biography that focuses on Froebel as a person; the peculiar character who established close ties with family members and associates but at the same time alienated them, both within the Keilhau community and the kindergarten movement. Thus, who was Froebel as a person? *Finding Froebel* is our attempt to approach this question.

This book wouldn't have been possible without the support of many friends and colleagues.

Our research depended on many libraries and archives, which were helpful in many ways. We are especially grateful to the *Bibliothek für Bildungsgeschichtliche Forschung* (BBF) in Berlin, which maintains the extensive letter edition Friedrich Fröbel. Whenever we had a question, they replied as quickly as possible. We would also like to thank the Friedrich-Fröbel-Museum in Bad Blankeburg for always supporting us and providing many of the images in this book. Thanks to Susan Breitung for translating an earlier draft of a biography of Froebel by Ulf and Michael, some sections of which made their way into this book. And very special thanks to Sacha Powell from the Froebel Trust and Tina Bruce for reading early versions of the manuscript and providing us with helpful feedback.

Denise Dewey-Muno of Dewey-Muno Language Solutions was immensely helpful in editing the manuscript. Her careful reading, corrections, and insightful suggestions have greatly improved the book. Thanks so much again for all your work.

Thanks are further due to our team at Bloomsbury, especially Mark Richardson and Elissa Burns, who supported our book idea from the beginning and guided us patiently through the process.

Helge would like to thank Elena Nitecki and Mi-Hyun Chung, who read earlier versions of the manuscript and gave helpful feedback. Thanks to all my friends who hosted me when being Germany, and very special thanks to my parents, who always supported me. And, of course, and most importantly, thanks to Caro and Oskar, who made this book possible in so many ways.

Ulf and Michael would like to thank Helge. Without him, the project would never have come to that glorious end: Thank you for all your efforts!

Introduction

Adolph Diesterweg, one of the most respected pedagogues of his time, was in the midst of a passionate speech to the attendants at the teachers' assembly in Gotha[1] on 3 June 1852 when suddenly the door of the assembly hall opened. The latecomer was a peculiar older man with long, parted hair. He looked fragile and sickly and needed the help of a much younger woman to walk to the front. The look in his eyes was penetrating, though. When those present realized who was standing before them, they rose to pay their respects. When Diesterweg's speech ended, the assembly's chairman Theodor Hoffmann welcomed Friedrich Froebel, and the assembly greeted him with three cheers.

The story of how Froebel finally received the recognition he had always craved for is well known because it fits nicely into the narrative of Froebel's life: a pedagogical genius who came up with a brilliant idea that would change the world of early childhood education forever but was misunderstood and mostly ignored during his lifetime. While this story has been told often, others are less known, and some have been ignored entirely because they don't fit into the grand narrative of Froebel the educational mastermind and inventor of kindergarten. While early biographies understandably tend to glorify the person of interest (and Froebel is no exception here), this approach comes as something of a surprise more than 150 years after his death. One would expect Froebel, the 'father of kindergarten' – whom Peter Weston has described as 'probably the most influential educationalist of the nineteenth century'[2] and Fritz März called 'the most significant pedagogue of German tongue after Pestalozzi'[3] – to be a well-known and well-researched figure. This is only partially true, though. There is quite a bit we don't know about Froebel. As Jürgen Oelkers (1988) pointed out almost twenty-five years ago, Froebel still is an unknown character hidden behind the cult that surrounds him. To this day, Froebel remains nothing more than a 'roughly drawn figure,'[4] at least if one expects credible, well-documented, and critically reviewed data. Myths and glorifications prevail and dominate the story about Froebel. While contemporary German studies[5] have expanded the knowledge about Froebel's life, and Froebel's letters can now be accessed easily – a fact that the most prominent Froebel researcher, Helmut Heiland, already called incredibly enriching for any biographical research on Froebel back in 2008 – a modern, critical, and well-researched biography is still missing. This is even truer for the English-speaking world in which Froebel is even more of an unknown figure.

With this biography, we aim to close this gap. While the story we tell is, of course, also based on previous biographies and research (meaning that none of what we write is entirely new[6]), we are especially interested in Froebel's personal life and relationships, in his way of looking at things as deduced from his personal letters and diary entries. These sources are highly interesting as most, not to say almost all of them, have never been translated or analysed in any depth in German research. They paint a more realistic picture of Froebel as a person and allow us to present him as a human being, not just as a mythical pedagogical genius.

And it is exactly herein that our interest lies and what this biography will mainly be about. Thus, we will discuss Froebel's ideas that have shaped modern thinking about young children and their institutionalized education only briefly[7] and instead strive to present Froebel's life somewhat differently to past biographies that have at times been in danger of glorifying Froebel. All too often, what Froebel has chosen to share about himself in his writings has uncritically been taken at face value, prompting certain stories and myths to be told time and time again and shaping how we think about Froebel to this day.

This is to a certain degree inevitable. For retelling Froebel's life is a challenge. First and foremost because he simply wasn't famous during his lifetime. In the end, he was a 'dime-a-dozen', and not many cared about his life.[8] Only very few people took contemporaneous notes or wrote accounts of meetings. Especially about his early years, little is known apart from what he was willing to divulge in his letters. And while these are essential sources, they were also his attempt to shape the story of his life. They always served a (second) purpose: to convince the audience and justify his misdoings. Froebel might have claimed to be honest and open, but certain aspects of his life have been omitted, mentioned only vaguely, or remain obscure. He was never entirely truthful in telling the story of his life. Thus, it isn't easy to gain a realistic picture of who Froebel was as a person.

Who *was* Froebel, though? Froebel has certainly fascinated many. 'Froebel's pure love for the children, his tireless sacrifice, his great frugality and unpretentiousness,'[9] wrote Ida Seele, the first kindergartner, were traits he lived by. Many agreed with Seele because one of Froebel's talents was to convince people that they were taking part in something unusual and better. But at the same time, he could be harsh, unyielding, unforgiving, and quick-tempered. He was self-absorbed, with narcissistic traits and a tendency to hubris. More than a few called him a fraud.

But, really, who *was* Froebel? Was he a pedagogical genius or a hoax, as many have claimed? A born educator or a 'pedagogical wreckage'?[10] Was he a loving and caring or a ruthless and obstinate leader of the Keilhau community? Did he value family, the united living family, above all else, or were his feelings for his nieces inappropriate? Did he support the female kindergartners in finding a place in the professional world, or did he merely use them as pawns to spread the kindergarten movement?

The answers to these questions aren't black and white, though. Indeed, one might say that all of these statements hold true and only actually give a comprehensive picture of who Froebel really was when considered together. Writing about someone born more than 150 years ago whose life hasn't been documented in detail certainly offers the temptation to speculate. While we can't but do this too, we do try to let Froebel speak for himself through his letters and diaries as much as possible. To keep Froebel's specific idiom alive, our translations[11] are as close as possible to the German original, even if it means to present him in his idiosyncratic, flowery, and often difficult-to-understand language. It simply is how Froebel wrote. Thus, our biography is neither a hagiography nor a condemnation of Froebel, but rather an attempt to create a realistic and vivid portrait of Froebel that acknowledges his achievements but doesn't conceal his complex character traits and improprieties.

Only when we believe it necessary (and especially when sources are ambiguous) do we add explanatory remarks. We moreover strive to exercise caution in our interpretations of events and present Froebel in his own words to help substantiate our idea of who we believe he might have been. We hope in this way to grant those still interested in Froebel's pedagogical ideas new insights.

As these introductory remarks imply, this book is not intended for a specific audience, but rather for a general readership. Hence we refrain from an overly detailed academic reference apparatus. Regarding well-known facts, we inexplicitly refer to standard biographies as well as to informative literature regarding specific periods of his life. However, controversial or mostly unknown claims are backed up with detailed references. Specific references are also given for all quotes and statements from primary sources, such as Froebel's letters or diary entries. We hope this approach enables and encourages readers to engage in independent study should they be interested in a specific period in Froebel's life.

Ultimately, though, it's all only another story. One that we believe is more grounded in what came to pass in Froebel's life, though.

It's our story of Froebel – the man who invented kindergarten.

Part 1

The Young Froebel

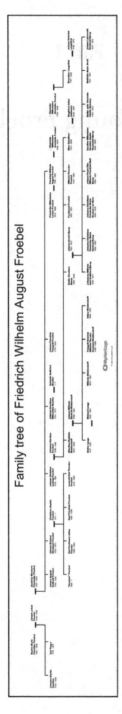

Figure 1.1 Family tree.

1

An Unfortunate Childhood

The world Friedrich Wilhelm August Froebel entered on 21 April 1782 was in upheaval. Indeed, the European world and its political, societal, economic, and cultural order were in flux. The French Revolution, the most dramatic event of the time, occurred when Froebel was seven years old. And while the revolution and its associated ideas of liberty and equality didn't impact Froebel's life the way it did many of his slightly older contemporaries, the wide-ranging changes that happened during Froebel's childhood and adolescence were by all means noticeable. New currents such as Liberalism, Conservatism, Nationalism, and Romanticism surfaced, and the relationship between secular life and religion changed; religious traditions were shaken up. However, Christianity continued to be a dominant force for many, including Froebel. Not the experience of a faraway revolution, but growing up in the pastoral milieu of a rigid Protestant pastor shaped how he thought about the world.

Friedrich Froebel was the sixth and youngest child of Johann Jakob Froebel and Jacobine Eleonore Friederike Froebel (née Hoffmann). His eldest siblings, Christoph and August, were considerably older, born in 1768 and 1766, respectively. Traugott, the closest to him in age, was four years older.

Friedrich was born in Oberweißbach, a small village named after a body of water in the principality of Schwarzburg-Rudolstadt that was first mentioned in documentary records in 1370. While small, the town possessed excellent potential for economic prosperity: After the Thirty Years' War, the pharmaceutical oil trade, the production and processing of essences, creams, and oils from medicinal plants became Oberweißbach's economic hallmark. In the eighteenth and nineteenth centuries, the village also became known for its glassblowing. Thus, the little town attracted traders, who brought prestige, world knowledge, and prosperity. Though new products, innovations, and news from Europe reached Oberweißbach quickly, it remained a small village in a rural area. Life was hard and shaped by religion and traditions, and famines were common.

Today, Oberweißbach is still a small town in the German state of Thuringia. However, neither Thuringia nor Germany as a unified state existed during Froebel's time, hence if we speak of 'Germany', then only for simplification.[1] Froebel was in fact born in the Holy Roman Empire of the German Nation, a heterogeneous entity consisting of three hundred territories that included large states such as Prussia or Austria as well as tiny ones like Schwarzburg-Rudolstadt. The empire was separated by countless political, cultural, economic, and religious dividing lines. There was no single ruler, effective sovereignty, or even a single church, as the territory was divided up between Catholic and Protestant rulers. The political conditions were volatile, and a state's policies often changed entirely after a monarch's death. Thus, the lifestyle, habits, and culture differed in each home state; there was no 'German' way of life as such. Some sovereigns were thrifty, others wasteful, and many oppressed their subjects.

The Napoleonic Wars changed this. To quote Thomas Nipperdey's famous words: 'In the beginning was Napoleon.'[2] Indeed, Prussia's catastrophic defeat of 1806 led to reforms and, in the long run, modern Germany. Secularization and mediatization changed the German territory irrevocably. After the Congress of Vienna, German territory suddenly consisted of 'only' forty states and four free cities. Still, a unified state didn't exist but rather only the German Confederation, a loose alliance of sovereign states with Austria as an essential part.

Germany existed, if at all, only as an abstract idea. People were loyal to their state, but not to a vague notion such as Germany, and many never left their home state or spent most of their lives there. This was true for Froebel as well. After growing up in the tranquil Thuringian area, he returned to the region after a few years away in Frankfurt, Yverdon, Göttingen, and Berlin. And following his time in Switzerland, Froebel again came back to the same area. Deep down, Froebel was a rather provincial citizen of Schwarzburg-Rudolstadt, loyal to the principality, and uninterested in the revolutionary ideas of his late years. If Froebel thought of himself as German, then only as an afterthought.

Oberweißbach belonged to one of the numerous German dwarf states, the principality of Schwarzburg-Rudolstadt. It was a relatively small and unimportant principality of approximately 100 square kilometres in size with no more than 60,000 inhabitants. During Froebel's childhood, Schwarzburg-Rudolstadt was reigned by Prince[3] Ludwig Günther II (1708–1790), Friedrich Karl (1790–1793), and Ludwig Friedrich II (1793–1806). Because the treasury was empty, Ludwig Günther II emphasized austerity. Ludwig Friedrich II and his wife, Karoline von

Hessen-Homburg, were highly educated and interested in the arts and sciences. Ideas from Enlightenment and Idealism were widespread in the principality and must have influenced Froebel's upbringing, at least to a certain degree. Nevertheless, such thoughts didn't play an essential role in Froebel's early years. What mattered to Froebel was the daily life in Oberweißbach, which was shaped by two aspects: his mother's early death and his father's dogmatic Christianity.

A Dramatic Loss: The Mother's Early Death

Jacobine Eleonore Friederike Froebel was just thirty-eight years old when she died on 7 February 1783, nine months after Froebel's birth, due to 'the consequences of a hard birth' and 'fiery consumption'[4] (probably meaning pulmonary tuberculosis). Biographers and Froebel himself have relentlessly emphasized the significance of her early death on his life.[5] In Froebel's own words:

> Early on I received the consecration of the painful and forceful life struggle, an artificiality and a deficient education wielded their influence on me. Soon after my birth, my mother became sick and after she had dearly cared for me for three quarters of a year, she died. Through this loss and hard life fate, my entire life's outer appearance and development were determined; I feel that this occurrence more or less determined the appearance of my outer life.[6]

Later, Froebel repeatedly claimed that his mother's early death had shaped not only his life but also his personality. For him, his mother's death was the reason he became an educator (of humankind). Even fifty years later, he felt the need to emphasize that the tragedy had been central to his personal fate and had assigned him an enormous task to unite 'life and death, union and separation, invisible and visible; my special profession became thereby to dissolve the largest of the contrasts (*Gegensätze*), of the oppositions (*Entgegensetzungen*) in one's own life and by one's own life into its consistency'.[7] This is a typical Froebel statement. He also used her death to justify his wrongdoings, again referring to the sacrifices he had to endure.

Many biographers have followed Froebel's lead and pointed to the traumatic early years as *the* reason for his later passion for educating young children and women as their first teachers. Some truth does indeed lie in this, but Froebel's words should be taken with a grain of salt, nonetheless. While his letters in the 1830s were a sincere way of reflecting on his life, he also used them to justify his struggles and failures, his character flaws, all his (wrong) doings, and why his chosen path had been the only one possible (and, of course, correct one). By connecting all that happened in his life, it all made sense to him.

However, in those days it was relatively common for children to lose their mother – and they certainly did not all become interested in education. To take this as the only reason for Froebel becoming an advocate for the education of young children and the training of mothers and kindergartners would therefore be an oversimplification. Still, his mother's death was by all means decisive, as it marked the start of a childhood that can only be called unhappy.

Growing Up in the Parsonage

After his mother's death, Froebel's father Johann Jakob Froebel assumed sole responsibility for his youngest son's upbringing and care – a role he certainly didn't aspire to. Johann Jakob Froebel was born in 1730 as the first of several children to a forester and the daughter of a tailor. Enabled and supported by his parents, he became a Protestant pastor. After working as a subdeacon in Rudolstadt, he became the pastor in the farming village of Elxleben and was then appointed as Oberweißbach's pastor in 1775. Four years later, the twelve-year construction of a new church was finally completed; bad harvests, famines, and epidemics had delayed its construction. The *Hoffnungskirche* (church of hope), nicknamed the 'Cathedral of South Thuringia', was the pride of the region as it was the biggest village church in Thuringia with room for 2,000 people. Johann Jakob Froebel even wrote a short book about the church, and Friedrich was baptized here.

Little is known of the couple's marriage; however, it must have been affectionate and the two loved each other. The mother was friendly and humble, with a calming influence on her husband. After the death of his wife after eighteen years of marriage, Johann Jakob became even more withdrawn and sullen. He now had to care for six children. The oldest, August, had just turned seventeen and would soon leave home. August didn't play any role in his brother's life; Froebel never mentioned him; and August appears to have died young in Russia. At the time of their mother's death, Christoph was fourteen, Christian twelve, and the only daughter, Juliane, eight. Four-year-old Traugott and Friedrich were the youngest.

It was a tremendous burden for the busy father. While he no longer had to oversee the church's construction,[8] he needed to provide pastoral care for the 5,000-strong church community. Neither had he time nor the necessary disposition to take care of the infant, hence Friedrich was first taken care of by a 'simple and female person, so pure and youthful',[9] a warm-hearted yet young girl who did as she was told. Later, he was mainly cared for by the servants or his older siblings – everything but a caring environment.

The father was well respected, but cold-hearted and ill-tempered. Authoritative, obstinate, and easily angered, he was constantly in discord with his parishioners as he took decisive action against widely held superstitions and customs. He also clashed with the village schoolteacher, his servants, and his older children's tutor. To put it simply: the villagers didn't like him. Oberweißbach was rife with rumours about the pastor, his parsimony, and his churlishness towards the servants and tutor.

Froebel didn't have fond memories either. He remembered his father as a hardworking Protestant pastor with a rigid and dogmatic faith and no time or inclination to consider the Holy Bible in any way other than its literal interpretation: 'My father was a theologian of the old days, who respected knowledge and sciences less than faith, but nevertheless tried to progress with time, if possible.'[10] While Froebel certainly respected his father, later calling him highly qualified for the position of rural pastor and a 'scholarly and experienced, restlessly active man',[11] the relationship between father and son was distant, and the father had no patience for educating the slow-developing and idiosyncratic Friedrich. Because his older brothers had already left home, Friedrich was without supervision or spent time with the servants, who used Friedrich's naiveté and trust for their feud with the father. It wasn't a pleasant start to life.

However, the most defining force during Froebel's childhood was his father's understanding and living of Christianity. What he heard and experienced in the parsonage greatly shaped Froebel's religious and pedagogical thinking. Like everyone in the family, Friedrich had to listen to the daily morning and evening devotions. On Sundays, he attended the service, often both and always alone in the sacristy. This was a rather odd decision by his father, one that probably led to more rumours. Many citizens must have wondered why the pastor's son was not allowed to attend the sermons in public. The sermons terrified but also fascinated the young child and moulded Froebel's understanding of faith and religiosity. Listening daily to the catechism and torments of hell, to sin and punishment as essential parts of Christianity, to the dualistic idea of a sinful world and godly afterlife, of the gap between God and men, such thoughts were ubiquitous in Froebel's childhood. Christianity, or why a church is needed, was never questioned, and churchly piety was taken for granted.

Such a religious upbringing was typical at the end of the eighteenth century, though, especially in pastoral households. Indeed, religion remained a fundamental part of the nation's psyche despite the growing criticism and rejection, and the nineteenth century was marked by a resurgence of religious practices.[12] Religion – and the 'alliance of throne and altar' – remained crucial to the state, society, and culture and significantly influenced how people viewed their world, life, and community. This was the case for Froebel both during his childhood and beyond, and his writings and pedagogical practices are prime examples of how religiosity remained a given for most people.

Despite developing a different religiosity over the course of his life, Froebel was never able – or interested – in freeing himself from his religious upbringing. He remained a profoundly religious person throughout his life. Living in 'unification' with God was always the ultimate goal of his educational endeavours, the purpose of kindergarten, or the gifts and occupations. It is in fact only against the background of his religious enculturation that Froebel's pedagogical thinking makes sense. Religion was what mattered most to him.

The Next Disappointment: A New Mother

Froebel's childhood seemed to change for the better when his father remarried in 1785. This time, it wasn't a love match. The 55-year-old pastor was looking for a new woman to take care of the household and children and found her in a 33-year-old merchant's daughter. His new wife, Friederike Sophie, née Otto, knew what she was getting into, namely marrying a fearsome man who was constantly at odds with his servants. It was 'well-thought-out on both sides'.[13]

The stepmother initially met Friedrich with heartfelt affection and, for a short time, Friedrich was happy. However, Friederike quickly became distant, also because the servants turned Friedrich against her. Friederike was soon tired of the demanding Friedrich, and when her first son, Carl Poppo, was born in 1786, Friederike only showed affection to him. Thus, the 4.5-year-old Friedrich found himself alone again; in a way, it was the second time he lost a mother. The situation rapidly deteriorated, and Friedrich was prohibited from addressing her with the informal 'you'. Friedrich was unsettled and confused by his stepmother's behaviour, and his father, who supported his new wife, was no help.

While it is fair to say that the new marriage did not give the neglected Friedrich the warm and caring mother he had longed for, one shouldn't judge Friederike too hastily. She had to find her place in the family, and her husband gave her the freedom to do so. That doesn't mean she was a 'cruel stepmother'.[14] She did show affection for Froebel by convincing his father to pay his debts to free him from the campus prison, for example.[15] And while Froebel didn't address his father politely in a letter sent from prison, he ended by greeting his 'dear mother and Siegken',[16] the latter his nickname for his stepsister. Froebel also didn't cut ties with her entirely after his father's death, and Froebel was anything but a forgiving person. Instead, he reconciled with Friederike, even if the two never corresponded, and he had a good relationship with his stepsiblings. After the war of 1813, Froebel visited his stepmother and brother in Rudolstadt, where he enjoyed a warm welcome.[17] While Friederike could never replace the mother he lost, one shouldn't describe her as overly cruel. We simply don't know much about her, apart from the little that can be found in Froebel's letters. Friederike died in Rudolstadt in 1836; Froebel's reaction when he learned of her death is unknown.

We do know, however, that Friedrich's childhood continued to be miserable.[18] 'I grew up without a mother, my bodily care was neglected, and because of this negligence, I developed some nasty habits.'[19] For his father, Friedrich must have been nothing but a disappointment. Instead of showing love or understanding, Friedrich's father punished and insulted him; sometimes, he even had to go hungry. As Froebel later explained, his parents' behaviour hurt him as a child because he never felt all his behaviour was entirely wrong or at least deserved such severe punishment. One evening, Friederike locked him in the dark, damp basement and, because they forgot about him, Friedrich spent the whole night there. The following day, he claimed that his dead mother had fed him – the tendency to such mystic delusions probably didn't help. However, his parents' disciplinary measures weren't successful. On the contrary, Friedrich's behaviour worsened – at least that's how his frustrated parents perceived it. The young child began to hide harmless actions for fear of getting punished, or he lied when asked about alleged misbehaviour. 'It was enough to say that I was considered evil early on in my life, and my father, who did not always have time to look into things, kept an eye on matters which were presented to him.'[20] To make things worse, he became Friederike's scapegoat whenever anything went wrong playing with Traugott and Carl Poppo, and she called him a 'hellion'. Because he now kept his distance from the servants, they saw him as arrogant and ignored him. Undoubtedly, Friedrich was lonely.

The emotional and physical abuse, especially by his father, traumatized Froebel for the rest of his life. In his daily papers from 1820, Froebel wrote that his father violently and mercilessly punished him, later supported by his 'step

(<u>stiff</u> – hard) mother', which drove him to misbehave. The fear of his father's punishment created a lifelong fear: 'So the fear of my youth was a model/pre-image (*Vorbild*) of the fear that oppressed me throughout life.'[21] The mistreatment and the non-existing relationship with his father probably caused Froebel's later inability to develop close relationships or trust people. 'As fear of man fear of man judgment and opinion dwells in me and my soul, so, on the other hand, weak trust in God in my soul.'[22] However – and this is what makes Froebel's life so fascinating – he developed a very different religiosity and thinking about young children. There was no sin and punishment; instead, he met children with respect and understanding and gave them freedom. His educational creed was the opposite of what he had experienced.

A Lonely Child

It's one of the best-known images of Froebel as a child: the time alone spent in nature that enabled him to already sense the divine law of the sphere – an idyllic picture that Froebel carefully romanticized until the end of his life. However, Froebel's solitude wasn't entirely voluntary, but rather another form of punishment. After Friedrich returned late to lunch after playing outside, he wasn't allowed to leave the parsonage without reason anymore until his tenth birthday. Hence, he couldn't mingle with the village children and was forced to stay alone in the parsonage and garden. Froebel's later description of the parsonage, emphasizing the walls, hedges, and the massive rock face in the back of the house, gives an almost prison-like impression. Outside 'was a different world'.[23] Despite Froebel's later romanticization, one shouldn't forget what it meant in reality: a young child deprived of meaningful relationships and the opportunity to engage with peers. Froebel never experienced empathy, nor learned how to solve conflicts and refind trust, nor practised his social skills within a peer group – hence he also lacked the latter as an adult.

In retrospect, and most biographers follow this argumentation, Froebel portrayed his solitude in the parsonage's grass, vegetable, and tree gardens,[24] which were also his father's pride – gardening seems to have been one of the rare activities that the two enjoyed together – as a prerequisite for his deep connection to and understanding of nature. From early on, Froebel later claimed, he developed what he called a premonition (*Ahnung*)[25] of the spherical law, the relationship between nature, humankind, and God, the law that lies within nature as well as in everything that is and lives, including himself. The 'unexpressed self-observation, self-reflection and self-education',[26] Froebel wrote, formed the basis of his life from an early age. The 'early and ongoing self- and life-observation taught me ...: the human being must ultimately find the reasons of his life's appearances, his life's fate in himself, as the one essential and dependent (*bedingten*) factor, in his own life, his feelings, his thinking, desire, and activity'.[27]

Froebel's reasoning shouldn't be dismissed too hastily. Already in 1811, when he wasn't trying to shape the image of himself with the same vigour as in the 1830s, Froebel wrote in his journal of an unspeakable joy when observing tulips, a 'most intimate joy for their regularity' and a 'most intimate joy at the sight of geometric figures and bodies'.[28] And in 1807, he stated that he had lacked the necessary love and care and suffered from the punishments and 'blows that penetrated me and my mind from the outside'.[29]

Today, we can only speculate whether such statements are realistic descriptions or merely Froebel's justifications. Either way, Froebel made his early suffering a theme of his correspondence, using autobiographical self- judgement – purposefully coarsely formulated – to make a virtue out of it. A typical example is the long letter from 1832 to the community in Keilhau and his statement that he had to fight from an early age until today for 'humankind's rights, humankind's truth, and humankind's essence'.[30] The 'adverse impact' of his surroundings and treatment must be seen as the 'key for all appearances of the development of my life'.[31] While the aim of such letters might have been honest self-reflection, it was also an attempt to shape his image as the philosopher of the law of the sphere, especially during his personal crisis in Switzerland. By referring to his unfortunate childhood, he consistently explained, justified, and refuted the various criticisms of his character and his often cold and cruel behaviour towards the Keilhau community. It might have been true, but it was also an easy way to deny all responsibility.

The Next Punishment: Attending a Girls' School

What is clear, though, is that Friedrich's childhood continued to be miserable, mainly because his father constantly humiliated and mistreated him. The situation increasingly deteriorated as Friedrich's father interpreted his self- centred, self-sacrificing behaviour as defiance or malice. In his biography, Halfter describes Friedrich's upbringing in detail, and even going by the child-rearing norms of the time, it must be classed as emotional and physical abuse. The only one who defended Friedrich was Christoph, who was studying theology and visited the parsonage occasionally. Froebel later felt that only Christoph and Christian, who was learning the weaver's trade and was away too, cared for him. Juliane primarily took care of the younger stepsiblings, and the relationship with Traugott, who was closest in age, was never warm. While Froebel later valued the 'indestructible (*unvertilgbare*) family and in particular sibling love', during the difficult first years, his siblings weren't of much help to him.

What disappointed his father probably the most were Friedrich's learning difficulties. He saw Friedrich as slow of mind, stupid, and a humiliation. While he had taught all his sons until they were old enough to attend grammar school, his attempts to teach Friedrich to read were unsuccessful and frustrating for both. Soon, he lost interest in his son's education and gave up. Unlike his older brothers, Friedrich wasn't allowed to attend grammar school when he turned seven and was instead sent to the village school. It was a drastic decision, for at the end of the eighteenth century, village schools only taught the absolute basics, such as praying, reading, writing, arithmetic, and singing. It meant that Friedrich wouldn't receive a sound academic education. His father went even further, however. Within the village school, the cantor Scherr taught the boys, and the organist Schubert the more than one hundred girls. Johann Jakob Froebel had witnessed an extremely unsatisfying school inspection in 1776 and had been at odds with Scherr ever since. As he was sceptical of the cantor's pedagogical talents and school leadership, he sent Friedrich to the girls' teacher – at least, that's Froebel's explanation in the letter to the women in Keilhau. It's speculative if Johan Jakob really wanted to protect his son from the cantor's teaching, if it was intended to be another humiliation, or if his stepmother simply didn't want him to study: 'That I should not study had already been determined earlier by the explicit will of my second mother. Since two of my brothers had already devoted themselves to their studies, she feared that new costs would deplete my father's fortune too much.' The result, however, was the same. Friedrich attended the girls' school as the only boy until he was 10½ years old; hence, he was denied a classical and well-rounded education.

The curriculum at the girls' school consisted of reading the bible, memorizing passages of his father's Sunday sermon and sacred songs. While Friedrich felt out of place in the girls' school, he appreciated its cleanliness, quiet, and discipline, feeling the impact on the development of his inner self: 'It was quite appropriate to it.'[32] It also might have given him some insights into the female world and the idea of caring.

However, his father's decision is telling. A pastor's son was expected to attend grammar school, and a pastor could make that happen. That Johan Jakob didn't push for it and even sent him to the girls' teacher speaks volumes about the complicated father–son relationship. Friedrich certainly wasn't a great learner, and he later admitted his struggles. Learning to read had been a 'torment', and he had often been accused of 'obtuseness' (*Beschränktheit*).[33] The only subject in which he showed promise was arithmetic. Therefore, while perhaps not entirely unjustified, his father's decision shows his unwillingness to support his son or make things happen for his benefit.

Whatever the reasons, the impact was huge. Throughout his life, Froebel lacked a systematic, well-rounded education. Among others, it's why he failed his studies in Jean and Göttingen. Froebel neither possessed the basic knowledge and language skills of contemporary (educational) thinkers, nor was he familiar with traditional philosophical concepts. While Froebel was interested in contemporary philosophical concepts, he could never fully understand the complicated ideas of Kant, Fichte, Schelling, or Hegel. Later attempts to overcome his limits were only partially successful. Many contemporaries have mentioned that Froebel lacked the academic knowledge to design *Gymnasium*-adequate lessons.[34] Froebel must have often felt inferior, even if he tried to demonstrate the opposite to the outside world. He would always be an autodidact with the tendency to only absorb what already fit into his thinking and ignore what wasn't easily comprehensible. It's also an explanation for his verbose and overcomplicated writing style.

A New Life: Living with His Uncle in Stadt-Ilm

Things changed in 1792 – and this time for the better. On 4 October 1792, Johan Jakob received a letter from Johann Christoph Hoffmann, the brother of Friedrich's late biological mother. The two siblings had been very close, and his sister had been his favourite, a wonderful person, as Froebel's uncle later told him. His uncle had visited the family of his beloved sister earlier, and now, after the birth of Friedrich's stepsister Johanna Sophie on 21 September 1792, Hoffmann made the unusual offer to take Friedrich in.

Hoffmann held a position far more powerful than his brother-in-law, namely that of superintendent of the church district of Stadt-Ilm, Thuringia, a day's walk from Oberweißbach. The Hoffmann family came from the bourgeoisie; their ancestors had been mayors, pastors, or tutors. Friedrich's uncle had been the tutor to Prince Ludwig Friedrich II at the court in Rudolstadt, and the two must have had a close relationship. In 1774, Hoffmann was appointed as the deacon in Stadt-Ilm and served from 1784 as the church district's superintendent. A beloved, father-like figure, Hoffmann was widowed early and had just recently lost his only child. He was now living alone with his mother-in-law in the spacious yet empty and quiet parsonage. It was probably a mix of obligation towards his late beloved sister and his living situation that made him send the letter.

Still, Hoffmann knew his irascible yet proud brother-in-law needed to be coaxed. Hence, he carefully formulated a letter, pointing out that the 'cheerful, maybe sometimes absent-minded (*flüchtig*)' but 'kind-hearted, obliging and helpful (*zutätig*)'[35] child would bring joy to his lonely home and cheer up his mother-in-law. Furthermore, Friedrich could learn much more at Stadt-Ilm's town school than at the village school. And anyway, his father was probably very busy with all his pastoral work after the birth of his daughter. He felt it was necessary to end the letter by emphasizing that Johan Jakob shouldn't take offence at the offer.

The carefully chosen phrases were probably not needed. After all, his offer was beneficial to all involved parties and, two weeks later, Johan Jakob accepted the offer even though he didn't consider it a 'benefit for the boy'.[36] That said, he made clear that Friedrich wouldn't be studying, but instead helping him with his clerical work in the future. With some luck, Friedrich would even abandon his 'juvenile mistakes'.[37]

It was a win-win-win situation, and no tears were shed when Friedrich's father took him to Stadt-Ilm on the first Sunday in Advent of 1792. For Friedrich, the move was a relief. In Stadt-Ilm, 'a new, entirely opposite kind of life now began when I was 10¾ years old'.[38] Friedrich would stay with his uncle for the next 4½ years and only see his parents during the long holidays. None of them minded.

For Friedrich, his new life seemed the complete opposite of his former one. 'This house gave me almost everything that my father's house would have given me in an opposite-equal way'.[39] The term 'opposite-equal' is, of course, a later term taken from his concept of life unification. However, it must indeed have felt like this. The same was true of his uncle's behaviour: 'If severity reigned in my father's house, here indulgence and kindness; if I saw mistrust there in relation to myself, here trust; I felt coercion there, freedom here'.[40] His uncle treated Friedrich warmly, and the sudden care positively impacted the child who had been neglected for such a long time.

Friedrich thrived in the new environment. Suddenly, he was allowed to explore his surroundings by himself as long as he returned in time for meals[41] and to mingle with his peers as he liked. The company was refreshing, but also frustrating. 'I was often deeply insulted by the frequent disregard in games.'[42] The clumsy Friedrich couldn't keep up with the other boys, who 'were so versatile and practiced in all their games' – boys who looked so big and strong: 'I looked up at them like giants.'[43] Despite his best efforts, Friedrich remained an outsider, 'Oberweißbacher Friedrich',[44] a peculiar boy who didn't fit in. It is not known whether he made any real friends during this time, but it doesn't seem so. At least he never mentioned anyone from his almost five years in Stadt-Ilm.

In Stadt-Ilm, Friedrich attended the town school. It was a more advanced primary school, and even if his uncle didn't push for it, Friedrich was soon promoted to the best of the three boys' schools in town and into the top class. This school wasn't good, however. While better than the school in Oberweißbach, the subjects still consisted of little more than reading and writing, a little bit of Latin, singing, geography, and mainly religion. Latin must have been taught miserably and, according to Froebel, the children learned almost nothing. Friedrich wasn't an outstanding student and showed no extraordinary talent in any subject other than mathematics. Most importantly, academic study and appropriate preparation for university were still lacking.

Religiosity, on the other side, continued to be of uttermost importance. His uncle, though, taught and lived a different kind of religiosity: 'My uncle's person and life were like his lectures – gentle, mild, loving.'[45] Friedrich also enjoyed the instruction from his religion teacher Temper whom he admired and 'whose remembrance is still in my good memory',[46] as he wrote more than fifty years later. As a member of the first boys' school, he was regularly tasked with reading psalms at the beginning of the afternoon service, parts of catechism, about Jesus's life, or creeds to the community and served as an altar boy – tasks that he enjoyed deeply. As his uncle was 'dearly loved and respected by his community'[47] and at the centre of town life, Friedrich listened to what was going on in the community and the world at his uncle's table. His uncle wanted to educate Friedrich, who was prone to rapture, to develop an active but not pious Christianity. The highlight, 'the most beautiful and most important year of my youth',[48] as Froebel wrote later, was his confirmation. The event aroused the soul of the now fourteen-year-old Friedrich intensely. When his uncle gave him his blessing, he became enraptured, which irritated both the community and his uncle. The teenager's often difficult behaviour had bothered him for a while, and his uncle now made clear what he thought of such eccentric behaviour. His words hurt Friedrich, who once again felt misunderstood.

Nevertheless, in retrospect, Froebel had fond memories of his time in Stadt-Ilm. 'From the autumn of 1792 to the spring of 1797, I lived a vigorous, free-spirited and, even in relation to teaching, at least for in a few directions, a more appropriate boyish life.'[49] Fourteen years later, he even asked the countess to appoint him as a teacher in Stadt-Ilm.[50]

For the moment, however, the question was what would come next. Becoming a student was out of the question, not only because of the stepmother's financial worries but also because Friedrich hadn't shown much talent, and the father didn't think Friedrich possessed the necessary academic skills and abilities. His uncle, getting old and fragile, didn't want to care any longer for the idiosyncratic teenager, and his father didn't want him back either.

Finally, both his uncle and father agreed that Friedrich should begin an apprenticeship as a scribe in Stadt-Ilm. The probation period didn't go well, however, primarily because the immature Friedrich couldn't cope with the tasks and didn't get along with the scribe and his wife. 'A longer stay in my house does not seem to be advantageous for Friedrich's education', his uncle wrote to Johann Jakob. 'Perhaps he will learn to obey better elsewhere, and to think more seriously about the removal of some bad habits.'[51] On St John's Day, he used even harsher words: 'To tell the truth, it won't be any good for him here anymore. Since Pentecost, when he left school, he has been almost completely idle.'[52] In September 1796, when an ugly, itchy rash broke out on Friedrich's body, both the scribe and Friedrich's uncle, fearing the gossip, had had enough and sent the sickly Friedrich back to Oberweißbach. This was yet another humiliation for Friedrich, who was again perceived as lazy and feckless and must have felt worthless and like no one wanted him.

His father was at a loss. He even tried to convince the scribe to keep him on by offering to pay for Friedrich's board and lodgings, but the scribe refused. For the next nine months, Friedrich stayed in Oberweißbach, mostly in apathy, without showing any interest in his future. His only idea for the future was to become an 'economist',[53] a profession he thought to be a mix of a farmer, administrator, huntsman, fosterer, and surveyor who lived in the countryside. Surprisingly, his father agreed. He probably was at his wits' end. After a lengthy search – the fees charged by real economists for an apprenticeship were too high – the fosterer Witz, who also worked as a surveyor and assessor, agreed to take Friedrich on. The two-year apprenticeship contract stated that Friedrich would be taught forestry, assessing, geometry, and land surveying. Friedrich, who still didn't care, was pleased that he would be in the countryside.

Everyone was relieved when Friedrich left. His father's parting words made clear that he didn't want to hear any complaints. This time, Friedrich took him seriously.

The Failed Forestry Apprenticeship

The apprenticeship is usually described as a second awakening to nature. The two years in Hirschberg, as the story goes, helped Froebel develop his deep love for and understanding of nature and also suspect that there was more to nature than just the empirically observable: 'a field, meadow and forest spirit', as Froebel wrote to his brother Christoph in 1807, 'in short something higher, inexplicable seemed to live in them, seemed to breathe on me out of them, to waft towards me'.[54] This statement is interesting because, in 1807, Froebel wasn't yet constructing the image of himself as the educator of humankind. Thus, there must be truth in it.

At the start of his forestry apprenticeship around mid-summer of 1797, Froebel was 15¼ years old, still young and immature. Witz was based in Hirschberg/Saale, a two-day walk from Oberweißbach.[55] It wasn't an entirely different world, yet at least something new.

The little known about the apprenticeship comes from Froebel's letters. He spent many months alone with the surveyor's wife as Witz was often away. Even if he was knowledgeable and capable, Witz wasn't a good teacher or interested in this part of the apprenticeship, at least according to Froebel. When Froebel wasn't in nature, he studied books about forestry and geometry. In addition, he drafted a map of the surroundings and created collections of stones and dried plants, activities that the fosterer's wife perceived as feckless idleness. She made his apprenticeship life sour with messenger walks, floor-scrubbing, shoe-polishing, and farm and stable work. When her husband returned, she complained about the withdrawn adolescent.

Little is known about Froebel's (social) life during these two years. It seems he wasn't interested in socializing; later, he never mentioned any friends or amorous passion. Once, after attending a play of a touring company in the one-hour-away royal castle, Froebel contemplated such a career while walking home during a starry night. He wrote enthusiastically about it to his father, who, unsurprisingly, called such ideas 'most culpable'.[56] It was the end of such dreams.

The second significant event was the acquaintance with a doctor from a nearby village. The doctor lent Friedrich books on botany and encouraged him to consider studying the natural sciences, claiming that he would cover the costs of the first semester – at least, that's how Froebel remembered it later. The doctor's enthusiasm led Froebel to begin thinking about the future and what he wanted to be, dreaming more and more of becoming a student.

After two years, the apprenticeship came to an end. Witz wrote a positive reference, probably expecting that Froebel would become his assistant. Froebel, though, didn't give it a thought: 'Now I was looking for a place where I could find this for me highest human knowledge united, and where those who possess it were also teachers. For me, this could be no other place than a university. Jena, it had to be.'[57] When his contract ended, Froebel left immediately.

It didn't play out as he had hoped, though. Witz wrote an angry letter to his father, complaining bitterly about Friedrich's character flaws. When Friedrich visited Christoph in Eyba on his way home, his brother, who had been forwarded Witz's letter by their father, confronted him with the accusations. Friedrich showed Christoph his private notes and explained the surveyor's failure while shyly mentioning his dream of studying in Jena. Convinced by his brother's arguments, Christoph decided to help Friedrich. However, he wanted to know why Friedrich had kept silent about the injustice. Friedrich explained that their father had told him not to complain.

Despite his support, Christoph was aware of his brother's character flaws: 'Of course, it is true that he has not yet completely abandoned his adverse nature and is more fierce than it is decent for a person of his years, especially when it comes to assertions of his opinions', he wrote to his father. 'That Friedrich is somewhat taken with himself, I also believe.'[58] To lose his hubris, Christoph explained, Friedrich must spend time with older, wiser people. And Jena would offer such an opportunity.

A Shattered Dream: Jena

Back in Oberweißbach, his father and stepmother made clear to him that he was nothing but a good-for-nothing in their eyes. Once again, Friedrich isolated himself and spent time alone in his room. It must have been a very unpleasant time that luckily ended when his father needed someone to take money to Traugott in Jena. Friedrich happily volunteered and, even if he didn't mention his dream of studying in Jena yet, asked if he could stay longer to find a vocation.

His father agreed. Impressed by the city's vibrant intellectual life, Friedrich finally asked if he could stay until the end of the summer semester. Traugott wrote some supporting words and, because only eight weeks were left in the summer semester, their father agreed.

Friedrich enrolled in lectures on surveying and topography taught by Dr von Gerstenbergk, and Professor Stahl's mathematics lectures. To do so, he needed to pay a fee and buy expensive surveying tools, money he borrowed from Traugott. Before he had even started his studies, Friedrich was already in debt.

Friedrich enjoyed his time in Jena, nonetheless. It gave him his first glimpse into the academic world and what such a life could be like. However, he also became aware of his insufficient education: 'My knowledge has no grounds, I have no theory at all, and now I can neither live for the benefit of human life nor honour myself.'[59] Still, he wanted to continue studying even if he knew his father wasn't willing to pay for it. However, like his siblings, he had a right to his mother's inheritance, a fact he hadn't realized so far. Thus, he asked his legal guardian, an uncle in Königsee, if he could use the money to study for one year.

Johann Jakob was probably not amused that Friedrich had contacted his legal guardian behind his back. However, and again with Christoph's support, the father gave in. He was probably relieved that it wasn't him who had to pay for what was in his eyes a pointless endeavour. All parties agreed that Friedrich could study for one year using his mother's inheritance, to be paid out in instalments. His father wrote a letter that certified Friedrich's ability to study cameralistics and gave him a bill of the total amount for the first semester.

On 22 October 1799, the now seventeen-year-old Friedrich enrolled at the University of Jena as a philosophy student. At the time, seventeen was a normal or even old age to start one's studies, so age wasn't the issue. However, Friedrich was poorly prepared for life as a student and was already overwhelmed by being a philosophy student. In his eyes, philosophy was something higher, entirely out of his range. Now, he was a philosophy student! And not only that, he was in Jena!

At the turn of the century, Jena was in its heyday, its golden years, and *the* place to be. German Idealism was at its peak, and Jena was at its centre. Since Schiller's inaugural lecture in 1789 on the nature and value of universal history, the then 4,300-inhabitant town in the Saale valley had become *the* centre of intellectual life in Germany.[60] After the well-respected Kantian Carl Leonhard Reinhold had left for Kiel in 1793, the new star of German Idealism – Johann Gottlieb Fichte – arrived. For many, Fichte was the first to complete Kant's Copernican Revolution. Attracted by Fichte, many followed, including Friedrich von Hardenberg, who was better known as Novalis, or Friedrich Hölderlin. Then there were the Schlegels – the renowned poet and translator August Wilhelm Schlegel and his wife; and his brother Friedrich and Dorothea Veit – the daughter of the famous philosopher Mendelssohn – who lived together without being married. The latter was a scandal. Nevertheless, or maybe for this exact reason, their salon was the city's centre. Intellectual life was constantly evolving. Novalis was working on *Heinrich von Ofterdingen*, while Friedrich Schlegel was writing *Lucinde*, the scandalous novel of the time. In 1798, shortly before Froebel arrived, the philosophical wunderkind Wilhelm Schelling became a professor of philosophy. Even though Fichte had left after the atheism dispute in 1798, Jena was still *the* intellectual place to be, and now Froebel was part of it. At least he was living in the same city.

Friedrich was enamoured by the city's intellectual, social, and cultural life. While officially enrolled in philosophy, he had much leeway and was more interested in the natural sciences. He attended various lectures on applied mathematics, arithmetic, algebra, geometry, botany, mineralogy, natural history, physics, chemistry, cameralistic studies, topography, and surveying. Interestingly, Froebel ignored what captivated Jena's students the most: Schelling's rousing lectures, even if Schelling's notion of a 'world soul' should have appealed to him. In general, Jena's theoretical-philosophical discussions didn't interest him much. Such concepts were probably incomprehensible for Friedrich anyway, as he was neither skilled in contemporary philosophical thinking nor familiar with basic ideas of German Idealism, not to mention the fundamental concepts of Plato, Spinoza, or Leibniz, which profoundly influenced Schelling's thinking. However, even if he never attended the lectures, it doesn't mean that he didn't become familiar with, or at least heard of these ideas. Given their prominence, one could hardly avoid them. Students talked about them over wine and beer in the pubs at night, and Friedrich must have absorbed some of it. The same is true for some of the natural science fundamentals that were circulating.

While Froebel enjoyed being a student, he was never fully immersed in student life, and there was no one to help him find his way at the university. He never made any notes and, though eager, never studied seriously because he lacked the necessary preparation and skills. If at all, he only absorbed what already aligned with his thinking.

Shy and reclusive as he was, Friedrich also didn't fit in. As Halfter puts it: 'He wasn't a real student.'[61] Students' lives were loud and often wild; there were celebrations and fencing practice, and many dreamed of and lived free lives. They had their judiciary, which looked benevolently upon the drinking orgies, brawls, and even the rape of maidservants. Due to the increasing awareness of his intellectual inferiority, peculiar character, and shyness, Friedrich often sat quietly at the tables – if he went out at all. While he frequently met a few Hungarians, nothing is known of Froebel's friendships during this time. As far as is known, he also had no contact with the opposite sex, even if this was common for students. He must have been the opposite of his fun-loving brother Traugott, and the two saw each other only occasionally.

Despite all the difficulties, in the first two semesters, Friedrich's studies were somehow successful. He especially enjoyed the chemistry lectures by Göttling, a warm and virtuous teacher who consulted Goethe and thus helped shape the idea behind Goethe's novel *Elective Affinities*. Then there was August Karl Batsch, the 'marvelous Batsch, my dear teacher',[62] and his natural sciences lectures. He quickly became Froebel's most important teacher. Batsch was an inspiring teacher who founded Jena's nature society (*Naturforschende Gesellschaft*), a significant society that even Goethe was a member of. In July 1800, Froebel was unanimously appointed a full member, thanks to Batsch's support.[63] Within the society, Friedrich helped with the collections' arrangement. When Friedrich went to visit Christian in Osterode at the end of the second semester, the future didn't look too dark. His financial situation was already problematic, however.

Despite his modest lifestyle, Friedrich ran out of money in his second semester. The cash-strapped Traugott had wanted his money back and asked for a loan which Friedrich had given him. Naïve as he was, he probably didn't imagine that he wouldn't see his money again. Traugott left Jena without paying his brother back, however, and Friedrich had to pay the fees for the numerous courses and purchase of books. Soon, the maternal inheritance was gone and, without any income, the debts began to pile up.

Little attention has been paid to date to the relationship between Froebel and Traugott and how poorly the older brother treated him. Froebel also kept very quiet about it. The brothers didn't stay in touch, though Froebel did try. In a letter to Christoph dated 26 June 1810, Friedrich mentioned that he was pleased that Traugott was happily married but hurt that Traugott had never replied to him or informed him of his marriage and that he had become a father. Froebel wasn't resentful, though: 'He certainly believes that I am a stranger to him, and yet this is not the case, I love him no less than all my siblings. One has to let him go his way, he will accept it one day.'[64] It remains unclear, though, why the two were so distant and never reconciled.

At the beginning of the third semester, Froebel's financial situation worsened. Neither his father nor his uncle wanted to pay for the next semester, but

Friedrich insisted on staying, assuring that a 'good friend from Hirschberg'[65] would sponsor his studies. However, the reference to the doctor in Hirschberg was only a figment of the naïve Friedrich's imagination.

Since he hadn't been able to pay tuition in the second semester, Friedrich now owed his professors money. Ashamed, Friedrich didn't attend any lectures and even avoided Batsch and the nature society meetings. Quickly, he became more reclusive and fell into a depression. Nevertheless, he still needed to eat and drink. Soon, he owned the innkeeper Fleischer 30 thalers. Afraid he would never see his money again, Fleischer contacted the university senate that wrote to Friedrich. Friedrich ignored the warning, though, and Fleischer contacted Johann Jakob Froebel to ask him to vouch for his son. Furious, his father refused, and Friedrich became disrespectful towards the innkeepers. The whole situation worsened – unnecessarily so, as Friedrich's father could easily have resolved the issue – and the senate threatened to imprison Friedrich. Both his father and his legal guardian refused to act however, leaving the senate with no choice: At the end of March 1801, Friedrich was incarcerated in the notorious campus prison.

Friedrich remained incarcerated for nine to ten weeks. In the meantime, both his father and uncle continued their stubborn fight, quarrelling over formalities, suspecting deception, no one willing to pay the debts. Friedrich wasn't particularly bothered about spending time in the campus prison, though. He primarily concerned himself with the rising costs and drafted a geometrical work sample. Ultimately, Friedrich's father demanded that Friedrich waive his fatherly inheritance, else he wouldn't pay for his debts. Friedrich agreed: 'I therefore do, under the father's self-imposed restrictions, waive everything from my father, however it may have come. Therefore, you can keep this letter to avoid further disputes.'[66] While Friedrich didn't care for the money, he felt misunderstood and unfairly treated and was probably also ashamed that he had proven his father and stepmother right. The disputes continued for a while, both between his father and legal guardian as well as between his father and the university tutor (*Studentenvater*). Finally, after the creditors waived parts of the debt and the amount still due was paid, Friedrich was released from the campus prison.

Once again humiliated, Friedrich returned to Oberweißbach at the end of May 1801. Until this point, his life had been nothing but a failure. His relationship with his father was worse than ever; neither wanted Friedrich to be back in Oberweißbach, nor did his parents want him around. Friedrich had no choice, though, as he had nowhere else to go.

Into an Uncertain Future: The Travel Years

Friedrich mostly spent the few weeks he stayed in Oberweißbach alone and hiding from the locals. The relationship with his parents was tense; his father felt his son was idle and wasting his time with worthless activities. It wasn't long before his father sent Friedrich to his stepmother's relatives, who owned Weitersroda, an estate close to Hildburghausen. It was another failure and embarrassment, as Friedrich didn't have enough money to buy proper shoes, so found himself in debt again. Friedrich talked about emigration for the first, but not the last, time: 'America also or Russia, shall become the finding places (*Findorte*) of my living.'[67] Emigration seemed to be the only hope left.

In October 1801, the now critically ill father called his son back to help him with the written official duties. Friedrich was reluctant but complied and took care of his father's affairs until he died in February 1802. He never regretted this, as it allowed him to reconcile with his father somehow. Later, Froebel was quite lenient when speaking about his father: 'May his transfigured spirit look down on me with calmness and blessing as I write this; may he now be at peace with the son who loved him so much.'[68] Still, his father's death was probably a relief.

Froebel knew that he wouldn't stay in Oberweißbach. Before he left, Froebel went through his father's papers and found the christening letter written by his godmother Johann Christina Friederika Kämpfin. The letter, which had been kept from Froebel, was very different in tone and style from the Christian orthodoxy that he had experienced. The words moved him:

> Shouldn't my heart be very happy to be able to do something this day that sets you, lovable godchild (*Patgen*), to a heavenly blessing and me in exquisite honour? So get up, my friend! My beautiful, come here and rest in my arms, on which I hold you in front of the sacred baptismal font to Jesus; from now on, this our Saviour will acquaint himself with you in justice, grace and mercy. Listen, son! Look at it and hold onto your best soul mate with immovable loyalty, who is now yours, until he will call you to his eternal rest at the end of your days. Follow the faithful and well-intentioned admonition of your tenderly loving godmother.[69]

Froebel kept the letter his entire life, calling it his 'Creed'. Froebel left the family home soon after the father's funeral at around Easter 1802 with the letter in his pocket and not much else.

Years of travel followed.[70] Froebel now had to earn a living, so he began working as an actuary in the forestry office in Baunach situated in the Prince-Bishopric of Bamberg. Baunach was a Catholic province, and to attend a Protestant service,

Figure 1.2 Map of travelling.
Based on map data of the IEG-Maps project (Andreas Kunz, B. Johnen and Joachim Robert Moeschl: University of Mainz), supplemented with Froebel's places of activity by Ulf Sauerbrey.

Froebel had to walk to Rentweinsdorf every Sunday. His supervisor at the forestry office was profoundly Catholic, but friendly towards Froebel.

Having previously only lived in Protestant regions, this was a new experience for Froebel – and one essential to his spiritual development as he learned to navigate between two confessions and also experienced religious tolerance.

The work wasn't particularly hard, so Froebel had plenty of spare time. As usual, he spent his time in nature but also used his supervisor's library to study subject literature and read easy literature. Over the following weeks, Froebel collected sayings and aphorisms in a little book he carried with him. He also socialized more, took walks, and went for the occasional wine or beer. As Froebel had to deal with other people, he became more mature and gained in confidence, as is seen from the numerous entries in his album (*Stammbuch*) from this time. For the first time, Froebel became closer to the female population, especially with Dorothea Papp, whom he began to meet frequently. Later, when both were living in Bamberg, they saw each other regularly. It might have been his first love interest, even if the relationship seemed more like one between siblings. At least he mentions her in his autobiographical letters. He became more involved with the Protestant community in Rentweinsdorf, too, especially with pastor Johann Schneider. At his supervisor's house, he made the acquaintance of a well-educated, ambitious, and purposeful tutor named Kulisch. Even if Froebel felt inferior, he enjoyed talking and mainly listening to Kulisch's lofty ideas, but showed little interest in Kulisch's educational work.

Froebel didn't stay in Baunach long. The Principal Decree of the Imperial Deputation had given the Prince-Bishopric of Bamberg to Bavaria, meaning that comprehensive land-surveying was needed. Surveyors were in demand, and Froebel wanted to become one. There was only one problem: Froebel was in debt again. This time, he asked Christoph to vouch for him, and his brother complied.

In Bamberg, Froebel was quickly hired by an official surveyor. The position wasn't very demanding, and when the new government wanted to hire surveyors permanently, Froebel submitted a work sample. While he was applauded and even paid for the work, he wasn't hired. Instead, he was paid privately to survey a small estate. One of the estate's owners was Dr Reibel, a student of Schelling, whom Froebel had met briefly in Jena. Reibel introduced Froebel to Schelling's idea of the world soul (*Weltseele*). Schelling's notion – the idea of unity and the overall context of God, nature, and humanity – was somehow similar to Froebel's naïve natural philosophy of a 'field, meadow, and forest spirit'. Froebel, so it seems, wasn't impressed, though; at least it didn't change his thinking.

While in Bamberg, Froebel published a job application in the *Reichsanzeiger* on 15 October 1803. The journal had a broad audience, and Froebel was open to anything, even Russia or Poland. He included work samples and soon received a variety of offers. Finally, Froebel accepted the one from the privy councillor von Derwitz in Mecklenburg-Strelitz, who lived on an estate in Groß-Miltzow. Before leaving for Groß-Miltzow, he spent January 1804 in Ahnrschwang, where he had to organize the business invoices of the privy councillor von Bölderndorf. All told, it was a promising start to his professional life.

On his way during a freezing February, Froebel chose a zigzag course to visit relatives, though not his stepmother. The album (*Stammbuch*) entries show how surprised and delighted many were to see how much Froebel had matured since leaving Oberweißbach. After visiting his uncle and legal guardian in Königsee, Froebel went to Stadt-Ilm where Traugott was now working as a doctor. More importantly, he visited his uncle whose health had been deteriorating and talked about his late mother and youthful misdoings. When Froebel left, his uncle wrote in his album:

> Your pious heart is always your greatest good.
> This will increase your pleasure, this will reduce your pain,
> this is your rank, your pride, your greatest happiness on earth.
> Otherwise, everything, except this, can be snatched from you.[71]

Seeing his beloved uncle touched Froebel's heart. Had he known it was the last time he would see him, he would have been even more moved.

Afterwards, Froebel visited Christoph in Griesheim. It was a sobering trip. Christoph had become the pastor substitute under his indebted and tyrannical father-in-law and was constantly short of money. Worse still, the marriage with the strongheaded Christiane was unhappy; at least, that was Froebel's impression. Next, Froebel visited his sister Juliane in Großkochberg, where her husband was working as a pastor. Finally, he went to Jena to apologize to the former innkeepers, the Fleischers. After a short trip to Leipzig to visit another brother of his late mother, he arrived in Groß-Miltzow in March 1804.

The work in Ahrnschwang had prepared him well for the new position and, after a short time, it became routine. Both von Derwitz and his strict wife were pleased. Staying in an elegant estate and society was new to him, but Froebel had become more confident and found socializing easier. One can find many entries in his album of this time. Nevertheless, many considered him to be quite peculiar.

Through some local pastors, Froebel was invited to join a reading society. Froebel became more interested in contemporary literature and ideas, but again not in pedagogical questions. During meetings, they discussed the philosophical questions of the time, and concepts such as a primal force, identity, and unity or a rationale nature must have fascinated Froebel. Three books especially enthralled him: *Anthropologische Abhandlungen* (*Anthropological Treatises*) by Pörschke, Novalis' *The Novices of Sais*, and Ernst Moritz Arndt's *Germanien und Europa*

(*Germania and Europe*). However, even if the readings (especially Novalis) unsettled him, they didn't change his thinking. It is also unclear how much Froebel actually read and understood. In retrospect, Froebel would give imprecise information about the title of his readings (not only regarding Schelling), so an in-depth study is unlikely. Froebel lacked the stamina to study the challenging work of contemporary thinkers seriously. Even a sympathetic biographer such as Halfter doesn't conceal this fact. His letters or writings show no evidence that Froebel ever read such works systematically. Readings always served more as stimulation for Froebel's spinning thoughts; conversations and oral reports were more important.[72] And while Froebel was interested in the philosophical ideas of others, he preferred to cling to his world view. If he made excerpts, then more to consolidate what he already thought. Froebel was never an open-minded reader.

The years of travel were significant, though, for Froebel matured and changed as a person, a transformation he wanted to emphasize with a name change. 'And from that moment on, I only called and wrote of myself as August, because I felt from different angles that a completely new, higher life was beginning for me, so I no longer wanted to use my old name to which so many adverse memories, especially of my early youth, were attached.'[73] Froebel would use this name for more than a decade.

Still, he wasn't ready to settle. After less than a year, he asked Kulisch about opportunities to work as an architect in Frankfurt. Kulisch offered to meet him and help him with his future there. Froebel was excited, but there was one problem: since he still had to repay debts owed in Bamberg, he had no money left. Froebel still wasn't able or willing to show financial responsibility. In despair, he contacted Christoph again, despite knowing his brother had no money. The answer, however, was a shock. His beloved uncle in Stadt-Ilm had passed away in February, and the childless man had bequeathed his assets to the children of his dear sister – Froebel suddenly possessed the means he needed after all.

For Froebel, it was a sign of fate. He resigned from his job and left Groß-Miltzow at the end of April 1805. On his way to Frankfurt, he made a short stop in Krumbeck in the Uckermark to meet a friend, inspector Meier. When they parted ways, the two exchanged words in their albums. However, Froebel didn't want to use well-known phrases, as it was common. Finally, after thinking long and hard, he wrote:

> May the benevolent fate give you a quiet rural dwelling, an honest, faithful woman, always cheerful mind and inner peace; I am driven restlessly through the world and only allow as much time to rest and relaxation as is necessary to

be able to recognize my point of view towards the world and people. You give bread to people; my striving is to give people to themselves.[74]

Those words have led to speculation. Did Froebel have some inner, unconscious premonition of what the future would hold for him – becoming an educator of humankind? In hindsight, it's easy to find such meaning in these words. There is, however, not the slightest indication that Froebel had already thought about a career as a teacher at this point. When he left for Frankfurt, his dream was still to become an architect.

Things turned out differently though. Indeed, the move to Frankfurt brought the decisive turn in Froebel's 'external and internal life' – suddenly becoming a teacher.

2

Suddenly, an Educator

Biographers have called the first months in Frankfurt a 'pedagogical calling'[1]. While it probably was, this happened by chance and simply by being in the right place at the right time. It was also no coincidence that it happened in Frankfurt. At the turn of the century, Frankfurt was the centre of the 'then so eventful time',[2] as Froebel later called it. For the first time, Froebel witnessed the effects of the French Revolution. Due to Napoleon's politics, the city was on its way to becoming the capital of an independent grand duchy. It was the seat of German liberalism, a modern and progressive city. Among others, Jews were granted civil rights here, and the city walls fell. Civic foundations and, instead of courtly pomp, liberal civic spirit characterized cultural life in the city. In addition, new large buildings were expected to be built, and architects were needed. That's why Froebel wanted to be there.

But Frankfurt was also interesting for educators. Many influential upper-class families were deeply committed to (progressive) education; indeed, education had acquired a new standing and begun to take on a similar rank as religion had in previous centuries. For many, a child's upbringing was seen as the elevation and redemption of humankind, the real way to find wholeness. Education was no longer just about raising children for the present, but also for the future. Such thoughts were prominent in Frankfurt, and genuine efforts were made to reform the municipal school system.

Froebel felt comfortable in Frankfurt, and the city was, as he later emphasized, essential to his personal development.[3] However, finding a position as an architect wasn't easy, even if Kulisch arranged the first acquaintances. And while some showed interest in Froebel's architectural talents, the *Reichsanzeiger* hadn't returned his drawings and credentials. Without them, no one wanted to hire Froebel. To earn a living, Kulisch wanted to introduce him to the patrician von Holzhausen family and put him in touch with the director of the progressive

Musterschule (model school). The family was looking for a new private tutor, and Kulisch, who had previously tutored the children and knew the family well, thought Froebel would be a good fit. However, when the two visited their city estate, they learned that the family was holidaying in Bad Ems, so Kulisch left a note.

The *Musterschule*, which had opened just a few years earlier hoping to change the educational landscape in Frankfurt, was always looking for new teachers. The school's head was the 27-year-old Gottlieb Anton Gruner (1778–1844),[4] who had studied in Göttingen and Jena and worked as a private tutor in Copenhagen. Afterward, he visited Salzmann in Schnepfenthal and spent three months with Pestalozzi in Burgdorf. While initially critical of Pestalozzi, Gruner had immediately been fascinated by Pestalozzi's educational ideas and was now eager to spread them. His publication about Pestalozzi's method and institution, *Briefe aus Burgdorf über Pestalozzi, seine Methode und Anstalt* (*Letters from Burgdorf about Pestalozzi, His Method and Institute*), was well received by Pestalozzi, who thought highly of Gruner. As one of the rising Pestalozzi supporters, he had been appointed as the school's head only three months earlier.

Pestalozzi was the name everyone was talking about, not only in Frankfurt. His elementary method was considered the most progressive and promising educational idea. Pestalozzi became known following the publication of his novel *Wie Gertrud ihre Kinder lehrt* (*How Gertrud Teaches Her Children*) – a novel as well as a parenting advice book – in 1801 and a similar yet more precise work, *Buch der Mütter* (*Book of Mothers*), in 1803. His educational institutes in Burgdorf, Münchenbuchsee, and now Yverdon had only increased his popularity. The idea of his elementary method was to follow children's progress in learning from simple elementary units gained through perception to more complex concepts and operations. His concept, known as the ABC of perception, was didactically oriented to such 'natural' learning: contents of reality were radically reduced in their complexity to elementary units (in particular number, shape, and word) so that children at the elementary stage of development can grasp the world. Many followers believed that his method offered the possibility to help the Enlightenment to succeed. Pestalozzi was *the* educator of the time, and when Froebel arrived in Frankfurt, Pestalozzi was well known and his ideas widespread. Anyone who called themselves a Pestalozzian at the time was considered progressive, modern, and revolutionary.

The *Musterschule* founded in 1803 was inspired by Pestalozzi's ideas and was supposed to serve as a model school. The school largely bore the character of a citizen and secondary school, with considerable attention accorded to the technical subjects and French. In religious terms, tolerance prevailed. Instead of the usual religious instruction, non-denominational lessons were held, also because several students were Jewish. However, the school struggled in the first few years due to incompetent leadership and was constantly searching for new teachers. Gruner preferred young men with the same passion for reform ideas – and Pestalozzi – as himself. It didn't matter if a candidate lacked pedagogical knowledge; Gruner liked inexperienced young men he could shape. In this sense, Froebel was a perfect candidate.

Gruner regularly attended a soiree for young educators, and it was here that Kulisch introduced Froebel. Surprisingly, Froebel wasn't as shy as usual and instead participated in the discussion. Listening to Froebel's words, Gruner felt Froebel was a kindred spirit. When Kulisch mentioned casually that his friend was looking for a teaching position until the start of his architect career, the excited Gruner allegedly proclaimed: 'Construction is nothing for you. Froebel, you must become a schoolmaster.'[5] It is not known whether this actually happened, but the story sounds good. Either way, Gruner immediately offered Froebel a position and, encouraged by Kulisch, the reluctant Froebel agreed by handshake. Becoming a teacher wasn't his dream. However, when it became clear that the proof of his previous work had been lost during shipping, Froebel embraced the opportunity. There wasn't anything better waiting for him anyway, so why not become a teacher?

The new field of activity enthralled Froebel from the first day on, and he soon wrote to Christoph:

> It was as if I had been a teacher for a long time and was actually born to this business … . I am when I am in the lessons – to speak with my usual expressions: as in my element. You cannot believe how pleasantly the hours go by for me; I love all the children so dearly and often long for their lessons.[6]

Passionate as he was, Froebel immediately claimed that the education of humans was one – if not the most crucial – task in his life.[7] There was only one problem: Froebel didn't know the slightest thing about education, teaching children, or children's development, and he also lacked any experience of working with children. Gruner, who quickly discerned Froebel's lack of pedagogical knowledge, was patient and encouraged Froebel to read Pestalozzi. These early readings fascinated Froebel, and he resolved to use the autumn holidays to visit Yverdon to learn more. Without any money, such a trip was impossible, though. Luckily, he found a sponsor: Caroline von Holzhausen.[8]

Finding a New Calling: The Pilgrimage to Yverdon

The von Holzhausen family was one of the city's oldest, most esteemed patrician families. Between 1311 and 1806, sixty-seven of the city's mayors were from the family. At the beginning of the nineteenth century, the family was one of the wealthiest due to their extensive estate. The parents, Georg and Caroline, were invested in and concerned about their three boys' education. When Caroline heard from her brother-in-law – who had just returned from Switzerland – about Pestalozzi's method, she wanted to learn more. After returning from Bad Ems, Caroline read Kulisch's note and invited Froebel to get to know him and hear about his thoughts on education. It probably helped Froebel that they hadn't met previously. As a new teacher, he now felt more confident speaking about education. Caroline must have liked what she heard because she offered to pay for his trip to Yverdon soon after if he would 'give account like a son'[9] of his visit.

Froebel travelled the 460 kilometres to Yverdon on foot, almost like on a pilgrimage. Thanks to Gruner's note, Pestalozzi welcomed him warmly. Froebel was allowed to observe the educational institute freely for the next two weeks. The curious but uneducated Froebel was fascinated yet overwhelmed. He must have tried to articulate his impression in his letters to Caroline,[10] but couldn't reflect critically on what he saw. Looking back many years later, Froebel wrote: 'What I saw had an uplifting and depressing, awakening, and numbing effect on me. My stay lasted fourteen days. I worked and processed what I could, and to which I was specially called by the accepted obligation to give a faithful account in writing of how I saw the whole, what impression it would make on me.'[11] Regarding Pestalozzi's school pedagogy, the visit probably clarified almost nothing.

Still, the short visit was a success. 'We were pleased to meet Mr. Froebel', Pestalozzi wrote to Gruner. 'He has participated with all his ardour in everything we do, and I hope much of his head and heart for the advancement of our common cause'.[12] Froebel was forced to return home after just two weeks due to the political turbulence caused by Napoleon's Third Coalition War. He accompanied Lotte Lutz, Gruner's future bride, to ensure safe passage. The two must have discussed Pestalozzi, education, and what it meant to be a teacher. When Froebel returned to Frankfurt, he was in high spirits and eager to pursue his 'newly begun life'.[13]

A New Profession: Struggling with the Everyday Life of an Educator

Back in Frankfurt, Froebel signed a three-year contract with a salary of 700 Rhenish guilder. An apartment above the classrooms and firewood, which was an expensive resource at the time, were also free. Froebel, who now saw himself as a Pestalozzian, threw himself eagerly into his work. His teaching load consisted of arithmetic, drawing, geography, and German; he was furthermore required to attend the weekly teacher meetings where school regulations or current issues, such as the dissatisfactory French lessons, were discussed. Froebel was soon asked to draft ideas for lesson plans and school organization, which he presented at a meeting. Since the school struggled to find appropriate teachers or discipline the pupils, the teachers began to experiment with field trips once per week. Froebel went into nature, teaching geography while outside, which helped cover up his didactical gaps.

Still, the first evaluation, which came relatively soon, went well, even if the lack of pedagogical knowledge was evident to the evaluators. Gruner saw it similarly, but continued to be tolerant, giving Froebel freedom to allow his development. Froebel continued his self-education by reading Pestalozzi, Kant, Fichte, the Fichtean Johannsen, the philanthropist Salzmann, Herbart, and Schwarz, or educational journals. Especially Ernst Moritz Arndt's *Fragmente über Menschenerziehung* (*Fragments about Humane Education*), which he called his 'bible of education', impressed him. Froebel was now constantly thinking about education and liked to discuss the topic with colleagues. Without question, aware of his shortcomings, Froebel wanted to learn as much as possible about his new profession to become a better teacher.

In addition to working at the *Musterschule*, Froebel began to tutor the von Holzhausen children for two hours a day in arithmetic and German. The youngest son, Adolph, also attended the *Musterschule* for a few weeks and often stayed with Froebel for lunch. Froebel became closer to the family,[14] which pleased Caroline. The more she learned about the young teacher, the more she became interested in him as a possible new private tutor.

Regardless of his enthusiasm for the education profession, Froebel struggled tremendously in both positions.[15] Froebel was quite aware of his deficits, as the letter to the famous philosopher Karl Christian Friedrich Krause from 1828 shows:

> But the first time I appeared before my thirty to forty boys aged nine to eleven (this class was given to me) I felt very good, I felt as if I were in my long-standing missed element, and as I previously wrote to one of my brothers, it was just like the fish in water; I was unspeakably happy. However, now, from the very first moment, because I was supposed to be effective immediately in my new profession, what a sum of sacrifices! – what a rich activity! – I was to give information, decision, advice on things I had not yet believed necessary to pay attention to, and here, too, in a very strange place, I stood cut off alone.[16]

Aware of his deficient abilities, Froebel began to study subject literature. However, changes in his teaching method weren't successful, and he soon returned to Pestalozzian ways, also without much success. Especially teaching German was – and would always be – a challenge due to Froebel's insufficient knowledge of German grammar. For the same reason, he struggled with learning foreign languages such as French. To make his teaching life more manageable, Froebel often opted for long walks in nature with the children.

Still and despite all his efforts, Froebel was didactically, content-wisely, and personally overwhelmed. In retrospect, Froebel was honest enough to recognize it, stating in a letter: 'I have made an infinite number of mistakes, have made things sour for myself and my students and, as they say, dry; my demands on my students were absolute calmness and attention, I was relentless, and yet the children loved to be in no lesson than in mine.'[17] Or in another letter: 'I know how inexpressibly poor I am in auxiliary knowledge.'[18]

After a few months, Froebel began to wonder if he had made the right decision, or if the *Musterschule* was the right place for him. Still, he now began to see himself – probably without knowing what it meant and would look like in reality – as an 'educator of humankind'. His superior also noticed his struggles. 'Gruner knew enough about people', so goes Froebel's honest self-evaluation, 'to see that a man so excited as I could not work well in an institution like the one he was in charge of'.[19] In March 1806, Froebel finally asked for his contract to be terminated. Gruner accepted without trying to convince Froebel to stay, as long as he would find a replacement. Froebel recommended one of his acquaintances, the tutor Sänger, and was free to leave.[20]

Later, Froebel became a master of subtly cultivating his image as a competent educator.[21] Thus, many biographers have described him as a 'born and masterful teacher'. As described above, such an ascription is questionable and more glorification than truth. However, to be fair, Froebel's pedagogical struggles were inevitable. For a young man who lacked the necessary academic and pedagogical knowledge and skills, the challenge of suddenly being responsible for thirty to forty students and tutoring the three children of a wealthy family was insuperable. In addition, his attempt to overcome his limits by reading about and reflecting on education must be acknowledged. Froebel now wanted to be a teacher – and a good one. He was probably less fascinated by the real teaching experiences than the active involvement with Pestalozzi's pedagogy. Becoming part of the reformatory movement surrounding Pestalozzi thrilled Froebel, and it should be seen as the central requirement for his reception of pedagogical ideas. That's what Froebel now wanted to be: an educator who would influence not only children and human beings but also humankind. It would probably nonetheless be fair to brand his first educational experience a 'pedagogical wreckage'.[22]

On 21 June 1806, Froebel officially left the *Musterschule*. He later claimed that 'my farewell day was a day of mourning for the whole school, and the children proved this to me in the most striking ways, almost everyone was crying, and the teachers assured me that they saw boys crying whom they would never have believed capable of tears'.[23] Again, we don't know if this actually happened.

Froebel made the claim in a letter to his brother Christoph. It's the first of their correspondence that was preserved, a correspondence that was of uttermost importance for Froebel. Until Christoph's death in 1813, Froebel elaborated on his developing educational thoughts and discussed his personal and financial struggles and plans with Christoph. Christoph was the first in the line of essential correspondents. While Froebel must have corresponded with Christian and Traugott,[24] Christoph was his confidant: 'See, you are the only man – think about it and feel it, the only man I can express myself against.'[25]

A New Life: Private Tutor for the von Holzhausen Family

The decision to leave the *Musterschule* wasn't particularly difficult because the von Holzhausen family had offered Froebel the position as the family's private tutor in the spring of 1806. Not that such securities ever mattered greatly for Froebel. Caroline – who felt her children had been 'neglected' educationally by the previous private tutor, a French Abbé – wanted Froebel, who was already on friendly terms with her two youngest sons. Even if he struggled to bond with the oldest son Carl, Caroline had high hopes for Froebel.

Figure 2.1 Caroline von Holzhausen, portrait medallion, around 1810.
Private Property of the von Holzhausen family.

Caroline von Holzhausen[26] must have been an extraordinary woman: interesting, amiable, witty and beautiful, influential, and one of the centres of Frankfurt's society.[27] Born as Caroline Friederika Louisa von Ziegesar on 12 February 1775 in Biebrich as the eldest of three siblings, Caroline had received a well-rounded general education. She was intelligent and familiar with contemporary literature and modern languages.[28] 'My fortunes, which led me happily on the whole, introduced me to Frau von Holzhausen, a lady who must be known to have her simple and bright, comprehensive and pervasive mind, her noble high soul, her noble dignity as women and wife, and with all this, unpretentiousness, to be duly appreciated',[29] Froebel wrote to Christoph.

Caroline had married her cousin – the baron Johan Justinian Georg von Holzhausen, who was four years her senior and the representative of the affluent patrician von Holzhausen family – in 1793. The couple had seven children: *Carl* Anton Friedrich Wilhelm August Rudolph (*16 June 1794); Theodor (*2 February 1796, died 27 August 1796); Friedrich Ludwig Carl, called *Fritz* (*6 July 1797); Johann *Adolph* (*25 December 1799); Sophie (*17 November 1801); later, Caroline (*17 January 1807) and Hector (*18 March 1812) completed the family.[30]

Georg had studied in Göttingen, but had been forced to abandon his studies when his father died in 1793. At this time, only twenty-two years old, Georg became responsible for the family and administering the considerable estate. The family mattered in Frankfurt and their salon was large, befitting their social status but far from being cold, with Caroline at the centre. Georg was an art enthusiast, collector, and man of the world. However, he neither shared his

Figure 2.2 Portrait of Johann Georg von Holzhausen by Georg Karl Urlaub. Städel Museum, Frankfurt am Main.

wife's intellectual interests nor her passion for progressive education, especially Pestalozzi's reform ideas. Due to his social position and wealth, Georg often appeared self-confident and distant and didn't always show much empathy towards his children.

Biographers have claimed that the marriage wasn't affectionate anymore when Froebel came into their lives. This is, if at all, only partially true. The couple's relationship was based on genuine affection. Caroline had fallen in love with her charismatic cousin and loved him throughout her life, even if disagreements and tensions existed and the relationship may not always have matched her ideal of marriage.[31] In her *Gedankenbuch*,[32] one can find reflections on what it means to be a wife and to love a husband, on friendship and marriage, and the remarks show her struggles with it. However, these were thoughts and reflections indicating her intention to make the marriage work. For Caroline, a profoundly religious person, fidelity was a given of a pietistic life. Furthermore, her aristocratic ancestry obliged her to live according to the moral norms of her class and act as a role model. While she had high hopes for Froebel as her children's tutor and felt a spiritual connection with him, that doesn't mean their relationship ever went beyond what was acceptable.

Both parents were deeply interested in their children's education. Even though it was mainly Caroline's responsibility, she didn't have free rein. In a family such as the von Holzhausens, a mother couldn't make important decisions – like who would become the children's private tutor – without her husband's approval. If Georg had objected, Froebel would never have been offered the position. Both Caroline and Georg instead carefully considered the decision. In the end, Georg trusted his wife, even if he hadn't much sympathy for the awkward enthusiast of Pestalozzi's reform ideas.

At the time, a position as a private tutor constituted a typical stage in the career of a young intellectual. Indeed, Lenz, Kant, Hegel, Fichte, and Schelling all held such positions. For it granted highly educated young men an opportunity to earn a living, often while also continuing to further their own education.

Surprisingly, Froebel was hesitant. While the salary of 500 florins was by all means decent, Froebel knew how burdensome such a position would be. The patricians of Frankfurt were particularly supercilious, and while working for and living with such a family would grant him access to critical social circles, it would also mean greater dependence. Moreover, as a lowly tutor in an aristocratic family, he wasn't allowed to use corporal punishment, meaning he would have to rely on other forms of pedagogical influence. This is in fact exactly what Froebel would do later.

However, the main reason for Froebel's hesitation was that he wanted to be more than a mere tutor. As a self-proclaimed 'educator of humankind', he wanted autonomy. Froebel discussed the offer with Gruner, who told Froebel that the role would keep him from his personal development: 'You will lose everything, you are searching for and expecting.'[33]

The negotiations dragged on, as Froebel wanted written assurance that he wouldn't have to live in the city house, preferring *Auf der Öde*, the family's small moated castle estate near Eschenbach. Froebel insisted he would only accept the offer if the family agreed to this.[34]

It's surprising to read of Froebel's bold demands today. They speak for his courage and clear vision of his role as the family's private tutor. Neither salary nor prestige was crucial; otherwise, he would have accepted the gracious offer immediately. However, it is even more surprising that Caroline convinced her husband to grant the demands. Thus, Froebel, the 24-year-old 'destitute and unqualified-uneducated natural talent',[35] still more a youthful hothead than a stable personality, became the tutor of the children of one of Frankfurt's most influential patrician families on 24 June 1806.

Again, someone such as the immature Froebel was an unusual choice. Other private tutors such as Hölderlin and Hegel were mature personalities with university degrees. Others such as Kant, Schwarz, and Campe had studied at least while working as private tutors. Froebel, however, was an uneducated nobody. He was neither a typical intellectual, nor did he have a university education. One can only speculate why Georg agreed to hire the awkward, eccentric, and stubborn Froebel who lacked the social skills of the world the family lived in. It speaks for the family, especially Georg, that they ignored Froebel's eccentricity. Instead, they recognized his efforts to build genuine relationships with their children, an unusual educational approach at the time.

Froebel and the three eldest children immediately moved to *Auf der Öde*; the youngest daughter Sophie joined them later. When not in the city, the parents lived in a different house separated by a garden. It had been one of Froebel's demands: 'The being of my boys and the circumstances of their parents make it necessary that I live with them separately from their parents.'[36] Therefore, the children did not see their parents daily, especially their father, which was another of Froebel's demands. Froebel despised the aristocratic lifestyle and accused it of being responsible for the children's character flaws: 'I hate the aristocrats' being (*Sein*) and life as much as evil itself and the father's pedagogical principles are not mine, or actually because the father doesn't even know what it means: to be a father.'[37]

Thus, it's no wonder that the relationship with the parents was complicated from the start. Froebel disliked the father but respected Caroline as 'a pattern of high dignified femininity',[38] even if he felt she was too weak to stand up against her husband in supporting the children. Though Froebel rarely saw Georg, he saw Caroline almost daily, and the two bonded quickly. The two shared similar spiritual interests, especially the educational reforms inspired by Pestalozzi. Froebel, who had experienced a lot of loneliness throughout his life, furthermore savoured Caroline's affection, and he soon grew to adore Caroline as a woman and a mother. After a while, the inexperienced and eccentric young man, who had never been in a relationship and lacked any sexual experience, might have been in love with her. Caroline, though, didn't reciprocate Froebel's feelings in the same way. She was a steadfast woman, self-aware and self-secure in her role in one of the city's most esteemed families. She was probably flattered by the adoration of the awkward and insecure Froebel, maybe even a bit flirtatious. Still, it's unlikely that she had romantic feelings. Her affection towards Froebel instead shows her warmth and empathy.

However, what mattered was the boys' education. The task was challenging and demanded a lot from Froebel, emotionally and pedagogically. The three boys differed in their dispositions, abilities, intellectual capacities, and specific needs. Twelve-year-old Carl caused Froebel the most trouble. He was often hostile towards his private tutor and generally behaved like a little lord: he has, in Froebel's words, 'already all the properties of the noble fine world', and they are 'growing like stinging nettles in the desolate, undeveloped place'.[39] Nine-year-old Fritz was a good-natured, affectionate boy without any unique talents. Froebel was most enthusiastic about the seven-year-old Adolph, though, who 'inhabits an unspoiled mind, pure heart and assertive mind'.[40]

Not only did the children benefit from their new tutor. Living with the children was an essential experience for Froebel as it enabled him to grow both as an educator and as a person. It allowed him to implement his pedagogy, reflect on it, and make modifications accordingly. For example, he countered Carl's perceived character flaws and 'inhumanity' by showing supportive attention, praising him, and using severity when appropriate. Froebel valued relationships – again unusual for the time and the opposite of his experience. Being around the boys constantly also enabled him to practise the art of observation, a skill that Froebel mastered carefully for the rest of his life. The precise pictures of the children he sketched during this time[41] – in which he described the children's life circumstances, their and his own struggles, and their learning progress – show his commitment. Based on those precise observations, Froebel reflected on the being of humans and education. His letters show that he deeply cared about all three children.

To succeed in the demanding task of educating the children, Froebel sought to get closer to them: 'I am still a teacher but not just a teacher; I am far more than this, I am an educator and foster father of three boys'.[42] For a while, he saw himself as their surrogate father, an attitude that certainly complicated the relationship with the children's parents. However, Froebel quickly gave up on this idea when he realized that replacing their father would be pointless.

However, his teaching methods were unusual for the time and are an early example of Froebel's innovative and child-centred educational thinking. Instead of lectures, drills, and memorization, he took the children on hikes, focused on gardening and physical exercise, and paper-, cardboard-, and wood-working. He wanted to accustom the children to natural occupations, to learn and understand through experience. Froebel also had a different understanding of their relationship; he didn't see himself as a rigid tutor, but more as a well-meaning partner. He was empathetic and interested in their lives and needs. While this might be considered normal today, it certainly wasn't in around 1800. Already as a tutor, Froebel was ahead of his time. And his efforts were successful. He forged a close bond with the children, and even Carl slowly started to trust him. This irritated their father, who felt that his children were not learning anything and constantly criticized Froebel's pedagogical efforts.

Froebel, for his part, didn't hide his opinions either. After a few months, he began with what became a lifelong attitude: sharing educational reflections in correspondence. Apart from the letters to Christoph, the letters to Georg von Holzhausen stand out. In a lengthy letter written at the end of 1806, Froebel candidly describes the children's character flaws. It's more of a report than a letter, open and blunt, showing that Froebel wasn't even willing to mince his words when it came to his powerful employer. That Froebel dared to write this letter is astonishing. Froebel deliberately waited a few months because he neither wanted to say anything untrue nor unnecessarily hurt the family's feelings. Now, however, he didn't hold back, mentioning the 'unfriendly, unbrotherly being of the boys'[43] or Carl's 'lovelessness and carelessness towards his parents'[44] and his 'extremely unbrotherly and loveless behaviour towards his brothers'.[45] Fritz, in contrast, is 'much weaker in body and mind than Carl'.[46] Froebel concludes that Fritz's main problem is his absentmindedness due to 'his eternal preoccupation with vulgar stuff and his constant chattering of meaningless and thoughtless words'[47] as well as his 'quick-tempered heat'.[48] He even criticized Adolph because of his 'irrepressible irascibility and vehemence' and his quarrelsome, unbrotherly, brutal behaviour when confronted with discipline.

Throughout his life, Froebel kept such blunt honesty. When convinced of anything, he stuck to it and defended his 'truth' no matter the consequences. While it helped him develop and spread his educational ideas, especially the kindergarten movement, it did also cost him friendships and support.

Today, one can only wonder why Georg von Holzhausen allowed such openness. Whatever he thought of the peculiar Froebel, he must have respected his work; otherwise, he would have thrown him out. While Georg continued to mock Froebel openly, he must have valued his eagerness and honesty. It's telling the father allowed Froebel to speak frankly, which meant criticism of his children, his family, and, implicitly, the parents.

Thus, it seems unfair that Froebel and biographers have portrayed Georg so negatively.[49] One example is Liebschner, who calls Georg a 'rather insensitive and overbearing man'.[50] Such a judgement doesn't seem justified, for Georg not only ignored many of Froebel's peculiarities but also often acted generously.

Who Am I? Froebel's Self-discovery

While the boys' education was time-consuming, Froebel still had sufficient time for his own studies and self-development. In this sense, the years in Frankfurt, and later in Yverdon, were equally important. They helped Froebel develop as a person and an educational thinker.

The most important influence was Caroline, who familiarized Froebel with contemporary literature and philosophy. As an autodidact, Froebel depended on such external stimulations. Their dialogues enabled him to educate himself and develop his independent pedagogical thinking. Not only did she serve as a role model for women and motherhood, Caroline further showed the insecure Froebel what it meant to live an educated and cultured life. Due to Caroline's warm personality, he opened up and became more confident.

While the conversations with Caroline were essential, Froebel also educated himself through an astonishing variety of (educational) literature. Among his readings were Goethe, Schelling, Herodot, Kant, Herder and Fichte, Jean Paul, Sailer, Salzmann, Herbart, Schwarz, and Sailman. Froebel also continued to be fascinated by mathematical and scientific content.[51]

Today, it is difficult to say how intensive Froebel's studies were and if they broadened his horizons. Speaking to others and getting inspiration from selected readings was always more important for Froebel than studying seriously. He also searched for reassurance – ideas he could easily assimilate into his thinking without changing them. While in Frankfurt, he was probably more open to new ideas compared to later years. Still, he lacked the prerequisites and stamina for a thorough reading. Thus, he paid a young man to prepare excerpts three times per week so he didn't have to study the entire texts – a very costly undertaking.[52] Also, building an extensive collection, even if he lacked the money, was more important than studying the works. That he possessed Kant's writings doesn't mean he read them. Even the well-meaning biographer Halfter calls Froebel a 'naïve philosophical onlooker'.[53] His later writings show no evidence that he studied contemporary philosophy in any depth.

This doesn't mean Froebel didn't want to develop and further himself as a person, though. For example, he studied French, English, Latin, and Greek, though unfortunately without any success. Then there was mathematics, the field he wanted to study comprehensively as he felt it would be essential to understand humanity and the world. Lastly, he wanted to write an 'encyclopaedical table of all teaching' – another project that never came about. There was always something new, always the next idea, always something to explore. Still, Froebel lacked the stamina to work on any topic systematically. This is a trait that would accompany him for the rest of his life. Throughout his life, Froebel was immoderate in his overzealousness.

The enduring question, however, was: what should he do with his life, and who did he want to be? Froebel increasingly saw himself as an educator, not only of children but also of humankind. What that meant, though, was less clear.

While thinking – or, better put, dreaming – about the future, Froebel came up with the idea of a (German) educational institute for the first time. In a long autobiographical letter to Christoph in March/April 1807, Froebel not only reflected on the past 1½ years with the von Holzhausen children and education in general but also outlined a concrete plan for his future.[54] In retrospect, it all sounds rather bold and ambitious. The goal was to stay in his current position until September 1807, then study for one year in Heidelberg or Göttingen, live with Pestalozzi for one year in Yverdon, and then become responsible for an independent private or public educational institution.

To make it happen, he sought a partner and found one in his half-brother Carl Poppo. Unlike Froebel, Carl Poppo was well educated. Christoph had taught him Latin and Greek; from 1805 on, Carl Poppo studied theology in Jena. A collaboration only seemed natural to Froebel: 'Carl and I would united summarize that in us, what is needed to the education of my purpose and the implementation of my plan; we would both be united form a whole, that what one misses, the other would replace, so with united strength we would marvellously gain our goal.'[55]

His idea, the first of many notions, never came about, though. Just one month later, Froebel told Christoph that he would continue as a private tutor.[56] There were probably different reasons for his change of mind. One was that Carl Poppo had lost interest in the undertaking. Instead, the only 21-year-old Carl Poppo married Johanne Sophie Dorothea Scheibe, the daughter of the wealthy princely court manager Johann Heinrich Rudolph Scheibe in Rudolstadt. Thus, he was set for life. After receiving his doctorate in secular wisdom in 1807, he started as a teacher at a grammar school in Rudolstadt.

Froebel's reaction foreshadows another of his later character traits: his vindictive cold-heartedness towards anyone who, at least in his mind, had betrayed him and the greater cause. The brother might be rich now, Froebel wrote to Christoph, but he would never be a good husband and father and his life would be wasted. Froebel blamed his stepmother:

> Certainly, something good could have turned out of Carl, if he had had more confidence in himself and without presumptuousness, if he would have followed me, now he's lost forever for something better, it's a pity for him, and he elicits sympathy from me as he will now hardly swing aloft to a higher worldview. I think I wanted to hear the news of his death rather than his marriage.[57]

Froebel's harsh words became true. Carl Poppo died in Rudolstadt on 15 March 1824. He and Sophie, who also died young, had five children.

In the months that followed, Froebel regularly considered leaving the von Holzhausens, a thought that he first voiced in September 1806.[58] Despite all his doubts, Froebel stayed. He probably felt responsible for the children, and especially Caroline, who valued his efforts and wanted him to continue despite his pedagogical struggles. Froebel, however, dreamed of living with the boys in Yverdon. Caroline was supportive of the idea and tried to convince Georg, initially without success. In April 1807, Froebel announced that he would leave, only to quickly change his mind again.

Many biographers have assumed that Froebel stayed because he learned of Caroline's pregnancy. The assumption is mainly based on a letter to the women in Keilhau in which Froebel stated that he realized her pregnancy in the summer of 1807:

> The impression of this remark had a striking, I would like to say magical effect on me; for this woman, although previously highly valued by me as a wife and mother and friend of mine, now appeared before me as a newly expecting mother in a completely transfigured form; she became a higher, more spiritual, noble being for me; I suddenly looked at her with completely different eyes.[59]

However, Froebel's memory is mistaken. Caroline Silvia Louise von Holzhausen was already born on 17 January 1807.[60] That also makes it unlikely, not to say impossible, that he was her biological father – another insinuation sometimes made[61] mainly based on a few entries in his 'diary' (*Tagebuchblätter*). There, he wrote on 31 July 1811: 'Farewell to you, beloved soul, spouse who is given to me by god and eternity and for all eternity … give the child a kiss and the blessing of the parting father … hand me your lips and your forehead in parting.'[62] Apart from this entry, there isn't anything that speaks of his paternity. When Caroline became pregnant, Froebel wasn't working as the boys' private tutor. Froebel probably felt spiritual paternity for Caroline, and his words in 1811 were his way of expressing his feelings.

Nevertheless, why did he make up the story in the letter to the women in Keilhau? It probably served his narrative, but it is also likely that he was simply mistaken. Froebel's memory was often unreliable. One of his favourite stories, Caroline's second birthday, is another example. The event, 'my highest idea and my purest thought of family life',[63] had a profound impression on him that he described enthusiastically twenty-three years later as a 49-year-old man. According to his memory, he and the boys had created a little patch with a lily next to a watering pond in the centre of the dining room.

> Green, blooming and fragrant houseplants formed on large tables in the corner of a room, their pots artificially covered a garden in the middle of which a free green space, and in the same a rounded, raised bed in which a many-budded lily stood a tub filled with good earth overturned and a watering can in the position of sprinkling, watering, a ray of sunshine fell from a cloud onto the lily from heaven, and in this clouds emerged, as it were, through the refraction of sunlight, the words: God's garden.[64]

If this did in fact happen, Georg must have watched the scene shaking his head.

Again, Froebel's memory is mistaken. Caroline's second birthday was in January 1809, when Froebel and the boys were living in Yverdon. If at all, he might have remembered her first birthday, though this was in the winter and not in the summer. Therefore, Froebel might have imagined the event as it fitted nicely in his later reasoning. The lily – the symbol of purity and motherhood – was one of Froebel's favourite symbols, and the fact that he and the children had lived it only made the story better. Froebel later used the described scenery as the head vignette for his weekly journal *Die Erziehenden Familien* (*The Educating Families*) and the cover of *The Education of Man*.[65] Whether it actually happened is another story.

Living with the Master: Yverdon

While it's unlikely that Caroline's pregnancy changed Froebel's mind, she probably did ask him in the summer of 1807 to stay.[66] Furthermore, Froebel probably realized that the breach of contract and trust would suggest the opposite of the moral person he wanted to be.[67] Finally, there were financial reasons. Froebel was once again in debt, and it made sense to stay and act pragmatically. At least, that was his explanation to Christoph.[68]

The boys' education remained challenging, especially Carl's, whose development Froebel called 'pathetic'. It was, of course, not his fault: 'Under these circumstances, how should I be able to affect a boy who was so depraved when I received him at the age of eleven that he hid his depravity so deeply in himself, that it was impossible for me to take action against it.'[69] Instead, he blamed the boys' father. 'However, how should it work – the boy has no father, only a person in the form of a man who calls himself father is standing there, and according to the authority that this word gives – secretly without me knowing and suspecting it, is destroying everything I build.'[70] Caroline was never blamed for the boys' flaws, however.[71]

In the spring of 1808, Froebel desperately wanted to leave for Yverdon. Not only for the children's sake – even if he saw it as essential to take them away from their father's influence – but also because *he* wanted to learn from the master. Caroline was supportive, but Georg was still reluctant. Only when his brother Friedrich, who had revisited Pestalozzi's institute in 1807, came to visit did he change his mind. In his personal notes, Georg outlined his plan for his children's future.[72] Froebel should go to Yverdon in September 1808, where Carl would stay until the end of his eighteenth year and then study cameralistics. After accompanying Carl to university, Froebel was supposed to return to Yverdon until Adolph were old enough to study law. For his part, Fritz would leave Yverdon at the age of fifteen to learn at a forestry.

We don't know whether Froebel was consulted about these plans. It's unlikely, but it also didn't matter. Froebel was delighted when he heard the news.[73] In July 1808, he cheerfully wrote to Christoph that they would all move to Yverdon to live there until Carl began his studies. To support Carl, Georg demanded that Froebel study Latin. This made Froebel even happier for he had always wanted to learn Latin. Very generously, the family had agreed to continue to pay his salary, even if Froebel wouldn't be responsible for the children's teaching and wasn't needed in Yverdon. Such arrangements weren't uncommon; children of affluent and aristocratic families sometimes brought their educators with them. Nevertheless, Froebel was excited when he learned of the decision. On 10 July 1808, he wrote to Pestalozzi: 'Mr. Holzhausen has decided to let me live in your institute with his three sons – if you allow us – and to let me work for them, supported by your fatherly advice and blessing, instruction.'[74]

On 27 September 1808, the von Holzhausen family left for Yverdon. Caroline and Georg stayed only briefly to see where their children would live, then left Froebel alone with the three boys.

The plan had been to stay in the boarding house run by von Türk. However, Froebel and von Türk didn't get along. Surprisingly, Georg supported Froebel, calling him a 'brave man',[75] but soon Froebel and the boys moved into Landry's private house close to the castle. They slept here, but took their meals in the castle's dining room at the table of the mathematics teacher Joseph Schmid. Frobel had no teaching obligations beside teaching the children during their free time. Pestalozzi had offered him the opportunity to teach geography; however, Froebel had declined, leaving him free to observe and learn from the master.

In 1809, Yverdon was in its heyday, even if the place had been an odd choice as Pestalozzi neither spoke French well nor had any affinity for French culture. Hence, the German-speaking institute was a kind of enclave in the canton of Waft. The castle was rather gloomy, but the surroundings – the grassy landscape and the open spaces – were welcoming. Since Fichte had mentioned Pestalozzi in his *Addresses to the German Nation*, Pestalozzi had become extremely popular; Pestalozzi stood for progressive education, and Yverdon was a pilgrimage site. Around 165 students aged six to sixteen attended the institute at this time. They were taught by thirty-one teachers, among them Niederer, Schmid, Nägli, and Krüsi – the core group that shaped the institute and influenced Pestalozzi. There were many student teachers; for example, Prussia had sent trainee teachers, and Therese von Brunswick – to whom Froebel would write one of his most important letters in 1842 – was also visiting in autumn 1808. It is possible that the two met. Therefore, Froebel's visit wasn't unique, and Pestalozzi didn't make any fuss about Froebel; indeed, Froebel isn't even mentioned in the volumes of Pestalozzi's work.[76]

Life in Yverdon was hard and strict. The von Holzhausen boys were kept busy, but they found it easy to follow the lessons, which pleased Froebel. Only in geography were they behind. The day began at 6 a.m. and ended at 8 p.m.; the children received up to ten hours of lessons each day and often got no more than five hours of sleep. The classes were modern, including group work. Outdoor activities and physical exercises were an important part of the daily routine. Neither the students nor the teachers had much time for themselves, and there wasn't much space for individualism.

Froebel used his ample free time to observe lessons, study Pestalozzi's method carefully, and learn from Pestalozzi. He sought to understand the elementary method that had made Pestalozzi famous. While Pestalozzi's belief in something

Figure 2.3 Pestalozzi from the time in Yverdon, by Francisco Javier Ramos (1746–1817).

like a universal method wasn't unusual for the time, what was unique was his firm conviction that he had discovered the basic elements that underlie the universal order of objects in the whole world, which is simultaneously composed of such elements. Thus, number, form, and word formed the central didactical triad of Pestalozzi's pedagogical approach. Pestalozzi believed that children learn content from the world that surrounds them best when the world is presented in a structured way. Activities such as counting, recognizing shapes, and naming objects were seen as central learning means in Pestalozzi's method, with which children can perceive, remember, and order impressions from their environment with all their senses.[77] Therefore, competent sound, word, and language teaching; number teaching using addition, subtraction, multiplication, long division, and fractions; and form teaching by means of writing, measuring, and drawing formed the main learning activities.

Many of Pestalozzi's ideas, such as the copy-what-I-say style of teaching, seem strange and outdated today. However, they must be viewed in their historical context: Pestalozzi's method was unique and innovative, and he developed a psychology-backed approach to the step-by-step teaching of content. Pestalozzi's ideas can be seen as the birth hour of the educational question of what 'elements' are *fundamental* for children's successful learning.

Froebel was initially enthralled by the method. 'What is generally known about Pestalozzi's teaching method, let alone Pestalozzi's educational method, is nothing, is a shadow against what is now being presented in Yverdon, how far one has now come in the perception and presentation of the idea.'[78] Being close to Pestalozzi and talking to his wife fascinated Froebel. 'Pestalozzi is my advisor and friend and our loving father.'[79] The time with Pestalozzi, whom Froebel would call 'his spiritual father'[80] for the rest of his life, and observing his teaching had a tremendous influence on Froebel's educational thinking.[81] He drew much inspiration from Pestalozzi and adopted the basic principles from Pestalozzi's educational concepts for his own.

Like many other visitors, Froebel wanted to spread Pestalozzi's ideas to his home country. However, it was difficult to explain the advantages of the new method clearly; therefore, Pestalozzi's method wasn't met with enthusiasm. Froebel wrote to Christoph – who was an influential figure in the educational system in Griesheim as pastor – to convince him to send teachers to Yverdon so they could later implement the elementary method throughout the country. 'God, what luck it would be for Stadt-Ilm's school and for the whole city, if Pestalozzi's pupils would teach there.'[82] And a few months later: 'Brother, dear brother, please do what you can to spread the Pestalozzian method.'[83]

Froebel's plans, though, aimed higher. Between 1 and 21 April 1809, Froebel compiled the basic characteristics of Pestalozzi's method in a lengthy essay-like letter that he sent to Schwarzburg-Rudolstadt's Princess-Regent, Countess Karoline-Luise. The hope was to convince the countess to 'improve the education of children and school lessons'[84] by implementing Pestalozzi's method in the principality's schools. The detailed and profound description of Pestalozzi's principles shows that Froebel had practically acquired the corresponding pedagogical knowledge through observing Pestalozzi and studying his texts to educate himself. His pedagogical knowledge was catching up with his enthusiasm, and the letter can be seen as Froebel's first in-depth reflection on education.

Froebel's argumentation contained much praise. However, one can also find the first critical tones:

> Pestalozzi's basic principles of child-raising and education do not incorporate the absolute nature of humans, and his method does not set up human nature as its most important principle. Pestalozzi sees the person exactly as he is, and under the conditions, terms and relationships through and in which he exists; but he therefore places more importance on those principles dealing with practical worth.[85]

Although the letter was well received by the countess, it didn't lead to anything. She charged a commission, composed mainly of clergymen, with examining the proposal, but it took them more than two years to reach a decision. By then, Froebel's life and attitude towards Pestalozzi had changed significantly.

Going his own way: Froebel's emancipation from Pestalozzi

In the months that followed, Froebel became increasingly critical of Pestalozzi's method. While he still agreed with the fundamental aspects of Pestalozzi's idea,[86] Froebel slowly developed his own educational ideas. In this sense, Yverdon was essential for Froebel's development. A main area of disagreement was the universal application of the method. While Froebel felt Pestalozzi's method was appropriate for children of school age, he considered it unsuitable for younger children as they would need a different, more vivid, childlike, more natural schooling, something he called 'first schooling'. He also believed the method shouldn't determine a child's development, but rather the method should be adapted to a child's development. Furthermore, he found Pestalozzi's educational practice too 'mechanical' and artificial. Lastly, Froebel began to realize the educational importance of play, not by copying Pestalozzi's ideas but by contrasting and increasingly turning away from them.

Soon, Froebel began to express his criticism: 'Pestalozzi's teaching method is true', he wrote to Caroline, 'I can't say more about it, but it could have turned into the greatest untruth, the ugliest nonsense if you had applied it to the earliest age in the way Pestalozzi gave it to us.'[87] Contrary to Pestalozzi, Froebel valued observations, especially of the children's outdoor games:

> In these games, and what each one involved in terms of messages and balances, I must recognize the biggest main aspect as being that of moral life, possessing moral strength. The games I remember as providing me with a wonderful, mildly strong spiritual bath. Although I did not understand the symbolic sense behind the games, I still felt in every playing boy a proper spirit and bodily strength, which I was very thankful for.[88]

Froebel made careful interpretations based on these observations.

Despite all the criticism, Froebel valued Pestalozzi's pedagogy throughout his life. Pestalozzi remained his spiritual father, and Froebel always saw himself as a pedagogue in the spirit of Pestalozzi:

> It could very well be, and I must be sincerely grateful for this, that Pestalozzi's general view of mankind … has contributed to the betterment of my inner life through this inspiration. Already before and soon after my arrival in Switzerland, the thought filled my mind of the everlasting and continual development of the spirit of all persons, each spirit of whom is made by God and is fully mature.[89]

Nevertheless, Yverdon was a time of emancipation and new ideas. As an independent educational thinker, Froebel began to awaken.

Froebel felt increasingly estranged from Yverdon. He was lonely: 'Since I left Frankfurt I have been standing all alone and without any information, because even if many people are here, everyone has their own, as it were, closed world.'[90] The letter to Christoph, written over two days, is a rare source of self-doubt. The first part, written on 21 May, is rather typical. It starts with a detailed explanation of how Christoph should share the attached books by Pestalozzi and Schmid to implement Pestalozzi's elementary method before lecturing about education. The high self-esteem Froebel demonstrated in those letters is perplexing to read today. The childless Froebel, who had never been in a relationship, wasn't shy of advising his much older, more experienced, and better-educated brother regarding child-rearing or family life. He was also very demanding, asking his brother and – through his brother – the estranged Traugott to act on his behalf. Froebel, so it seems, took such help for granted and as natural, as he was the one who had found universal truth.

Two days later, the tone changed completely. Now, Froebel spoke of his loneliness and how misunderstood he felt.[91] His only friend, so he wrote, is

Schmid, the young prodigy and teacher, which was a wishful dream as the wunderkind wasn't interested in Froebel. Unsatisfied with his life, he confessed:

> So, I sometimes live a high, often a sad, depressing life, and there is also the fact that the world has had a terrible effect on me since my earliest years and has covered me up. It is unbelievable what effort it takes to make negligence and mistakes in earlier education harmless later, and after years of struggle and quarrel, if you let yourself go for a moment, you can sink into yourself that you are frightened for yourself.[92]

He was bearing his 'rotten, struggling life' only for others, and despite his 'deepest inner depravity', he had been able to maintain self-respect and the respect of others. Nevertheless, 'I am rotten'.[93]

Froebel was rarely so self-critical. Afterward, he stayed quiet for almost two months, struggling with his self-doubts and the quarrels within the institute in which he increasingly became involved.

He distanced himself from Pestalozzi, probably for different reasons. Now convinced of the importance of his thoughts on education, Froebel no longer felt valued at the institute, as important figures such as Niederer and Schmid, not to mention Pestalozzi himself, didn't take him seriously. At the same time, the institute suffered a significant crisis, with especially the quarrels between Niederer and Schmid proving damaging. Niederer, a systematist, was a profound thinker well trained in philosophy and adept in German Idealism. Just three years older than Froebel, he was one of Pestalozzi's closest colleagues and indispensable. While eager to spread the elementary method, Niederer wasn't always so skilled in explaining its essence. In contrast, Joseph Schmid had come to Burgdorf in 1803 as a poor fourteen-year-old boy of a farmer. He possessed extraordinary mathematical abilities, something that most teachers (including Pestalozzi) lacked. Schmid had become an assistant teacher after just a few months and was now one of the institute's driving forces. Though he had many admirers, Schmid was ambitious and often cold and knew how to take advantage of people's admiration. Niederer and Schmid were different in character and had different opinions about the method. To make matters worse, they were in love with the same woman, one of the female teachers, who ultimately became Niederer's partner.[94]

The quarrels erupted after an external evaluation in the fall of 1809. Pestalozzi had asked the state authorities to assess Yverdon in the hope of a favourable outcome. While Niederer had pushed for the evaluation, Schmid had opposed, feeling that the institute wasn't ready. The outcome was disappointing. Only

Schmid was praised, and disputes became the order of the day, especially between Schmid and Niederer. The aging Pestalozzi simply stood by helplessly.

Froebel, who disliked Niederer and had criticized his religion lessons in the past, supported the twenty-year-old Schmid who fascinated him: 'I don't know anyone of my age who would be dearer to me than him … . Should Schmidt [sic] one day feel the need to have a friend and would he choose me. Now he stands (it seems to me) alone as I stand alone.'[95] Besides feeling close to him personally, Froebel also admired Schmid's mathematical abilities.[96] Indeed, years later he still had a copy of Schmid's *Die Elemente der Form und Grösse* (*The Elements of Form and Size*) and referred to it in *The Education of Man*.

Pestalozzi supported Niederer, however. The disputes intensified over the weeks that followed, and Froebel felt it was his duty to point out the institute's weaknesses. Again, he criticized Niederer's religious lessons heavily. While Pestalozzi agreed with some of Froebel's criticism, he felt Froebel had gone too far. However, Froebel wasn't willing to compromise, even if Pestalozzi asked him to do so. Instead, Froebel intensified his sharp criticism of Niederer. He probably focused on Niederer as he didn't want to criticize Pestalozzi personally.

The quarrels ended when Schmid left in July 1810, and other teachers such as Raumer, Muralt, and Mieg followed him.[97] Seeing the institute falling apart rankled Froebel, who still believed in Pestalozzi. Still, he kept silent to the von Holzhausens and Christoph, whom he didn't write to for ten months. Instead, he became increasingly estranged from Pestalozzi. 'I now withdrew completely and lived with no one on a mutual friendship except Schmidt [sic!].'[98] Schmid was the only one he still admired: 'O! Schmid. You should know the 22-year-old Schmid', he wrote to Christoph after his return to Frankfurt. 'This is an excellent man, I am glad we are friends through equal pursuits, and we will both work together forever for one goal.'[99]

On 1 May 1810, Froebel informed the parents that it was time to leave. Froebel knew the disputes would become public in Frankfurt; thus, he included careful criticism of the institute, emphasizing that it wouldn't be beneficial for the two younger boys to stay. In addition, he offered his thoughtful plan for the three boys' future education, which again shows how seriously Froebel took his responsibility.[100] Most importantly, however, he suggested that he, as the private tutor, be replaced by a 'more knowledgeable man'.[101]

Meanwhile, the dispute reached its climax. Froebel felt it was necessary to explain to the parents what was happening, 'circumstances, proportions and influences … in which I have been living and working here for a few months'.[102] Pestalozzi was allegedly outraged when he learned of Froebel's plan to leave, accusing Froebel of withdrawing the children from him and acting unworthy. 'Pestalozzi says that – because I believe in having acted according to my highest and best conviction by suggesting to you to let your sons' further education be terminated from the parental home – that I have thereby returned your sons to unnaturalness.'[103] Niederer had allegedly called him 'a wicked, dishonest person' and 'that if he had been in Pestalozzi's place, he would have thrown me down the stairs six weeks ago'.[104]

A compromise was now impossible. 'It got fierce again and so we parted.'[105] Froebel finally had enough:

> I have Mr. Pestalozzi! thought over the whole thing with me: and it is impossible in the future for me to act differently than I have before. I am a free man and I ask you, Mr. Pestalozzi! as such to let me act according to my conviction. If I deserve it, I will therefore receive the most just punishment, I will not seek an opportunity to evade it, I also won't try to make its impact on me less tangible. I do not demand wages for my actions to acquire, but just the conviction: not to have acted against my dignity. By the way, I would like to say that I will soon be leaving from here.[106]

Today, it's impossible to say what actually happened. We only know about the quarrel from Froebel's letters to Georg; Pestalozzi never mentioned it. However, Froebel's letters only portray his opinion and were written to deny the allegations to avoid damage to his reputation. The correspondence shows a steadfast Froebel who defended his behaviour as justified. He would continue to tell the truth, Froebel claimed in pathetic words, even if it meant to 'die a moral and civil death'.[107]

The parents' reaction was unexpected. Caroline criticized Froebel heavily for his behaviour towards Pestalozzi:

> I received your letter of 29 May yesterday. I sincerely confess that, after having acted with the greatest sincerity under your eyes for so long for five years, that at this point in time, and under the circumstances under which and how I am now acting as the educator of your sons, that under consideration of all this, I would have expected such a letter from you.[108]

Caroline's words hurt. Froebel tried to defend himself by pointing out his indulgence towards Pestalozzi, who had 'complained against me with the greatest injustice'.[109] Georg, for his part, supported his private tutor. He might have been satisfied that the Pestalozzian reform nonsense had failed, as he had said from the beginning.

The fierce disputes changed Froebel's mind about the elementary method. In mid-June of 1810, Froebel followed up with a letter to Princess-Regent Karoline-Luise to correct the previously highly recommended plan: 'With regard to some earlier presentations of ideas about the generalization of a school- and child-raising (method) improvement, allow me here to correct some of these principles.'[110] The letter from 1809, he stated, had been an 'earlier mistaken attempt to present the Pestalozzi method'.[111] Ironically, the jury panel's majority agreed with his changed opinion. Pestalozzi's elementary method wouldn't be implemented in schools in Schwarzburg-Rudolstadt. Froebel's dream had vanished into thin air.

Finally, Georg von Holzhausen demanded their return. The time in Yverdon had come to an end.

A Bitter Homecoming: Leaving the 'Rune of His Life'

Froebel and the children arrived back in Frankfurt on 22 August 1810. It wasn't a pleasant homecoming. The tension was tangible, and Froebel was at odds with himself. There wouldn't be a Pestalozzian school in Stadt-Ilm, and the countess hadn't offered him a position at the city school either. But Froebel had already told Georg that he didn't want to continue as the children's private tutor, the ongoing disputes had tired him, and he also didn't feel fully supported by Caroline anymore. Thus, what would come next?

Surprisingly, Froebel told Christoph that he would stay until Carl began his studies in September 1812. Apart from the moral obligations to Caroline, he had more pragmatic reasons: the 'many years of struggle with this large-headed hydra – monetary debt'.[112] At least Caroline, who also hoped the friendship would be renewed, was pleased.

Such hope, however, was deceptive. Life in Frankfurt had changed. They were now all living together in the city house, and the tension that had overshadowed the last months in Yverdon still hung in the air. While Georg showed more respect and allowed Froebel to attend social events, his relationship with Caroline was marred. The two, at least that was Froebel's perspective, were alienated, and something that Froebel couldn't put his finger on was missing. The 'old, previous life' was 'paralyzed'.[113]

Despite his earlier promise, Froebel resigned in March but stayed until the end of May 1811, then moved to Göttingen. The children were sad and their letters to him show their affection. Surprisingly, Froebel didn't share the news with

Christoph first, but rather with his sister Juliane. Juliane, who reminded many of her late mother, was critically ill. Froebel, the godfather of her fifth child Ernst, had never been close to her, but he was disturbed by her approaching death.

The move to Göttingen has often been described as a sudden flight, with Caroline as the reason.[114] Caroline had always been more than just a 'gracious lady' for Froebel; they had been friends and soulmates, spiritual-educational kindred spirits. Not only had he idolized her as the image of the lost mother, but he had admired her and, maybe, even loved her from early on.

After the return from Yverdon came a breach of friendship, however. One reason was that Froebel had changed. He was no longer the same malleable young man, and he was now confident, not to say convinced of knowing what was right for him and life in general. In discussions, Froebel now stuck to his opinions and didn't give in anymore, which led to tensions. He was furthermore deeply hurt when he learned that Caroline had given away a gift, a copper engraving based on the painting *Johannes* by Zampieri, to a young clergyman whom Froebel disliked. Froebel was furious. In his eyes, it was a betrayal of their friendship, even if Caroline immediately replaced it with a copy. 'And if you buy a hundred copies, it's not what I gave to you.'[115] Allegedly, he couldn't look at the replacement even twenty years later.[116] When Caroline reminded him that he was only her employee, he was insulted. 'My disappointment, when I, who felt inwardly equal to her husband, was treated as a subordinate, a servant',[117] Froebel wrote in his diary three years later. That he continued to act as the children's 'spiritual father' – an attitude that went too far for many in the family – probably didn't help either.

However, the real reason for his departure was probably that Froebel had fallen in love with Caroline. Today, it is impossible to say whether the relationship turned into love, even sexual relations, if Caroline was only his emotional-spiritual partner, or if love only existed in Froebel's imagination. We don't know how Caroline felt and experienced their relationship. The sources are incomplete, and today much is speculation.

Nevertheless, something must have happened in the early months of 1811, at least for Froebel, and it impacted him so profoundly that in 1831 he spoke of a '21-year struggle'[118] that had almost destroyed him. Thus, whatever happened, it must have occurred in around 1810/11 and not in 1806. Caroline, Froebel later noted, was the 'rune' and the most dangerous fight of his life, a battle that only fully ended after their last meeting in Frankfurt in May 1831.

We assume Froebel was in love with Caroline but that his feelings were unrequited.[119] Froebel's affection can be seen in letters and diary entries between

1811 and 1815. Froebel secretly sent six letters to Caroline via Susanne von Heyden, Caroline's friend. It is unknown whether Caroline had sent letters to Froebel in the same way.[120] It speaks of secret correspondence, especially because some letters differ in their tone. In official letters, Froebel formally addressed Caroline as 'My gracious lady'. In five of his letters,[121] however, he used the intimate 'you' in German.

Froebel's diary reveals even more intimate language. On 31 July 1811, he wrote, 'give the child a kiss and the blessing of the parting father ... hand me your lips and your forehead in parting',[122] and ended the year by writing: 'I close this year with holy pure memory of you G.—, of you Ariadne, of you family, and with undying thanks for your love, your loyalty. Goodbye! We shall surely see each other again!!!'[123] He frequently used words such as 'girlfriend', 'lover', 'spouse', and 'child' in the diary and spoke of himself as 'father'. C. and G. were used synonymously – C. referring to Caroline, and G. probably to *Geliebte* (lover) or *Gattin* (spouse).[124]

However, it doesn't necessarily mean what we think today. Froebel never admitted Caroline had been more than a soulmate. In the letter to the women in Keilhau, Froebel argued that the relationship had changed because their characters had drifted apart. 'I want people to develop and become; – she wants to make and build religion, and she wants to make and build religious, pious people, and I want religion to develop and become, as I want people to develop and become religiously.'[125] The understanding of religion, not an impossible love, had separated the two, according to his explanation. But it would have been impossible to admit a sexual relationship in this letter anyway.

Today, it is impossible to say whether the relationship ever became sexual. It seems unlikely, though. Extramarital sexual relationships were uncommon at the time, though they did, of course, exist. Caroline, who was seven years Froebel's senior and a mother, was aware of her dignity and in no position to jeopardize her reputation. On the contrary, precisely her status as one of Frankfurt's leading ladies made it possible for her to respond to the insecure, struggling, and probably often exuberant Froebel with warmth and empathy. The confidentiality she granted was impartial because she was superior to him as a mother and a lady.[126] Thus, it seems more likely that Froebel, who was, as far as we know, entirely inexperienced sexually, started to toy with the fantasy of a solely spiritual marriage. Caroline might have tolerated such imaginations in the beginning, but no more. Froebel, though, stuck to his fantasies until 1816. The rational calm with which Caroline reacted to the often impulsive letters is another sign of her superiority. If anything close to love existed, then probably only in Froebel's mind.

It has also been speculated that the youngest von Holzhausen child, Johann Hector, born on 18 March 1812, was Froebel's biological son. Both Halfter[127] and Liebschner allude to this. This is also unlikely, though, and no evidence exists to support this claim. It seems more likely that Froebel became aware of the couple's renewed intimacy and considered this a breach of his spiritual marriage.

Nevertheless, Caroline was the key experience of Froebel's time in Frankfurt, and maybe his life. The relationship and its reprocessing impacted his episteme, pedagogical thinking, and thoughts on women and their essential role in educating young children. In and through Caroline, Froebel became aware of the importance of women and their unique abilities to support children and human beings in general. Caroline von Holzhausen was and remained the symbol of all women, of motherhood.[128] The loss of his mother and the fact that he had been raised without a mother figure probably complicated everything.

It took Froebel years to make sense of the relationship. 'Terrible, tremendous are the waves of raging and arguing in the human breast', he wrote to Christoph at the end of May 1811. 'How my inner could withstand the storms that filled it for months, I don't understand.'[129] Later that summer, in the same entry in which he spoke of giving his child a kiss, he formulated a death wish:

> Come death, if you will; I seek to pave my way, my bridge is built, and in spirit I see the far off hereafter, where it rests secure … . What more can I say to you, beloved soul, spouse, given to me by God from eternity and for all eternity. Rejoice, as I do; see my face serene, my eye bright, I go ahead to prepare the dwelling for you, to seek our joy, and in triumph to receive you when you come.[130]

Whatever happened in the spring of 1811, Caroline was undoubtedly the 'rune' of Froebel's life.

3

From Studies to War Then Back to Education

Over the next five years, Froebel was mainly occupied with finalizing his self-education, developing his episteme, and finding his place in the (professional) world. Interestingly, at least on the surface, the focus wasn't on education, even if Froebel never lost track of his vision of being an 'educator of humankind'. Instead, he wanted to learn as much as possible about humanity, humans, and the natural sciences –necessary prerequisites, in his eyes, for becoming the educator he envisioned. And in this sense, the time in Göttingen and Berlin was indeed a success.

Froebel enrolled at the University of Göttingen on 23 June 1811. On his way there, he visited Christian and his family in Osterode. Osterode wasn't far from Göttingen, and such visits became frequent; Froebel and his older brother grew closer.

Froebel had come to Göttingen to study and acquire the perceived lacking knowledge. To avoid distraction, he mainly stayed on his own. As far as we know, he didn't have any close friends in Göttingen. It was a big change compared to having been an intimate part of the von Holzhausen family for almost five years, and Froebel felt depressed. However, the solitude was necessary to cope with the last months: the quarrels in Yverdon, the separation from the boys, and, most importantly, the relationship with Caroline.

Göttingen's university was well established. The classical and linguistic studies as well as medicine, mathematics, and natural sciences had a good reputation, and students who wanted to study seriously could use the comprehensive library. Surprisingly, Froebel didn't enroll in philosophy or theology, the subjects in which educational issues were normally discussed at this time. Instead, he began with linguistic studies and natural sciences to merge both subjects into a higher unity that, so he thought, would help him understand humanity. However, Froebel was once more overwhelmed by the university environment, especially the tremendous diversity within his chosen subject. Since he still lacked the basic academic knowledge and skills, the workload was too much. Froebel began to study Hebrew, Arabic, Indian, Persian, Greek, and Latin, all initially with enthusiasm but without much success. While Froebel took his studies seriously – he lived a very secluded life, worked hard during the day, and only went out in the evenings for walks, avoiding any students' activities – he soon had to give up his linguistic studies. Instead, he focused on physics, chemistry, and mineralogy.

Froebel's goal was never to graduate in a particular subject to earn a living. 'I still declare to you that I do not train myself for any external purpose, neither to instruct others nor to get bread, but entirely for my own sake',[1] he told Christoph. Such an attitude wasn't uncommon; many studied because finding and perfecting one's self was seen as the ideal of humanity. Froebel thought similarly. He was looking for answers to the big questions: what is the world and humanity, and what is the human being? He wanted to bring order to his thoughts on education and humankind, and if that would bring any practical implications, then so be it. But it didn't matter much. His goal was to become an 'educator of humankind', whatever that would mean.

Making Sense of Life and the World: The Law of the Sphere

Froebel was convinced that linguistic studies and natural sciences would be beneficial for understanding humankind and the development, learning, and education of human beings: 'The study of nature, the research of nature seemed to me to be the foundation and cornerstone for becoming certain and clear about the laws and the course of human development, human education and human upbringing, only on a different level of life phenomena.'[2]

Froebel hoped his studies would allow him to develop a corresponding educational philosophy that would justify his educational actions. He had already developed preliminary thoughts on what he would later call the spherical law. Based on these ideas, he now envisioned a *Menschenerziehung*, an education of humankind, a real education that would help every human being to fulfil their potential.

Froebel had been contemplating the essence of such a law for some time, and he now drew the various ideas together. He later claimed he was inspired during nightly strolls in August at the time of the Great Comet of 1811, which he took as a sign of the greater things to come. He resolved to call the law *sphaira* or sphere; alternative names were *metallon* and *concordia*. Between July and October 1811,

Froebel reflected on the law almost daily in his journal in an attempt to find fitting words to express his feelings and views and the regularities he believed to have discovered in the world around him. He mixed insights from his natural studies and observations with reflections on himself; the friendship between Caroline von Holzhausen, Susanne von Heyden, and himself; and, of course, the 'spiritual marriage' with Caroline, along with remarks on masculinity and femininity, physical and spiritual-moral marriage, and pure, holy marriage. Halfter refers to these reflections as 'chemical observations for the illumination of moral consciousness'.[3]

What Froebel tried to achieve was to find suitable (mathematical) formulas and symbols to represent personal relationships and, ultimately, the one law that exists in the world. By formulating universal insights, he wanted to legitimize his existence, disentangle his feelings for Caroline, justify the relationship with her, and simultaneously develop universal principles that could serve as the foundation of his pedagogy. 'My ambition was and is to explain myself quite popularly and in a quite ordinary way of speaking about it: I wanted to know what it is about the human race (*Menschengeschlecht*) and humankind (*Menschheit*)',[4] he wrote on 17 October 1811. But he struggled to bring it all together and make sense of it. To find a formula for the one law that would serve as the basis for all outer and inner life was an impossible task, one that Froebel never solved to his dying day.

The entries show an often very confident yet also doubt-filled Froebel. 'That's why I would like to know from someone what would be the value or not value of the idea I have cultivated and that are now stepped out', Froebel wrote in a draft letter. 'I am gladly satisfied if you say to me at the end of your examination that you have set up partly delusions, partly commonplace things long known to the initiated and already forgotten again.'[5] External approval would have been welcomed. However, Froebel mainly wrote for himself, even if he envisioned a book called *Buch über die Sphäre* (*Book about the Sphere*). Two copy fragments show that he had started with a draft without finding a satisfying solution to the issues he was grappling with.[6]

Finally, he began to share his ideas. On 25 June 1811, Froebel outlined some key concepts in a letter to Christoph, a first attempt to express the profound thoughts he had felt more than understood in words. What makes the letter and many of the diary entries fascinating is that these thoughts would continue to be remarkably constant for the rest of his life. Examples are the theses he wrote down on 1 August 1811 or another draft from 15 October 1811, which can be seen as a development of the earlier theses.[7] While it would take years to publish his thoughts on the law, Froebel already established the critical ideas in Göttingen. Indeed months-long, Göttingen was a very fruitful time. Helmut Heiland has summarized the month-long process of thought and reflection very well. 'For Froebel, the spherical law of 1811 is the successful attempt to philosophically understand the connection between unity and diversity and, simultaneously, clarify his relationship to Caroline von Holzhausen in the image of marriage, of the polarity of attraction and repulsion.'[8] Drafting the law helped Froebel come to terms with the relationship with Caroline, find inner peace, and clarify his epistemology. The law of the sphere he developed in Göttingen shaped Froebel's thinking for the rest of his life. From now on, everything only made sense in the context of this law.

Trying to Prove the Law: The Move to Berlin

What still wasn't clear for Froebel, though, was what to do in the future. Should he become a teacher, a private tutor, or the director of an educational institute?

At least Froebel had some plans for the immediate future. He wanted to continue his studies in Göttingen until the end of the summer semester of 1812 and then move to Heidelberg or Berlin. The reason was his new focus: the natural sciences. Froebel had already attended lectures on theoretical chemistry, the chemistry of plants and animals, introduction to mineralogy, and experimental physics and had become interested in analytic or practical chemistry, mineralogy, and geognosis.[9] However, as he explained to Christoph while visiting Christian, almost as if he wanted to avert such a suspicion, while those subjects might have a practical benefit, it was only a secondary aim. The 'main aim is always to train me to be a teacher, and here my eye is steadfastly on Berlin and Prussia.'[10] The idea was still to understand humanity and become an 'educator of humankind', not a natural scientist.

Visiting Christian again was no accident. Family relationships became more important,[11] and Froebel regularly wrote to Christoph and Traugott, even though Traugott never replied. Froebel visited Christian's family frequently; for example, he spent the summer of 1812 in Osterode. Christian became the model of fatherhood for him, and Froebel respected him as the family's representative. The relationship with Christoph's family was more complicated; once again, money was the issue. After their sister Juliane passed away on 25 July 1811,[12] the family had to organize her children's inheritance and sold the last acres that had been their mother's in Stadt-Ilm. Since Christoph was in debt, the siblings agreed to loan him the interest from the inheritance. Christoph also had personal issues. His wife was sick, and living with his father-in-law was problematic. Thinking about his beloved brother and the unfortunate living situation he was in was painful for Froebel.

Froebel also needed money. With no income, he didn't know how to pay for the next semester and even considered earning money by publishing literary works. Once again, an unexpected death and inheritance changed the situation. An aunt, their mother's sister, passed away, and each brother received 350 thalers. Now Froebel could continue his studies, and he again saw this as a form of destiny and a sign.[13] While his uncle's death had allowed him to move to Frankfurt and become an educator, his aunt's death made studying possible. There were some quarrels about the inheritance, though. Christoph had already received 200 thalers as a loan and could only expect 150 thalers, and for this reason, Froebel wanted his brother to get as many clothes and as much linenware as possible. For himself, he only asked for small memorabilia. However, Christoph's wife disagreed and an auction therefore became necessary. Froebel and Christian became increasingly alienated from their sister-in-law.

Before he moved to Berlin, Froebel spent the autumn holidays in Osterode again. When he left, Christian wrote in his album:

> You go, oh brother! Towards the image of the frosty future – winter. But just as nature recovers in winter and gathers strength to emerge with the unstoppable strength of spring despite all storms and unfriendly weather with rejuvenated beauty; so the future will also brighten up and break out vigorously and beautifully and one day bloom and bear many fruits.[14]

At least the brother saw a bright future for him, and Froebel was convinced that this future awaited him in Berlin.

What Froebel wanted from Berlin was a better understanding of mineralogy and crystallography. Since he was still grappling with his spherical law, he hoped that studying the natural sciences would enable him to prove the law: 'The all-encompassing and comprehensive in itself necessary conditional inner regularity which I recognized everywhere confronted me with such clarity and power that I saw nothing in nature and in life, in which it would not have, even if in very different degrees of derivation and levels of increase are pronounced.'[15]

The new Friedrich Wilhelm University in Berlin, which had just opened in autumn 1810 as a result of Prussia's educational reforms, seemed a better place to be for his interests. Today, crystallography is the science of the structure, formation, or production of crystals, their properties, and their possible applications. However, for Froebel, crystallography was a chance to understand the world in its minor manifestations, which he hoped would help him finalize his philosophy of the sphere. While a natural history approach was taken to the study of crystals in Göttingen, a theoretical, systematic approach was taken in Berlin; in Froebel's eyes, this was a more promising approach. Furthermore, Christian Samuel Weiß (1780–1856), a widely known crystallographer at the time, held the professorship of mineralogy from 1810 and gave lectures on crystallography, mineralogical-physical theory, and crystalline structure in Berlin from 1811. Weiß was also responsible for the Royal Mineral Cabinet, a mineralogical collection. For all these reasons, it made sense for Froebel to move to Berlin.

Finding Friends during the Napoleonic War

Froebel arrived in Berlin in November 1812. While passing through the besieged city of Magdeburg, even the apolitical Froebel realized how serious the political situation was. Still, unlike many of those around him, Froebel wasn't yet impassioned by the uprising against Napoleon. Instead, he wanted to study. He listened to Weiß's lectures with enthusiasm and soon became one of Weiß's confidants. Froebel also attended lectures by Johann Gottlieb Fichte (1762–1814) and became familiar with Fichte's *Addresses to the German Nation*. To earn money, he worked at an educational institute founded by Johan Ernst Plamann. Plamann had published about Pestalozzi's method[16] and visited Pestalozzi in Yverdon, where he had heard Froebel's name. Froebel's friend Marsch, who had lived in the same house in Yverdon, had introduced the pair in Berlin. Froebel wasn't excited by the institute or his new educational position; for him, it was a way of earning a living. In general, education still wasn't his focus, even if the correspondence with the von Holzhausen children shows his educational abilities.

In spring of 1813, Froebel concluded his studies. Following Napoleon's loss in Russia and the German campaign of 1813 (*Befreiungskriege*), it proved impossible for him to escape the nationalist sentiments any longer. An encounter with the gymnastics educator Jahn, who was known as the *Turnvater*, led him to enlist with the Lützow Freedom Corps (*Lützowsches Freikorps*) volunteer force that Jahn was assembling in April 1813. While the first impression wasn't the best – Jahn thought Froebel a 'droll fellow' – Froebel joined other students who were enthusiastic about liberating the occupied territories from Napoleon.

Figure 3.1 Christian Samuel Weiss.

Biographers have claimed that Froebel expressed enthusiasm for nationalist ideas during the war, especially when it was helpful to present himself in such a light. He may have been influenced by his time in the Lützow Freedom Corps, which was loyal not to the king but to the fatherland; Froebel later stated that he was more interested in the German people and the German nation during the war.[17] This also explains his decision to call his institute the *Allgemeine deutsche Erziehungsanstalt* (*General German Educational Institute*). Froebel's enthusiasm shouldn't be overrated though, nor should he be considered a war-supporter. Instead, like many young men of the time, he felt the need to be a part of the war: 'Anyone who ever wanted to take part in people's lives as a person and could now go to war was not allowed to stay at home.'[18] Not least as a future educator, for one couldn't be an educator of children 'whose homeland and fatherland he had now not defended with his blood and life'.[19] Halfter summarizes Froebel's motivation well: 'His pride couldn't bear to be left out of it.'[20]

The decision to join the corps was also made easier by war-supporter Weiß's promise of an assistantship at the Mineralogy Institute after the war. Froebel had applied for this position in April 1813, and it was his dream to work under Weiß, who had already become his mentor. Weiß provided Froebel with letters of recommendation; with Weiß's support and the position in sight, it was easier to march into the war.[21]

The war was a frustrating and unsatisfying experience. The corps was ill-equipped – even uniforms were in short supply; untrained; and entirely unprepared for the imminent battle.

Nevertheless, the war changed Froebel's life. In the first days, on the march from Berlin to Dresden, Froebel met two young theology students named Wilhelm Middendorff and Heinrich Langethal.

> An exquisitely beautiful spring evening on Meissen's friendly banks of the Elbe and Meissen's magnificent cathedral brought me closer together with them, as with several other people; but it was actually the beautiful banks of the Havel near Havelberg, the charming location of the magnificent cathedral, Georg Forster's Rhine journeys, the same love of nature, and above all the same lively drive for edification (*Bildungstrieb*) that bound us together forever.[22]

Middendorff and Langethal would become Froebel's closest associates, maybe even friends, and at least Middendorff remained true to Froebel until the very end.

Jahn introduced Langethal to Froebel as a fellow countryman. The son of a craftsman, he was ten years younger and well educated with a serious disposition, studying theology under Schleiermacher. The pair bonded over their shared inner piety. Langethal then introduced Froebel to nineteen-year-old Middendorff.[23] The youngest son of Westphalian farmers, Middendorff grew up in the small village of Brechten in the greater Dortmund area. As a gifted child, Middendorff had been allowed to attend the gymnasium. His parents dreamed of seeing their son as Brechten's pastor. Middendorff had begun studying theology in Berlin in October 1811, where he listened to Fichte and Schleiermacher. He was a dreamer and often unworldly, but charming, amiable, and gentle – the opposite of the stiff Froebel. Middendorff's first impression of Froebel wasn't the best, thinking him 'a peculiar being, who walks his lonely ways and reads strange things out of stones and plants'.[24]

The three quickly grew close, nonetheless. Froebel was the oldest of the three and actively sought their friendship, especially Middendorff's. None of them was enthusiastic about the war, and they mainly discussed religious and pedagogical matters. Karl Heinrich Ludwig Bauer, born in 1785, also participated in the nightly discussions, and the four young men became friends.

For Froebel, the war mainly meant strenuous marches, idleness, and not much else. In May 1813, Froebel participated in the Battle of Lützen, but then a truce was called. The corps remained in Havelberg, where it finally received some military training. Froebel had been separated from his new friends and was mostly alone again. After only a few months of war, Froebel was disillusioned.

On 16 September 1813, the corps participated in a battle close to Lüneburg. Seeing all the dead and injured was a disturbing experience for Froebel. Afterward, they again had to sit idle. When the decisive Battle of Leipzig took place from 16 to 19 October, Froebel's corps was far away. The frustration grew both within the corps and in Froebel, who wrote to Weiß that they all were weary of it. The complaints about the corps' condition and the inaction in his letters became a constant theme.[25] Froebel asked for a transfer to the Garde Landwehr battalion in Berlin, but his request was denied because the Prussian authorities viewed him as a foreigner. Froebel had to stay, and the corps continued to mainly march first to Westphalia, then to Northern Germany in the winter of 1813/14. Constant marches, hunger, and a shortage of clothing, even of footwear, shaped the winter months.

It's interesting that Weiß, and not Christoph, was Froebel's main correspondence partner during the war, especially since Weiß never replied. It foreshadows Froebel's later behaviour. He assailed Weiß with over forty letters, mainly describing the war's progress. In addition, Froebel kept a war diary full of reflections on war, life as a solider, and geognostic observations. Froebel used the monotonous war to reflect on himself, the sphere, Caroline, and pedagogical questions and to think about his future as an educator. For this reason, Halfter refers to the war as 'months of self-education in the field'.[26]

Above all, however, the letters and diary show the monotony and miserable circumstances of the war.

And now I see a new and unfortunately the saddest and most frightening side of the soldier's life, which I knew only from hearsay – it is the one where the soldier considers everything as his property, what his eyes only see and what his greed only lusts for. The physical sufferings brought on by hardships and deprivation are often very oppressive and hard, but how much I would rather endure them than always be surrounded by actions against which the whole inner revolts.[27]

War and the soldier life weren't for Froebel.

The worst event of the war, though, was Christoph's unexpected death. Christoph had cared for soldiers with typhoid after the Battle of Leipzig and succumbed to the same illness. Froebel learned of his beloved brother's death while visiting Weiß in Berlin at the end of January 1814. He was utterly devastated. Interestingly, he never mentioned his brother's death in his letters in the months thereafter. This was typical behaviour for Froebel. Death was something he didn't want to write about.

Froebel left Berlin on 27 February and followed his corps until he finally found them in Aachen. There were endless further marches via Liège and Namur until they arrived in France. Froebel hoped to see Paris, but in May 1814, the war ended abruptly with a temporary peace agreement.

Froebel's time as a soldier also quickly came to an end. 'I liked being a warrior and I can say with all my soul, but I don't want to remain a soldier for long.'[28] On 3 June 1814, Froebel was discharged. He travelled through Belgium with Bauer before the two parted ways in Elberfeld. Next, Froebel visited Cologne, Bonn, Bingen, and Mainz. Weiß, who had given him more letters of recommendation, had suggested the visits. On 22 June, Froebel arrived back in Frankfurt. 'Today, to my great joy, in which I consider Frankfurt to be half a birthplace for me, I arrived here.'[29]

Of course, he visited the von Holzhausen family.

Once More: Caroline von Holzhausen

The war had changed not only Frankfurt but also the von Holzhausen family. The two eldest sons had now left home: Carl was now in the Austrian military, and Fritz had started his forester apprenticeship in Meiningen. Froebel had stayed in touch with the family over the years, not only through letters to Caroline but also by writing warm letters to the children. The family had tried to learn as much as possible about Froebel's whereabouts during the war and welcomed him as a friend. During his eleven-day stay in Frankfurt, he visited the family frequently.

But the familiarity of times past was gone. 'What can I say about [the family's, the authors] life, it was dead and even more disturbed by the war riots. Life dominated Frau von Holzhausen or rather, as she told me, she let herself be dominated by life on principle; I therefore saw little of her and actually spoke even less to her.'[30] The war experience hadn't only changed Caroline but also Froebel; it's also likely that seeing Caroline might have rekindled Froebel's old passion. Since he knew it was pointless to express his true feelings, he might have concealed them.

On his way back to Berlin, Froebel visited Fritz in Meiningen. It was a pleasant reunion, and when they parted company, Fritz gave his former tutor silver cutlery as a gift with the accompanying words: 'Meiningen, 8 July 1814. Take this, friend, as a souvenir of earlier times, for which I will forever owe you thanks. When using it, remember your faithful friend. Friedrich von Holzhausen.'[31] Silver cutlery was an expensive gift, showing the boy's gratitude and affection. Fritz's warm attitude confirmed to Froebel that he had treated and educated the boys well. In 1831, Froebel wrote: 'Yes! For the sake of this only person I would already consider myself happy to have become an educator and for the sake of this single blossom and fruit I would bless my entire educational life in Frankfurt with all its pressure and its night, its struggle and its pain.'[32] When Froebel wrote these words, Fritz was already dead. Friedrich von Holzhausen died young in 1820, and Froebel never saw him again.

Caroline von Holzhausen and Froebel also wouldn't meet again until 1831. According to Halfter,[33] it is possible that the two saw each other in spring of 1815 while Caroline was visiting a friend in Berlin. While such a meeting would explain Froebel's new and suddenly more intense passion towards Caroline in 1815/16, there isn't any evidence of this. Caroline, however, would matter to Froebel for the next fifteen years.

Back in Berlin: The Institute for Mineralogy and Maintaining Friendships

Before returning to Berlin, Froebel visited Christoph's family in Griesheim and Traugott. He also saw his stepmother again – 'Basically, she didn't mean it that bad. We just didn't understand each other.'[34] Afterward, he visited his aunt Hoffman in Leipzig, where he probably met his cousin, Muhme Schmidt, who would later become a vital correspondence partner during the time of the development of kindergarten.

In Berlin, Froebel soon learned that Weiß would keep his promise and that he would become an assistant at the Institute for Mineralogy at the University of Berlin. The position came with a small but decent salary of 200 thalers and a free apartment in the university building with costly firewood included. The only thing missing was furniture; hence, Froebel borrowed money from his friend Marsch for this. Without telling Froebel, Marsch asked Henriette Klöpper, the woman who would later become Froebel's wife, for the money.

As Weiß's assistant, Froebel was responsible for the rock collection, which he had to unpack, organize, and keep clean. He was often alone with the minerals but was satisfied with the task. The new position enabled Froebel to study the abstract, mathematical version of the spherical law in nature. His careful observations of the crystals helped him realize that the divine can be found everywhere, big and small. Froebel wrote in 1827:

> In the multiplicity of forms and shapes, I sensed and recognized, saw a law of development and design, modified and individualized in the most varied of ways … . What I had seen and recognized so varied in human being's life, in the course of God for the development of the human race, the same laws and phenomena met me here in the smallest definite shape (*Festgestalt*) of the only acting natural objects, then it came to me as never before, the divine before my soul, the divine is not only the greatest, no, the divine is also the smallest.[35]

However, the first months in Berlin were difficult. Weiß was away until November, and Froebel felt alone and depressed, as he later admitted. The situation improved slightly when Froebel met Bauer and then – to his delight – Middendorff and Langethal. The two had also returned to Berlin. They only saw each other occasionally, though, because of their different study subjects. Middendorff and Langethal were close friends, the two shared an apartment, and Froebel slowly became a part of their circle, as entries in Middendorff's diary show.[36] The two were also friends with Henriette Klöpper, Froebel's later wife, who had already supported the penniless students before the war. She now became a counsellor in all hardships, especially for the sensitive Middendorff, who was prone to melancholy and whose rapturous disposition rose to unfulfillable expectations, which the woman thirteen years his senior guided to appropriate forms.[37] A lonely woman in a loveless marriage, she felt enriched and more self-confident through the friendship, and she also learned of an older friend who fascinated both: August (Friedrich) Froebel.

In spring of 1815, with a new war against Napoleon looming on the horizon, the friends were faced with the decision of whether to volunteer. Langethal, but not Middendorff, had already been called up. 'Froebel advised with certainty: either I would have to follow Langethal or the inner voice that urged me to stay here.' Middendorff wrote in his diary:

> I knew that too – only this cold determination hurt me. Bauer had to feel this too – and asked Froebel, with vehemence, how he could advise in such a definite and contradictory manner in the matter of another. – He fully deserved this chastisement; this is a bad characteristic of his. Bauer and Froebel now got into a lively argument about religion and morality. Froebel dared to deny Bauern the latter in many cases.[38]

Middendorff's summary can be seen as typical. While the friends bonded, Langethal, Middendorff, and Bauer were at the same time often repelled by Froebel's peculiar character.

In the end, none of them had to join the war, as war veterans aged under twenty-five and people studying or in public service didn't have to participate due to there being so many volunteers. Since Middendorff hadn't wanted to rent a new apartment for what he thought would only be a short period, he now moved into Froebel's apartment on 30 May 1815. Both liked the arrangement – Middendorff because he could live for free and it was so quiet, and Froebel because he now had someone to talk to. Froebel was again actively seeking Middendorff's friendship, and the gentle but also naïve Middendorff became more and more fascinated by his older friend, despite 'all the often-repulsive peculiarity of his outward appearance as well as of his nature'.[39] Froebel, the oldest among them and the only one with a secure position, began to explain the world to his friends with certainty and started sharing his thoughts about the sphere with them. Soon, he began to cast a spell over them. Especially the contemplative Middendorff felt it increasingly difficult to withdraw from Froebel:

> It seems to me that he (Froebel) could, above all, most of all bring me back on the path if he would only approach me with calmness and love, help me to clarify my own ways, show me the wrong ways, allay the doubts as far as possible and lead me to an occupation which I must choose myself, with the consciousness of the whole man, as the one appropriate to me.[40]

Langethal, on the other side, was more steadfast. Froebel's name doesn't appear in Langethal's diary until 23 June 1816. At this time, Middendorff had already spoken several times jokingly of his 'Magister' Froebel. On 4 August 1816, Langethal wrote:

> Yesterday was the birthday of my intimate friend A. Froebel, whom I love with all my heart and respect even more; for through him I will have peace and clarity,

through him, the son of nature, who also wants so much to lead his brothers along this path, the only one that leads to salvation.[41]

Froebel, who had already announced that he would leave Berlin soon, was hoping his younger friends would join him in his next endeavour. But Langethal insisted on his independence and would never be as subservient as Middendorff.

Froebel's erratic behaviour stressed the friendship. Langethal and Middendorff describe a heated quarrel on Middendorff's twenty-third birthday in September 1816. Froebel had felt that Middendorff's behaviour was immature and must have been beside himself with rage, a form of ecstasy that disturbed the young men. Both felt insulted by Froebel. The quarrel only ended when Froebel, who had threatened to leave the friends, 'forgave' them and calmed down: 'Dear friends, what you have now seen, do not investigate further, you cannot understand it yet. But I will stay with you tonight; come, let us go in and eat.'[42] It was a pattern that wouldn't end for a long time. While Langethal and Middendorff were often disturbed by their older friend's behaviour and words, they were also fascinated by him.

A Secret Kept: The 'Spiritual Marriage' with Caroline von Holzhausen

While Froebel opened up to his friends about the spherical law and his plan to become an educator of humankind, he kept one secret: Caroline von Holzhausen.

Coming to terms with their relationship preoccupied him once again during these months. There are numerous entries in his diary between spring 1815 and summer 1816 in which Froebel reflects on their past. He also wrote many letters to her, often apologizing for sending the next one without waiting for a reply. On 28 May 1815, he wrote what Helmut Heiland has called an 'unequivocal love letter determined by passion and desire'.[43] Caroline presumably received the letter via their mutual friend, Susanne von Heyden, probably to conceal the correspondence. 'Since my last letters to you, my only one', Froebel started, 'my inner life has been developing with ever-increasing definiteness and has become ever clearer to me, it has been my firm resolution to express to you my innermost being and life and my love for you as clearly, as vividly, as truly as it stands before me.'[44] Froebel then speculated about what might have been and what their life together would have looked like. 'Your absence fills me with melancholy and painfully I feel the separation from you. How far must we go in the next days and weeks to progress in our refinement and in ever-increasing perfection if we now live a joint life ... . My soul thirsts for the love of yours and my self longs for its loving You.'[45] Froebel also included two controversial books: Schlegel's novel *Lucinde*, and Schleiermacher's *Vertraute Briefe über Schlegels Lucinde* (*Familiar Letters on Schlegel's Lucinde*). The books had already been published in 1799 and 1800, but Froebel probably only discovered them now. While he felt they mirrored his feelings, Caroline must have been horrified to receive these books.

But why did Froebel write a love letter now?[46] Had the passion been rekindled during the visit to Frankfurt? Or did he now feel the urge to resolve the relationship to detach himself from Caroline? We don't know.

Caroline reacted calmly, however, and replied with a sympathetic letter on 16 February 1816. She felt hurt by Froebel's long silence and was sorry for having hurt him so deeply. Still, she saw things differently: 'That which I think I have taken from you, or yet disturbed in you, is *your* faith. God forgive me, forgive me for it; if this word offends you, it is not my will, but truth against me speaks it.'[47] In her eyes, not any romantic feelings but rather the religious disagreement was the reason for their spiritual separation. Their feelings for each other – or, better, what they both thought their feelings had been – had been a misunderstanding. 'Burn all the letters you have from yourself, everything you have written down about yourself, don't write anything about yourself for yourself, to read it again after some time.'[48] Caroline wanted Froebel to move on and stop with the constant self-reflection.

Froebel must have perceived her words as an insult. Self-reflection was his life's essence, and giving it up was impossible. And the issue still wasn't resolved. He wrote in his diary in May 1816:

> As I knew what dying was, I soon knew what it meant to be a husband, a father of a family ... . The time when all contradictions disappear is the time of the lily. Then I'll be completely reconciled with my girlfriend ... . I asked her: And if the man's path went through night and death, through fear and hell, would you follow him? She confidently said yes.[49]

In August and September 1816, he again thought about Caroline almost daily:

> It is strange, it must be significant, that my letters, written with so much intimacy, well-intentionedness (*Gutgemeintheit*), repel the friend, have a painful, aggravating, woeful effect on the friend – and that again the friend, likewise with much intimacy, well-intentionedness, really excellent, true letters, rich in content and consequences, that again these letters have an embittering, angering, annoying, offending, painful, repulsive effect on me! Wherefrom this changeful repulsion?[50]

Time and time again, he tried to make sense of the relationship and why they had separated. In some entries, he blamed her:

> C. has revoked the reason for the high trust with which she loved me as a lie. Her and my love appears to her as a sin, which she has to repent and atone for to God ... . She didn't keep her word. She did not trustfully follow through death and hell. Did you keep your word?[51]

Today, we can't say with certainty what happened in 1815 and 1816 and what urged Froebel to write those lines. One should be careful with interpretations. Froebel's choice of words doesn't necessarily mean that 'love' existed or a sexual affair transpired. At the time, terms such as 'friend' didn't mean what they do today. Furthermore, if passion and 'love' existed, then only for the moment and only for him. Caroline always reacted amicably.

The passion, however, suddenly was over. The correspondence continued for a while, but Froebel mainly described the development of the law and later Keilhau to Caroline. Nevertheless, it would take fifteen more years for Froebel to came to terms with one, if not *the* most important relationship of his life. Only in 1831 did the 'most dangerous struggle of his life' – the '21 years long struggle'[52] – come to an end.

Finally, a Decision: Becoming an Educator of Humankind

At the end of 1815, Froebel still hadn't decided what to do with his life. He grew increasingly unhappy with his work at the Mineralogy Institute as he felt isolated from the world and people. The more significant issue, though, was that the almost same-aged Weiß did not treat him as an equal. Weiß had a different understanding of the crystals' system, and Froebel had to follow Weiß's guidelines when presenting the collection to visitors. For Froebel – who was convinced that he now possessed a profound understanding of the minerals' structure and universal truth – it was frustrating not to be allowed to share his ideas. Yes, the position secured his livelihood, but it wasn't the carefree life of study he had imagined in 1811.

Instead, Froebel began to think about education again. Encouraged by Middendorff, Froebel attended Schleiermacher's lectures with him, where education was one of the topics.[53] Since January 1815, Langethal had worked as the private tutor of the three children of the wealthy banker Anton Heinrich Bendemann, and Middendorff was the tutor of August Heinrich Bendemann's only son. Both were struggling with their position, and Froebel wasn't shy in his advice. Froebel himself gave lessons to the eldest daughter of a lieutenant.

However, what really captivated Froebel during these months was Johann Christoph Greiling's *The Life of Jesus of Nazareth*.[54] Middendorff had recommended the book, and Froebel later compared the reading experience to the earlier ones of Novalis and Arndt in 1805. Greiling was a theologian and popular enlightener, and his book influenced Froebel's thinking heavily. Later, Froebel often referred to the life of Jesus as the archetypal ideal of education. Reading the book was another reason why education was on Froebel's mind again.

Notwithstanding, around 1816, Froebel entertained the idea of a scientific career. Allegedly, he was even offered a professorship at a Swedish university.[55] It is questionable, though, whether this actually happened. Froebel also knew that he would never have been able to fulfil the demands of a professor's life as he lacked the necessary knowledge for an academic career and the prerequisites for higher natural sciences. The position as Weiß's assistant had no future either, though. Froebel later admitted that he would only have endured this occupation for two years.[56] Furthermore, the crystals had given him what he wanted:

> The world of crystals proclaimed to me loudly and unequivocally in a clear, firm form the life and the laws of life of humankind, and in silent but true and visible speech the true life of the world of humankind; there it drove me, leaving everything and sacrificing everything, back to people, to the education of people.[57]

It was time to move on.

However, what would such an education of people look like in reality? One possibility was to take over the responsibility for the education of Christoph's sons. Froebel had revisited the family in autumn of 1815. The second oldest son, Karl, has described his uncle's arrival:

> It was towards evening when my uncle arrived. He wore long hair and a black, not exactly new-looking hat that had suffered a little even in its shape. He seemed tired from the long journey on foot, asked about my mother and followed me into the house between two gardens. I still remember that, after the first greetings and a few questions, he suddenly hit his forehead with his hand and threw himself on a chair. After some silence, in which my father's death and the situation of the family he had left behind seemed to grasp him, he freed his covered face. And soon a hopeful breath seemed to blow through the house. The next day I heard that on the last day of his trip, my uncle had bought bread with

his last penny in Erfurt. That hurt me; I felt little of pity, however, and soon I thought my uncle was a very rich man who could help us all.[58]

As so often, the peculiar Froebel had made an impression. And the boys needed an education, so why not from him, just as he had promised Christoph many times?

The thoughts about the future and being an educator of humankind led to new sphere-philosophical reflections in the daily papers (*Tageblätter*). This time, the focus was on education. They're a fascinating reading which show just how profoundly Froebel thought about education. Froebel now recognized education as anthropologically necessary; to become human beings, humans need education. Education is needed so that humans can form their consciousness, recognize their spherical being, and live accordingly, so Froebel concluded.[59] Froebel wrote down these thoughts between 22 February and 23 July 1816, planning to later publish them in what he wanted to call *Sentenzenbuch* (*Book of Sentences*). Both in 1816 and 1823, he thought about such a publication.[60] On 11 September 1816, Froebel wrote: 'To the touchstone (*Prüfstein*) sentences: To test our past and present actions, to guide, direct, signpost our present and future action.'[61] And then on 4 July 1823:

> For the furtherance of my livelihood, I could therefore perhaps have the truths recognized in front of the spirit, which have risen from the spirit, have them printed: 'Branches, twigs, buds; leaves and blossoms and fruits from the tree of my life' collected, broken and communicated by Manthanoh[62] (the learner).[63]

Froebel probably used the earlier daily papers as preparatory work for the 'book of sentences'. They provide deep insights into Froebel's spiritual workshop of the time; the ongoing struggle to understand and combine the laws of nature, society, and God; the connections between individuality, manifoldness, and unity; and deriving pedagogical conclusions from it. As usual, however, following Froebel's leaps of thought is challenging, and much is incomprehensible today.[64] The sentences are essential, though, as they show that Froebel indeed had decided to become an educator (of humankind), first on 29 April 1816, and finally concisely summarized on 7 July 1816: 'My striving is to be an educator, a builder of human beings – a nurturer of human beings – an educator.'[65]

And it actually came about. On 9 April 1816, Froebel submitted a petition for release from the Mineralogy Institute. The request was rejected, though, because Froebel had conscientiously carried out his duties. In the summer of 1816, he submitted another petition for release, as he wrote on 7 September. 'I willingly renounce being any individual, scholar or artist to cultivate all this in a young mind. My aspiration is to be a sculptor (*Bildner*), sculptor of humans (*Menschenbildner*), caregiver of humans (*Menschenpfleger*), educator.'[66]

Finally, he was absolved from his responsibilities. Weiß couldn't understand his mentee's behaviour and thought Froebel was too erratic.[67] 'Froebel, if you leave here, you will become a beggar!' Weiß allegedly said this at the two's parting, a story Froebel later loved to tell.[68]

But Froebel had made his decision. Thus, aged already thirty-five and at an advanced age for the time, Froebel opted for a break in his biography and returned to the field of education – a profession he would pursue until his death.

Part 2

The Teaching Froebel

4

Keilhau's Rise and the Development of 'Developing-educating Humane Edification'

While Froebel might have always envisioned becoming an educator of humankind, he had never actively pursued such a path since leaving the von Holzhausen family. He had, though, promised Christoph that he would take care of his nephews' education if something should happen to Christoph. Despite Froebel's promise, three years had passed since Christoph's death without Froebel stepping up. But things were to now change. While one reason for this was certainly that his life in Berlin and academic career had reached a deadlock and no better options existed, Froebel unquestionably felt responsible for his nephews. Thus, he returned to his rural provinces, the principality of Schwarzburg-Rudolstadt. With the move, Froebel's years of travel ended. Over the next fifteen years, Froebel only left the area for short trips. First in Griesheim and then in Keilhau, Froebel finally became what he always had wanted to be – an educator of humankind in charge of an educational institute to his liking. Keilhau became a focal point in his life.[1]

A New Educational Adventure: The General German Educational Institute

According to Middendorff's diary, Froebel left Berlin on 4 October 1816. The friends had celebrated a joyous farewell with wine and champagne the night before. Middendorff accompanied his friend halfway to Charlottenburg. They said goodbye there, but both knew it wouldn't be for good. As usual, Froebel travelled by foot. On a foggy morning, he passed through the Schaale valley, which reminded him 'strangely strongly' of Rousseau's stay in the Jura. 'This is an educational valley', he thought, or at least that's the story he later loved to tell.[2] The name of the little village nearby was Keilhau. A few days later, Froebel arrived in Griesheim.

Griesheim was a lovely village situated on the banks of the Ilm between meadows, farmland, and wooded heights, with the gloomy mountain ranges of the Thuringian Forest behind it. Christiane Froebel, his sister-in-law, was still allowed to live in the parsonage as long as her father – pastor North, Christoph's predecessor – was alive. The parish property consisted of a little farmstead, and its yield made up an essential part of the family income. The whole family had maintained the farm,[3] which came in handy; Julius, the oldest son, was knowledgeable and talented with arboriculture and later created his own little garden with a nursery in Keilhau.

Since her husband's death, Christiane had been responsible for the boys' education. She was an intelligent, realistic, and strong-willed person, though a bit domineering. Another character trait was her insistence on pedantic cleanliness, which would lead to problems with the often-dishevelled Froebel. Christiane was political, a smart and passionate newspaper reader who got along well with all people, including highly educated men and women of the higher class.[4] The parents had raised their children in the spirit of rationalism, or in Julius' words: 'Brothers and sisters were given a free direction of the mind from earliest childhood. Our thinking, however, did not receive any revolutionary admixture from our parents.'[5] Her relationship with her father – who belonged to the Herrnhuter sect, a pietistic Protestant religious movement – was complicated, and disputes over religion were common.

Christoph's death had been a tragedy for the family. Christoph hadn't left much of value, only an extensive book collection which the boys had unfortunately partially destroyed while unsupervised. The rest, if not sold, was lost in a fire.[6] Hence, the future looked bleak for the family, even if Christiane did own some land whose yield might have kept extreme poverty at bay. However, it would never have been enough to raise and educate all four children, especially because the three boys were expected to study.

When Froebel arrived in Griesheim, Christiane and the children were living with their grandfather, who was wasting away, and the strict and somewhat morose grandmother North and her sisters. The situation wasn't pleasant for anyone, and tensions must have been high. Julius was away because he was living as a grammar school student in nearby Rudolstadt, sponsored by benevolent families. He was quartered with a theatre barber, where, according to his statement, 'a relaxed tone' prevailed: 'In winter, cards were played late into the night; in summer, when a troupe of actors engaged for the merry months worked on the aesthetic education of the people of Rudolstadt during the famous "bird shooting", some associated ladies came and went with us and also let me have a share in this educational benefit.'[7] The eleven- or twelve-year-old, who loved to entertain his friends with sausages, fruit, and sugar, had already fallen into debt, and his performance at school, according to his later self-judgement, was highly unsatisfactory. In short, the naïve good-for-nothing, as he later called himself, was about to go to rack and ruin.

The whole situation wasn't what Froebel had in mind for his favourite brother's sons. He wanted a well-rounded education and the best in an educational institute. To achieve his goal, Froebel thought more children would be beneficial, and he travelled to Osterode to convince Christian to entrust him with his sons. He had already resolved to open an 'institute', however. Hence, he informed his friends in Berlin, and Caroline von Holzhausen from Osterode, that he was to become an educator of humankind. The letters were also written in the hope that Middendorff and Langethal would join him.

Christian did indeed entrusted Ferdinand (*1807) and Wilhelm Theodor (*1810) to his brother's care. Finally, Froebel opened his educational institute on 13 November 1816; at least, that is the date he would mark as the opening day. The name 'institute' was somewhat misleading, as it wasn't much more than an extended family consisting of Froebel and his four nephews. Julius, whom they had spent Christmas with, became the fifth pupil. Froebel had made Christmas heartfelt for the children, and it was the first of the famous Christmas celebrations for which Keilhau later became renowned.[8] It had such a powerful effect on Julius that he had pleaded to stay.[9] 'In my uncle's enterprise, a sanatorium opened up for me, so to speak, in which the harmful effects of a premature genius period in dealing with theatre hairdressers and theatre princesses were to be eliminated.'[10] With his five nephews assembled, the educational work could begin.

Froebel moved into a rented farmhouse with Christian's boys and quickly bonded with them. Soon, even Christaine's boys regarded the place their home, telling their mother that they want to go home now.

The boys' enthusiasm for their peculiar uncle did nothing to improve the already tense relationship. The grandparents and aunts were also appalled because Froebel gave the boys a lot of freedom, which was very unusual for the time. They were allowed to go outdoors without a head-covering whatever the weather, and when they asked about daring undertakings, Froebel simply replied by asking if they were sure they could handle it. The boys loved their newfound freedom and began to idolize their uncle. 'I cannot imagine a happier

Figure 4.1 Friedrich Froebel, lithography by J. H. Sherwin (1888).
Bildarchiv Friedrich-Fröbel-Museum Bad Blankenburg (Picture Library Friedrich-Fröbel-Museum Bad Blankenburg)

youth than ours.'[11] That they were now allowed to do what they would have been punished for previously enthralled them. Karl recalled at the age of sixty:

> I felt in a new world of freedom. Although my activities were much more ordered, my time more precisely divided; but in everything I did, even in playing, I learned

something ... . We learned to shoot with a bow, to throw spears, to jump over a rope and other gymnastic exercises, and also to do cardboard work, paper weaving and cutting out ... . Froebel's lessons opened the view into a new world of order, beauty and regularity. We learned to speak correctly; mean expressions quickly disappeared because we were ashamed of them.[12]

In a sense, Froebel gave his nephews a childhood that was the exact opposite of his horrible experience.

The First Associate: Middendorff Joints the Institute

However, it was clear that the future wouldn't lie in Griesheim. What Froebel wanted was an actual educational setting with more pupils and allies. To achieve the latter, Froebel courted Middendorff and Langethal, subtly trying to convince them to work together for a better education of the future generation. Already at this point, it wasn't about an educational institute but a life mission – a movement to reform education and society. Especially Middendorff became his target, but he was reluctant. He had just passed his exams with distinction in spring of 1817, and saying yes to Froebel would have meant the end of his theological career. Middendorff knew that joining Froebel would greatly sadden his parents, who had pleaded with him not to do so. Still, after fierce struggles of conscience, he told Froebel that he would come. The father allegedly exclaimed heartily: 'Heaven has blessed us abundantly; one must be sacrificed to the Lord for it.'[13]

However, what Froebel really wanted was Langethal. The institute needed a teacher with extensive language knowledge, which Froebel didn't possess. Langethal, on the other hand, had such expertise. But for now, Langethal resisted, even if Froebel pestered him with letters. Langethal had other plans; he wanted to stay independent and find a parish or teaching position after graduation.

Nevertheless, he trusted Froebel enough to instruct Middendorff to take his younger brother Christian to Froebel. 'In beautiful May weather, we moved out and 14 May 1817', Christian Langethal recalls, 'was the strange day on which Froebel's young institution received its second teacher and its first foreign pupil.'[14] Christian was awed by the situation in Keilhau. He quickly became friends with the boys, especially with Ferdinand. 'For me, a child of the city, in the most beautiful season suddenly transferred from the sea of houses into the free nature, everything was new.'[15] The institute was growing – it now had six pupils and two teachers.

Figure 4.2 Portrait of Wilhelm Middendorff (1793–1853).

With Middendorff's arrival, Froebel's role changed. He spent less time with the children because 'he had neither patience nor peace enough for that' and instead encouraged activities that Middendorff supervised, examined, and then 'gave new thoughts and ran away again'.[16] Middendorff's role in Griesheim was completely passive; he mainly did as Froebel bid.[17] But he quickly bonded with the children by listening to their needs and ideas. Initially, he must have been more of a friend than a teacher.

For her part, Christiane observed the developments with divided feelings. Yes, the boys were happy, but it was a strange sight, and she also must have felt taken aback by the exclusiveness with which the uncle drew the children to himself. Soon, her relationship with Froebel turned sour. Biographers have alleged that the widow had hoped and almost expected that her brother-in-law would marry her and that she withdrew when it became clear that Froebel had no interest. This is very unlikely however and was later strongly disputed by descendants of the Griesheim Froebel line.[18] Froebel's manner didn't correspond to Christiane's practical, energetic nature; in her eyes, he was distant and extravagant, always unpunctual and unkempt. She might – but this is a big if – have contemplated a marriage alliance before his arrival, but the fact that this didn't happen wasn't the cause of the later conflicts.

A New Home: Keilhau

For now, though, Christiane supported her brother-in-law and made it possible to exchange 'his marching quarters for standing quarters'.[19] The move was necessary because Christiane's father had died, meaning she now had to leave the parsonage within a year. Froebel, who had been searching for the right place for his institute, convinced Christiane to sell all her property and buy what he longed for – a small estate in Keilhau.

Keilhau was exactly what Froebel had been looking for: an educational institute in nature, far from what he perceived as society's negative influence. But Froebel had no money. However, when he learned that an indebted farm estate in the 'education valley' that he had noted on his way to Griesheim was to be auctioned, he convinced Christiane to bid on it with her modest means. The estate had belonged to August Schilling, one of Keilhau's wealthiest citizens, who had amassed debts due to gambling and the construction of new buildings and lost the remainder of his fortune during the bad harvest of 1816.[20] In the words of Julius Froebel: 'My mother, who was enthusiastic about the educational purposes of her brother-in-law, bought for the sake of the cause with her small fortune in the village of Keilhau, made liquid by the sale of her land in the city of Ilm',[21] the small estate. Thus, one of the Keilhauer estates, whose homesteads had been inherited from father to children for three hundred years, fell into the hands of strangers.[22]

In 1817, Keilhau was a small, dreary village. It consisted of twenty houses, nineteen farms, seventeen estate owners, and around ninety people.[23] Located in the remote, narrow *Schaaltal* more than an hour from the next bigger villages, Keilhau was surrounded by high hills, covered with spruces, pines, and silver firs.

Keilhau was situated in the principality of Schwarzburg-Rudolstadt, which had been ruled by the lenient Prince Friedrich Günther since 1814. Life there was tough and many people had been living from hand to mouth since the late eighteenth century. The local forest was the primary source of income; however, the hills surrounding the village had been logged long ago, and heavy rains had washed the fertile soils away and covered the village's best food source with debris. Arable land was in short supply, and most people mainly lived on bread and water, along with a few vegetables and fruits from their small gardens. Actual livestock grazing was rare. The well water was at least clean, and the potatoes introduced in the 1780s had alleviated the worst famines. However, the eruption in 1815 of Mount Tambora in Indonesia[24] led to the Year without a Summer in 1816, a failed harvest, and the return of hunger to Keilhau. The effects were palpable when Froebel arrived.

Keilhau itself was run down. The pathways were neglected and the church in need of repair. There was a pond in the street, and five springs meant the village's roads were seldom dry. Sewage leaked onto the roads when it rained, and salamanders emerged from the houses' walls when it rained in the summer. The water lizards that inhabited the nearby flax forests could be heard at night. Winters in Keilhau were especially bleak.

Keilhau didn't only look medieval, though; the same was also true of the local customs. On Sundays, the whole community gathered in the church. The women wore heavy blue cloth coats decorated with gold braids, which had been passed down for generations, while the men wore the same long cloth shirts they wore when they went to the market in Rudolstadt to socialize over a herring, bratwurst, and beer.

The nature surrounding Keilhau was beautiful, however. Eagle owls lived on the bare rock faces of the Steinberg; there were foxes in the forests as well as songbirds, wood pigeons, thrushes, and – on the banks of the streams – kingfishers. Along the streams and springs that joined to form the *Schaalebach* were numerous flowers whose names the children soon learned. It was exactly what Froebel had wanted for his educational institute. 'Only in a completely spherical structured life fulfilled, a man reaches his highest destiny, he reaches his destiny in the most perfect way', he had already written down in his *Sentenzbuch (Book of Sentences)* on 20 July 1816. 'But which life corresponds most to this perfectly spherically structured life? – It is the country life.'[25] For Froebel, education and a united, spherical family life were only possible in the countryside, far from the city's alleged destructive influences.

The small group moved to Keilhau on around St John's Day in 1817. They decided Froebel would occupy the estate in Christiane's name and renovate the badly run-down and dilapidated property. Christiane, whose grace year hadn't yet expired, would remain in Griesheim with her sons until autumn. The departure, which is portrayed vividly by Christian Langethal, gave Christiane good insights into what to expect of Froebel. Although the departure had been set for early morning, Froebel had forgotten to order the wagon to transport the luggage. Now everyone was working, so they had to wait until the afternoon.[26]

> It was a very hot afternoon shortly before St. John's Day, which saw our little colony wandering into the treeless Teuwe. Froebel, his coat on his arms, walked ahead with sprightly steps, Middendorff followed, and we three children formed the end. Sadly, I looked back from the friendly little castle to Griesheim and with gloomy looks into the bare plain that lay before me.[27]

Christiane must have been shocked by her brother-in-law's ineptitude. The walk was arduous and the group only found shade when they arrived at Keilhau's spruce forests in the evening. When they reached the little village, it was already dusk. 'Everything here was so lonely, so desolate and dilapidated',[28] Christian Langethal described his disappointment. The next day, the mood was still sour: 'When I awoke the next morning, I was transported to a desolate courtyard of the old village of Keilhau, where I liked it very badly. And how could I like it in Keilhau!'[29]

It wasn't the most promising start to their new life.

Soon, however, the children's opinion of Keilhau changed – among others, because school wasn't to be thought of for a long time. Over the months that followed, everyone was occupied with the necessary renovations. The previous owner had started to replace the old, run-down house with a new one, but never finished the work. While it had a roof, with the exception of the only room on the first floor, windows, doors, and floorboards were missing. The old house was close to collapse and inhabitable, and building materials had been left lying around the estate's orchards. In the middle was an empty barn where field mice lived.

But Froebel had lofty plans. The goal was to have both floors of the new house extended by autumn while simultaneously demolishing the old house and building a new barn. Then, the old barn should be torn down and a schoolhouse built in its place. In the meantime, Froebel rented an apartment on the upper floor of a house owned by the Hänolds. The Hänolds, like August Schilling, had started to build a new home, but the apartment was run down and needed floorboards, doors, and windows; even the staircase was missing. With the help of carpenters, locksmiths, potters, and glaziers, they began with the renovations

Figure 4.3 The Keilhau Educational Institution in the Thuringian Forest.

of which Froebel, Middendorff, and the children did most themselves. Normal
lessons were out of the question. The first months in Keilhau were nothing
but chaos.

Still, Keilhau quickly became home. The first months were delightful for
the boys; there were no school hours or lessons, and Froebel mostly let them
have their way. Since there were no lessons, the boys spent most of their time in
nature doing all kinds of studies. They were also responsible for chores such as
harvesting hay, potatoes, and fruits, activities the children loved. Keilhau was a
schoolboy's dream.

When summer ended, Christiane still hadn't moved to Keilhau, hence Froebel
had to hire a cook. Caroline Froebel, Christian's wife, came to see how Ferdinand
and Wilhelm were getting on. The group had finally moved into the apartment
in the 'Hänolds' house', and Caroline helped furnish the apartment. She was
accompanied by her daughter, Emilie, and the two stayed for fourteen days, which
Froebel later called the most beautiful days of his life, the 'lily days'. Their stay
gave him an idea for the family-like environment he longed for at the institute.[30]

Finally, Christiane's entire family – the boys, her daughter, and her mother
and aunt, the 'two old aunts' – moved to Keilhau. The aunts lived on the lower

floor of what the community called the 'lower house' to differentiate it from the 'Hänolds' house', while Christiane and the children lived on the upper floor. More renovations were needed, but money was tight, even if Christiane supported the institute financially. Julius Froebel later wrote: 'However, in the first period of the Keilhau institution, in which not only the founder lacked all means, but also those of my mother were exhausted, who willingly sold all superfluous possessions to create the most necessary money, not infrequently economic distress took the place of pedagogical principles, without contradicting them.'[31] Again, only Christiane and her financial support made the institute in Keilhau possible in the beginning.

With Christiane's arrival, more serious school lessons began. When the weather became harsher, they spent more time inside, and Froebel and the children made building blocks that they used to create magnificent buildings. It was a happy time.

What made life in Keilhau unusual was how Froebel and Middendorff treated the children. The relationship was warm and caring; all children remembered the time with joy. Instead of fear, 'trust and love led the regiment'.[32] To increase the intimacy, Froebel had introduced '*Du*' (informal you), which was again uncommon (and what his stepmother had denied him) but corresponded to the spirit of Jahn's gymnastics community.[33] The sense of community was further reinforced by the common attire: all wore a linen longcoat with a bare neck and long hair – the style known as *altdeutsche Tracht* (old German dress). Well-to-do boys normally wore a neckerchief, cap, long stockings, and laced boots and walked beside their parents.

Thus, it is no surprise the boys adored their uncle.

> It was not only due to my uncle's system but the economic conditions under which this man, equipped with nothing but his reformatory thought and truly apostolic faith, dared to begin his activity aimed at the transformation of the German people in character, society and state, brought it about that his pupils were placed in intercourse with nature almost unknown to today's common education. In principle, the institution had to be located in the countryside and was to be protected from the Intrusion of urban life.[34]

Soon, Christiane's sons were more attached to him than they were to her. And while it filled Froebel with great satisfaction,[35] the whole scenario was probably disturbing for Christiane and the aunts. In their eyes, the Keilhau youths, who cavorted around outdoors without head-coverings and with bare legs, were nothing but a wild gang.

The Third Founder Arrives: Langethal Joins the Community

Langethal was still missing, however, despite Froebel's repeated requests. After finishing his theological studies with distinction, Langethal was immediately offered a pastor's position in the Rhine region, with him picking from one of three choices. It was an attractive offer; the position was in one of the best parishes in the country and came with a salary of 700 thalers. But Langethal turned it down and instead accepted the position as tutor in Count Stolberg's family in Silesia. In autumn of 1817, Langethal left the Bendemanns and came to Keilhau to pick up Christian to take him to Silesia and visit his old friends.[36]

Langethal probably knew Froebel would try to convince him one more time. However, he was determined not to join Froebel's enterprise. Allegedly, Froebel sat down with his friend the night before his departure and carefully asked about his future. Then, he raised his eyes and looked penetratingly at Langethal. 'You go to educate boys?' – 'Do you know the nature of children? – Then I advise you to keep your hands off education.' We don't know what was really said. Nevertheless, Langethal cancelled on Count Stolberg the next day and returned the travel money. In Osann's words, Langethal 'had ventured into the circle of the Pied Piper and lost the game from the beginning. Froebel had set his mind on drawing Langethal to him and achieved his goal.'[37] Langethal would spend the next decades of service in Froebel's sphere or, as Middendorff remarked, 'to share the agonizingly happy fate of high effectiveness with extreme effort and almost unbelievable deprivation.'[38]

Langethal proved a breath of fresh air for the institute. A handsome man of twenty-five, he afforded a very different character to both Middendorff and Froebel. He also possessed the classical and musical knowledge that Middendorff – and especially Froebel – lacked, making him excellently suited as a teacher for the older boys. This was also why Froebel had tried so hard to win him over.

Langethal's presence was by all means crucial, as he was respected in pedagogical circles in Erfurt, and by declaring Keilhau an excellent institution where he would teach, Keilhau gained in reputation. An Erfurt acquaintance's son immediately became the seventh pupil and another boy joined three months later, with two more following soon after. Thus, Keilhau also gained acceptance in Rudolstadt. Keilhau's development into more than just a family enterprise was unquestionably due to Langethal.[39]

With Langethal, school life in Keilhau changed. Froebel was the master of the whole, which was clear to everyone, protecting his method against arbitrariness

Figure 4.4 Heinrich Langethal.
Bildarchiv Friedrich-Fröbel-Museum Bad Blankenburg (Picture Library Friedrich-Fröbel-Museum Bad Blankenburg).

and often flaring up in the fight for his idea.[40] Langethal at least had some influence regarding the curriculum, though. 'There was no more talk of Greece; now we all wanted to be real Germans and Valhalla was stormed with all our might.'[41] The children indulged in the romance of knights, set up caves called castles in the forest and on the rocky mountain walls, and even spent the night there in summer. Toughening up was part of Froebel's educational system, and the boys wore their linen outfits come rain or shine. Langethal sent them on endurance runs, assuring them that this was nothing compared to what a soldier or knight had to endure in war.

Even their language changed. All foreign words were eradicated and replaced by German ones. 'We no longer ate boulettes (*Bouletten*), but meatballs (*Fleischklöße*); we no longer asked for sauce (*Sauce*), but broth (*Brühe*) and Froebel's nephews had suddenly lost their "uncle" (*Onkel*) and gained an *Oheim* instead.'[42] Through German words, Froebel sought to support the development and appreciation of the German character. The children took this seriously; whoever was caught using a foreign word or dialect pronunciation had to remain silent until he could point out a mistake by another boy; whoever spoke anyway had to catch a sinner in the act twice, and when it happened for the third time, he was ordered out of the room for ten minutes.[43]

However, the 'Germanification' of language didn't make everyone happy. Keilhau's peasants were astonished when they suddenly found themselves, mountains, and streams renamed because Middendorff claimed to have found the original names. The old aunts thought they had lost their minds. 'Tell your uncle that you and he are crazy!' One of them replied gruffly to Theodor after he had told her that she was no longer an aunt (*Tante*) but a *Base*. 'And whoever of you wild scamps calls me a *Base*, I'll throw the book at his head!'[44]

The old German garb with long hair and a bare neck further expressed democratic sentiments. It was considered offensive and almost criminal in the reactionary world, though this didn't bother the boys because they thought of the 'commonfolk' as despicable and pitiable anyway. 'Our way of life had a character that set us apart from the ordinary world, and we expressly learned to despise or pity "common people".'[45] The goal was to show 'manly virtue' by living a simple and natural life. Foreign drinks such as tea, coffee, or cocoa were frowned upon. Gymnastics were practised almost religiously, and the diet was simple and primitive. Newcomers were mocked when they were dissatisfied with the food on the table.

In general, the Keilhau boys were considered a wild bunch. They climbed trees, hiked many miles a day to bathe, caught squirrels, and discovered birds' nests, not to destroy but to examine them. Once they even brought home a young merlin – and another time a young eagle owl – and raised them. Long hikes and field trips were a frequent occurrence, even beyond Thuringia's borders. There were also agricultural activities to enrich the modest livestock. The 'gleaning' (*stopplen*), which involved beating the remaining fruits from the trees with sticks and stones, was popular in autumn.

The gleaning was of great importance to us: it was not only to conquer a favorite food of the children, but we also obtained material for roasting on the fire, and there were enough dry wood and juniper bushes in the forest to light the fire. When dusk approached, a fire was lit on the mountainside and how nice it was when we could roast fruit while the flames soared high, and the smoke swirled into the usually still November air! Potatoes were also roasted in the ashes, and we found them so much tastier than when they were boiled in water.[46]

And when winter came, they all sled down the *Hopperbahn*; sometimes even the serious Froebel joined in enthusiastically. 'Loud laughter rang out when someone turned over, which happened to Froebel not infrequently because the teachers also rode with us.'[47] The highlight was Christmas, which would become Keilhau's most joyful tradition.

It is not difficult to see why the boys loved being students in Keilhau. Life here was very different to the dry and often dull school life that most of their peers were experiencing.

Over the months that followed, Keilhau grew. Froebel was mainly occupied with overseeing the growth as well as refining and implementing his pedagogical ideas. At the start of 1818, an eighth pupil joined from Erfurt,[48] and in spring, the renovations of the estate and the Keilhau institute continued. The long garden, until then a meadow full of trees, was transformed into an herb garden according to Froebel's instructions by day labourers. Each boy received his own flowerbed and was encouraged to experiment with planting vegetables and flowers. The uppermost part of the garden was transformed into a flat square, which served as a gymnastics field. Soon, the new barn was finished.[49]

Life in Keilhau continued to be unusual. Langethal carved bows for the boys and showed them how to make arrows, and Middendorff found a place on the river Schwarza below Blankenburg that was reasonably suitable for bathing. They had to climb a mountain of 200 metres in height to get there, but no one cared. School learning still wasn't overly critical, and the pupils continued to be occupied with the renovations, planting and harvesting food, a little learning, and spending time in nature. The children's memories of the early years are joyful – and why wouldn't they be? They were a child's dream.

While many of the children's activities were necessary for the survival of the Keilhau community, Froebel justified them as educational. Already in 1817, Froebel had stated that life is 'more life than school' and gave the everyday errands an educational purpose: 'Whoever has not found the meaning of school … in and through life, school will never pass over into life, become life. School is the highest thing, but only if it is life.'[50] The quote later became well known in Germany. However, the statement didn't arise from a 'wise' insight of a pedagogue experienced in life and work, but instead served Froebel to justify his actions during a crisis-ridden and uncertain time in 1817. It wasn't really based on an educational plan; most of it was spontaneous. In the beginning, life and education in Keilhau were chaotic.

Finding a 'Mother': Wilhelmine Hoffmeister

Things changed when Froebel suddenly married. Froebel had wanted a 'mother' for the community for a while. He wasn't longing for an effective and loving relationship or sexual fulfilment; such feelings never played much of a role in his life, apart from his affection for Caroline von Holzhausen. But to become a real community with an orderly family life and a family-like environment and education, a woman was needed.[51]

> The construction of my house of education was not only decided but the preparation for it had already begun, the family was already formed, I would say, so everything had to come down to one point: to give the family a female head, the household a wife, the children a mother and the male life the second female half belonging to it, the striving thinking man, the caring feeling woman.[52]

This rationale explains the rather odd choice of courting Henriette (Wilhelmine) Hoffmeister (divorced Klöpper) – Langethal's and Middendorff's acquaintance from Berlin, a woman Froebel had only met once briefly. The logical choice would have been Christiane, but she wasn't interested in playing the role of the mother, and she had shown the utmost indifference towards the institution. Froebel also didn't feel that Christiane had the right skills and character traits, as he explained in a letter to none other than Henriette Hoffmeister: 'She is a very intelligent and eloquent, but not a domestic, leisurely, how shall I put it better than not a feminine, or perhaps better a housemother housewife'; Christiane would never be the 'orderly, calmly creating, gently nurturing housewife I need, which she can't be, at least doesn't want to be'.[53]

When Froebel started courting Wilhelmine, Christiane was already on the brink of leaving Keilhau for good. While it certainly didn't help that Froebel was courting someone else, what appalled Christiane was Froebel's way of doing business. Froebel's economic administration was disastrous, debts had piled up, and Froebel's incompetence as a farmer was obvious. Once he even ground the grain intended for sowing. Christiane feared she would lose all her money and demanded her share of the loan back, even if she wanted to leave her sons in Froebel's care. Her demand was a problem because the institute would collapse if she withdrew her money.[54] Ultimately, the two came to an agreement that wasn't beneficial for Christiane in the long term. Interestingly, the 'old aunts' stayed in Keilhau, but Christiane later regularly spoke ill of Keilhau and Froebel's pedagogy.

With Christiane not being an option, who would become the 'mother'? Froebel wasn't keen on getting married, 'but by no means did I see this demand here as coinciding with my educational striving; the thought did not even occur to me that I myself must give the circle what it lacks; on the contrary, I still held personal solitude as a condition for the higher attainment of my life's calling.'[55] It's possible that he still had feelings for Caroline von Holzhausen.[56]

Instead, he wanted his niece, the fifteen-year-old Albertine, to come to Keilhau. Not to marry her as he felt obliged to clarify in the letter to the women in Keilhau: 'This already excluded any view of my next family relationships in my choice; which view was already not permitted by another quite dark but just as deep as true voice of my innermost being.'[57] Not only did he see himself as too old, but he envisioned Albertine as Middendorff's future wife. However, Caroline Froebel objected, fearing that taking care of the abundantly wild youth, Froebel's feverish urge to work, and the increasingly tense reluctance of the Griesheim women was too much of a task for her daughter. Next, Froebel turned to Middendorff. The 24-year-old was frightened and passionately repelled by the idea of marriage. Still, a housewife was needed. At one point, Froebel must have realized that it was indeed his responsibility. 'Now I finally recognized it clearly as an indispensable duty to give, myself to give the circle that I had formed, I would like to say to give the needy family that was caused, what it demanded, as the point of heart and life, as the heart of a healthy, purely human life.'[58] However, where could he find such a woman?

Froebel's choice ultimately fell on Caroline Amalia Wilhelmine Henriette Hoffmeister. Born on 9 August 1782,[59] Henriette had been married to war councillor Klöpper briefly. Their childless marriage was soon dissolved, however, probably because of her husband's adultery,[60] or maybe because of Henriette's sickly disposition – or both. Henriette was deeply hurt by her first marriage, and mentioning it was taboo in Keilhau.[61] Following her divorce, Henriette returned to her father's house in Berlin. Divorce was considered a disgrace, especially in a dignified, Protestant family such as her own in which Kant's imperative of duty and Prussian discipline were crucial. Having fallen into disarray, Henriette devoted herself to an intellectual life and attended Schleiermacher's lectures in

1814/15. There, she met Langethal and Middendorff with whom she remained in touch, taking a motherly interest in their lives.

Shortly before Froebel's departure from Berlin, Langethal had suggested they all visit the mineralogical museum. There, Froebel and Henriette met for the first and only time. Froebel remembered the meeting as follows:

> You were fond of my stones, you above all showed great interest in their quiet, silent life, which I endeavoured to explain to you. Whoever loved my stones was worthy for me … . My eyes rested in yours, I must have been very excited at the beginning of the conversation as well as in general during this time; for I noticed the appearance rising like a bright dawn and clear sun, how my mind in the course of the conversation and resting in your eyes, my loved wife! I became calmer and peaceful, so calm and peaceful that I myself was amazed at this phenomenon in me, because it was so strange to me and had never been felt before.[62]

It obviously was neither passion nor love, but a feeling of calm and peace that attracted Froebel to Henriette. This was, his later explanation goes, what he wanted in a woman; he longed for someone who would support and calm him, not someone he could love passionately.

Froebel's decision to court a woman he had only met once seems strange today, even if marriages were arranged differently in those days. Henriette was in her late thirties, two years older than Froebel; in one picture, she appears pale, a little puffy, with a small, saddle-set nose and narrow eyes under her highly coiffed dark hair. A one-year correspondence began, and Wilhelmine quickly expressed an interest in joining Froebel and his mission. She was very modest, always belittling herself due to the disgrace of her first marriage. In an emotional letter on 14 February 1818, she once more emphasized her 'imperfection and defectiveness' and asked Froebel if he really wanted her and not better a 'girl of immaculate innocence and delicacy'.[63] At the same time, she averted her never-ending loyalty if he would really take her as his wife.

It was clear that the sickly Henriette would never be a mother. She might have had an organic disease, but it is also possible that her husband had infected her with gonorrhoea through his frequent affairs. Since no effective medication existed, she had probably become infertile in the further course of the disease. Henriette was open about it and wanted Froebel to be fully aware of the divorce and her health condition, which he had to discuss with Henriette's fiduciary doctor. However, Froebel was undeterred by the news of a possible non-sexual and childless relationship. He still felt Henriette was a 'mother' because she had adopted a little orphaned girl.[64]

There was another reason why Henriette was attractive. For the institution's sake, Froebel needed a wife with something to contribute, either through her personality and abilities, or financially. While Henriette was physically fragile and, due to her upbringing, hardly suited to the deprived, harsh life as a housewife in Keilhau, she had financial means. Her father, the war councillor Hoffmeister, was wealthy, and Henriette was expected to inherit it.[65] It's fair to say that Froebel's reason for courting Henriette was not romantic but rather strategic.

In October 1817, Froebel visited Berlin. While the official reason was his involvement in the living memorial to Luther to mark the tercentenary of the Reformation, he also asked Henriette's parents for her hand. The meeting proved an embarrassment for the unsuspecting suitor,[66] for Henriette's father considered one divorce enough and reacted coldly. He distrusted Froebel, a character so different to his own, and the feelings of his newly divorced daughter even more so.

Froebel didn't give up so easily, though. Yet, neither Weiß's letter of recommendation nor the verbal intervention of the pastor Wilmsen could convince Henriette's father that the gullible and dreamy Froebel was trustworthy or capable of taking care of his daughter. To make matters worse, Henriette's divorced husband demanded official proof that Froebel could support her. Froebel himself was also full of self-doubts, as he declared in an emotional letter to Henriette.[67] Ultimately, the pair married against the will of Henriette's parents on 11 September 1818. Her father handed her over 'with cold severity'. For Henriette, Keilhau was a new start and a new life – also under a new name: she already signed off with Wilhelmine before their marriage, on 4 July 1818.[68]

The boys had no idea that the marriage had taken place. Over the summer, most of them had stayed in Osterode, accompanied by Langethal. They had travelled through the Harz Mountains, and the trip was probably no coincidence, as the deserted institution made the beginning easier for Wilhelmine.[69] When they returned to Keilhau in October,[70] Wilhelmine was living with her foster daughter, Ernestine Crispini, and Froebel on the upper floor of the lower house. The boys were surprised. 'We were astonished to find Froebel no longer with the Hänolds, but with his wife in the pastor's lodgings when we arrived in Keilhau.'[71]

Soon, they no longer felt like the centre of attention. The men now spent time with Wilhelmine, and the children often had to play alone. But Wilhelmine's presence also changed Keilhau. Coffee, the disreputable drink of degenerate people and which every true German should avoid, was suddenly served on the gymnastics field! 'We couldn't let that go unrebuked', Christian Langethal recounted,

> and we held a great council among ourselves about what to do. The suggestion to nail a note to the door of the gymnastics field, which contained the words 'coffee house to the polluted gymnastics field', found general applause and was approved. Julius had the most beautiful hand; he should write it. Thought, done: we were all happy about the wonderful idea.[72]

The adults, however, didn't think it was a wonderful idea. Froebel wanted to speak to the boys, but to their surprise, they didn't receive the expected punitive lecture. Instead, Froebel appealed to their sense of honour and calmly asked: 'And this is supposed to be the thanks for our love for you, what you have posted out there?'[73] The boys were remorseful, shook hands with the educator 'tearfully', and promised to be better. And they kept their word, even if their life was changed forever. 'It never became like that again, the May month of our life in Keilhau was now over, although many beautiful summer months followed it.'[74]

Through Wilhelmine, Keilhau became the family-like institute that Froebel had envisioned. Wilhelmine was warm and loving, and gradually the children became accustomed to the 'Berlin *Base*' and the new conditions. Soon, the boys trusted and loved her. Wilhelmine, who had been raised in the comforts offered by salon life, also adapted to the new situation and the harsh conditions in Keilhau. It was a challenge for her, though. Wilhelmine wasn't the practical housewife that the institute desperately needed, and she often failed in practical matters; the food was often miserable and came at varying times. Soon, Albertine had to come from Osterode to help with the household.

Notwithstanding, Wilhelmine had a remarkable influence on the prosperity of the institution and made Keilhau and the learning environment more caring through tasteful furnishings. She brought much stimulation, orderliness, and unity to Keilhau, to which she became intimately attached.[75] As often as her housework allowed, she participated in educational activities. Wilhelmine also raised the level of conversation; the teachers no longer talked exclusively with the boys about knightly deeds and sporting activities and now separated themselves more often from the children. The famous Christmas celebrations in Keilhau took on a special glamour through her presence. The many letters she later wrote to the pupils from Switzerland show her motherly, caring feelings. Wilhelmine became the soul of Keilhau, especially by the womanly way in which she treated the so-often-peculiar Froebel.

Figure 4.5 Wilhelmine Froebel.
Bildarchiv Friedrich-Fröbel-Museum Bad Blankenburg (Picture Library Friedrich-Fröbel-Museum Bad Blankenburg).

And Froebel loved her in his way, even if it wasn't a love match. By marrying her, Froebel had to give up the idea of finding a spiritual partner, becoming a father, and living a passionate relationship, something he wasn't necessarily looking for anyway. The support he received was more important and that he now had a woman at his side, who gave him stability in an acceptable relationship with the outside world. The marriage probably also helped him overcome the still burdensome and unclear relationship with Caroline von Holzhausen. Later, it helped Froebel cope with his inappropriate feelings for his nieces. While he might have married Wilhelmine to secure the heavily indebted project and give stability to the household, he clearly loved Wilhelmine and the marriage was harmonious. In the beginning, the marriage was close to Froebel's idea of a holy family.[76]

One should also not forget, though, that without Wilhelmine, many of Froebel's accomplishments wouldn't have been possible. As a literary-educated, philosophically trained woman with versatile interests, Wilhelmine was an ideal friend and companion for the restless and unconventional man. Wilhelmine did everything she could to calm and lift his spirits, and her letters reveal her deep understanding of Froebel's aspirations which she supported fully. Wilhelmine always stood by him, both in good times and in times of sorrow and decline.

The Institute's Fourth Founder: Christian Froebel

Around 1819/20, Keilhau's future looked promising. The institute now had its mother, the most necessary renovations were complete, and more and more pupils were enrolling. Since the tercentenary of the Reformation in 1817, Froebel had been toying with the idea of creating a living memorial to Martin Luther by giving descendants a free education in Keilhau. Langethal had secured considerable sums through his Berlin connections, and they had finally found two boys descended from Luther's uncle, Ernst and Georg Luther, the sons of a cowherd in the village of Möhra.[77] In the spring of 1819, the two 'swains'[78] arrived, and in autumn, the eleventh pupil joined. The institute was flourishing, and whoever visited at the time was enchanted by the cheerful spirit that prevailed.

But the growth brought new problems. Above all hovered the financial woes. Since the lease with the Hänolds had ended, everyone now lived in the narrow space of the lower house, where the old aunts still occupied the lower room. Even after three additional bedrooms were created in the barn and the upper hall was converted into a teaching room, the space was extremely cramped. Due to the institute's low revenue – there might have been more pupils, but as in the case of the Luthers, most weren't paying any or paid only modest tuition fees – Keilhau lacked the means to expand the new teaching building. Without the expansion, however, the school's growth was in jeopardy.

Finally, Froebel, Langethal, and Middendorff resolved to charge a fee of 112 thalers per year. The fee was reasonable; still, Froebel often asked for less. He wasn't interested in money, but in admitting children whose parents believed in Keilhau's mission. Thus, the children of the pastor Bähring, including his daughters, the first female pupils, were allowed to participate in the lessons for free. The economic conditions in Keilhau worsened, and when Wilhelmine's father lent Froebel five hundred thalers against a receipt at the beginning of the winter of 1819, it only helped a little.[79]

It is, therefore, not an exaggeration to say that the institute would have ceased to exist if Christian Froebel hadn't stepped in.

Christian Froebel was a successful tradesman with a flourishing weaving mill. Froebel had been working on his brother for months to give up the business and join Keilhau with the entire family. His wife, Caroline, however, feared giving up the prosperous business and placing their future in the fragile educational work of his younger brother. In the end, though, Froebel was once again able to get what he wanted: Christian sold his business and property and moved to Keilhau on 11 May 1820 with his wife and three daughters: Albertina '*Albertine*' Mathilde (*1801), Emilia '*Emilie*' Dorothea (*1804), and Caroline *Elise* (*1814).

The only house that could accommodate the family was the washhouse, which would be their home for almost two years. Thanks to the new family, Keilhau was suddenly much more stable economically. Christian gave his brother a 'loan'[80] and thus brought in what the institution 'was lacking, namely money, or "funds", as the three friends always liked to call money'.[81] The new community members were furthermore instrumental due to their skills and expertise. The forty-year-old capable, intelligent, and skilled housewife, Caroline, and her daughters enhanced the housekeeping, which was soon running more smoothly. Wilhelmine accepted it and there wasn't much friction between the women. Wilhelmine and Caroline worked well together, making it easy for Caroline to support the community selflessly.[82] The letters that Wilhelmine later sent her sister-in-law show her affection. Caroline was soon admired by all the children and became an essential part of Keilhau.

Still, why did Christian give up his successful business and jeopardize the future of the whole family? Christian was likely disappointed by the narrow-minded, reactionary dictatorship of the great powers following the idealistic impetus of the Wars of Liberation. After the Wartburg Festival in 1817 and Kotzebue's murder in 1819, denunciations, press censorship, and the demagogue prosecutions made it almost impossible for independent-minded people to pursue their business and inclinations unmolested. Keilhau, on the other hand, was a place where young people were educated to become free, self-acting, self-thinking people, striving towards a common goal without mistrust and greed for profit. The community must have spoken to Christian's ideals, and he must have been convinced of the greatness and necessity of his brother's work. Otherwise, he wouldn't have yielded to persuasion. Christian's decision only makes sense as a rejection of the dominant society and a commitment to the free and patriotic spirit of the Keilhau community.

Christian and his whole family fitted in well and became essential to the community. Wichard Lange, who later married Wilhelm and Albertine Middendorff's daughter Allwine, called him 'the embodied archetype of beautiful, simple human greatness, a model of physical and mental health'.[83] Companions have stated that Christian bore very little resemblance to his brother, in both appearance and character. Christian Langethal described him as a 'handsome man with a sturdy and stocky build and a round, full face', a man with a clear mind and who was kind and mild and different from his brother and who 'was characterized by sharpness and brevity in nature and expression'.[84] One similarity, though, was that both knew what they wanted.

Christian quickly became an essential part of Keilhau due to his practical nature. He immediately painted and whitewashed the large parlour of the washhouse so that his family could live there. Furthermore, he took over the management of the small estate, which was soon providing the necessary means of living. Even more importantly, Christian's leadership relieved Froebel of the daily worries. Thanks to his practical skills and the help of many craftsmen as well as another advance of 1,000 thalers from Wilhelmine's father and Christian's own money,[85] the necessary renovations progressed very rapidly. In June 1821, the new school building was finally ready.[86] The boys moved in and the teachers soon followed, so Christian's family could live in the lower house.

One can agree with Christian Langethal's notion that Christian was 'the fourth founder of the institution'.[87] Not only wouldn't the institute have survived much longer without him and his money, but he also brought in a real sense of family life to Keilhau, which inspired Froebel.[88] Christian remained in Keilhau until the end of his life, a blind patriarch, well respected, and loved by many.

With the new space, the institute was able to grow. Regular field trips and journeys, for example, to the Fichtel Mountains in the summer of 1822, made the institute better known.[89] Froebel had initially thought of twenty-two pupils as the maximum and envisioned the new buildings accordingly, but soon the number far exceeded that.[90] What had started with a single room in 1817 blossomed rapidly and reached its peak in 1826 when fifty-six pupils attended the institute. The community now consisted of a classroom, a dormitory, a dining room, and a gymnasium; new living and utility rooms had also been built.

More pupils meant new teachers were needed, which led to problems. Language and music teachers came over from Rudolstadt and Herzog, a Swiss teacher from Lucerne taught history and German, and Schönbein from Metzingen instructed the pupils in the natural sciences. The older pupils, especially the nephews, served as teaching assistants and helped with the arithmetic, language, piano, and drawing lessons. Around 1826, the General German Educational Institute had grown into a full boarding school for boys (only a few girls attended lessons but never lived in Keilhau) with a familial character consisting of an elementary level and a secondary level that prepared for the transition to university. All adults shared the same ideas and attitudes, even if the unity was in jeopardy due to the new teachers. Keilhau was a real community. Visitors, among them Princess Karoline, praised the institute. After a visit, she wrote in May 1825 about the children: 'What they know is not a formless mass but has form and life and is immediately applied to life, if at all possible. Everyone is at home in himself; no one knows here about parroting and unclear knowledge.'[91] The princess in addition granted a 'loan' of 1,000 thalers, which she never claimed back. Keilhau's future looked rosy.

A Fruitful Time: The Concept of the Education of Humankind

The years between 1821 and 1826 were Froebel's most productive years. He devoted himself to the institute's establishment, even if he became increasingly less involved with the daily teaching. He also drafted his educational concept to justify Keilhau's practice. Here, in and through Keilhau, his school pedagogy gained its decisive expression, proper practice, and theoretical depth.

The productivity was made possible by Christian's arrival. Thanks to Christian overseeing the daily duties, Froebel no longer had to worry about such petty matters and could instead focus on formulating his educational and anthropological thoughts. Now, his independent theoretical activities started. What he wanted to achieve was nothing less than combining the law of the sphere, his religiosity, and Pestalozzi's elementary method into his concept of the 'edification'[92] of humankind' (*Menschenbildung*) to enable people to live a spherical life, to live in life unification.

Over the years that followed, Froebel was restless. From July 1820 until May 1821, he wrote down his thoughts in daily papers (*Tageblätter*). An extensive collection of ideas, the daily papers from 1816 to 1821 consist of around 1,780 pages.[93] The excessive writing was likely prompted by the irritations and emotions caused by his niece Albertine; manic writing was one way for Froebel to cope with personal issues throughout his life. He had done so in 1811 and 1816 and would do so again in 1831.

The daily papers allow great insights into Froebel's thinking at that time. They show his attempt to combine anthropology with educational thinking to develop a consistent world view. He wanted to create a metaphysically theologically founded anthropology. At the same time, his personal struggles become visible. The notes are also a remarkable piece of autobiography in connection with sphere-philosophical speculation, now with a stronger focus on Christianity. The educational work in Keilhau, though, plays less of a role.

Compared to earlier notes, Froebel's thinking changed. Now, the religious aspects that were deeply rooted in him since childhood became even more vital. He created a variant of his philosophy of the sphere by combining his thoughts about the spherical law with his image of Jesus Christ, thereby developing what can be called his trinity philosophy,[94] emphasizing the trinity of unity (*Einheit*), individuality (*Einzelheit*), and manifoldness (*Mannigfaltigkeit*), which can, according to Froebel, be found in all aspects of humanity, nature, and life in general. In addition to the second Keilhau pamphlet from 1821 titled *Durchgreifende, dem deutschen Charakter erschöpfend genügende Erziehung is das Grund- und Quellbedürfniß des deutschen Volkes* (*Education That Is Thorough and Exhaustively Sufficient for the German Character Is the Basic and Source Need of the German People*), the notes in the daily papers are the most concise[95] and comprehensible depiction of the spherical law; both texts were written almost simultaneously. The spherically based Christianity that Froebel created also clarifies why Christmas was the great festival in Keilhau.[96]

Froebel applied the trinity philosophy to all areas of life: love, obligation, fear, miracle, or prayer, but also family and marriage – Froebel looked at all from a trinity perspective:

> There are 3 purposes, or 3 reasons, or 3 causes for marriage; strictly and quite true to the innermost essence and meaning, for the earth or earthRelations (*ErdVerhältnisse*), these 3 reasons in their unification should make up the total reason, the total purpose of marriage … . The 3 main differences are: 1. External existence, external relations subsistence – external purpose. 2. Personal appropriation, personal possession – personal purpose. 3. Advancement, of the species, development, formation and further education of mankind – general purpose.[97]

These purposes are similar to individuality (personal purpose), manifoldness (external purpose), and unity (general purpose). One wonders today what Froebel made of his marriage, which didn't match such aspirations.

In the daily papers, Froebel also prepared what would be the essential idea for the rest of his life: human beings have to live in trinity – in life unification as he would later say – to become whole human beings: 'My aspiration, my calling, my destiny – our aspiration, our calling, our destiny is: to present unity harmony in the universe in the physical and psychic world through word and teaching and life, cognition and doing.'[98]

The daily papers also show Froebel's personal struggles. One can see his desperation. Often, he felt misunderstood, disregarded, and alone in his aspirations.[99] In his suffering, he compared his life to that of Jesus, pointing out alleged similarities or differences. 'Jesus died an agonizing painful bitter death, I have to live an agonizing painful hard bitter life,'[100] 'I must serve as Jesus served God,'[101] or 'My profession, my destiny is to develop the revealed religion according to the way and on the basis of the teachings of Jesus himself.'[102] Increasingly, Froebel saw himself not only as a mere educator but as a kind of religious founder and the undisputed community leader. Froebel had never been shy of such aspirations, but such tendencies increased in the 1820s, and with it also his claim to complete dominance within the community. Occasionally, self-doubt shimmers through, seen in the context of the trinity like the admitted faults of ambition, selfishness, and jealousy, which he relativized immediately since such qualities can also be found in the C (Caroline von Holzhausen) close to him, in W (Wilhelmine) the G (wife), in A (Albertine) or the Br (brother Christian). Fighting these three faults, according to his further thinking, is like Jesus's fight in the desert.[103] Froebel was no stranger to hubris at that time.

Froebel had planned to turn the notes into a book called *Das Streben der Menschen* (*The Striving of Humankind*). On 10 February 1821, he also toyed with the idea of a 'general comprehensive, exhaustive, sufficient educational writing' with the title (*Die Natur, der Mensch und das Leben oder) Der Mensch u dessen Erziehung oder Religion und Trinität Gottes der höchste u einzige Erziehungsgrundsatz* ((*Nature, Man and Life or) Man and His Education or Religion and Trinity of God the Highest and Only Principle of Education*). However, he abandoned the book project until he took it up again under the theme of an 'edification of humankind' after 1823.[104]

Instead, he used the daily papers for the six Keilhau advertising pamphlets, which appeared in rapid succession in Lorenz Oken's magazine *Isis* and as independent publications between 1821 and 1823. While the pamphlets were written to present the institute to a broader audience, they went far beyond that. In these writings, Froebel formulated the basic features of his pedagogy, advocating for the general education of the people, and developed his philosophical foundation – the law of the sphere. Froebel was restlessly active, always feeling misunderstood, and not valued enough, constantly trying to convince the world of the correctness and importance of his thoughts and principles.

The world, however, wasn't listening.

The first publication, *An unser Deutsches Volk* (*To Our German People*) from 1820, presented Froebel's thesis that a national renewal of the German people is necessary and possible through education. In a sense, he picked up the approach of Fichte's *Addresses to the German Nation* from 1806. Froebel didn't address a particular class or group of people but 'our German people' because he envisioned education as the right of all. Only the education of free and equal citizens striving for a unified nation state, according to Froebel, can meet the current social demands. In the second part of the writing, he described Keilhau's educational plan, which was still reminiscent of Yverdon but already emphasized the importance of a family-like education and occupations in the house, yard, and garden. In the third publication, *Die Grundsätze, der Zweck und das Innere Leben der allgemeinen Deutschen Erziehungsanstalt in Keilhau bei Rudolstadt* (*The Principles, Purpose and Inner Life of the General German Educational Institution in Keilhau Near Rudolstadt*) (1821), Froebel explained Keilhau's educational plan in greater detail by distinguishing between a basic, first level of instruction and a second level of traditional instruction in subjects. Both the fourth, *Die allgemeine Deutsche Erziehungsanstalt in Keilhau betreffend* (*Concerning the General German Educational Institution in Keilhau*) and the fifth pamphlet, *Über deutsche Erziehung überhaupt und über das allgemeine Deutsche der Erziehungsanstalt in Keilhau insbesondere* (*On German Education in General and on the General German of the Educational Institution in Keilhau in Particular*) from 1822, summarized the preceding writings. With the sixth and final writing, *Fortgesetzte Nachricht von der allgemeinen Deutschen Erziehungsanstalt in Keilhau* (*Continued News from the General German Educational Institute in Keilhau*) (1823), Froebel presented didactic innovations and reflected on the relationship between the boarding school and the parental home.

The most important writing in this series, however, was the second pamphlet from 1821. Froebel had begun writing it around 1819 and based it on drafts of the spherical law from the Göttingen period and the daily papers. The writing contains the spherical law in concise formulations, complemented by his thoughts on how the German people can be educated to their fullest potential.[105] It might be the most accessible writing to approach Froebel's philosophy of the sphere.

Froebel's Episteme: The Law of the Sphere

Until the end of his life, the idea of the law of the sphere and the related concept of life unification shaped Froebel's thinking, educational practice, and living. For Froebel, everything in his life was a logically necessary extension of his metaphysical-religious world view. Anthropology, general pedagogical theory, school pedagogy, and kindergarten practice derive from this specific view of the world, humankind, and the human being. He wanted to educate children according to the spherical law so that they could live a spherical life. For him, the united community of Keilhau was an expression of such life unification. Without understanding the spherical law, one can't understand Froebel's pedagogical thinking.[106] But what does it mean?

Froebel was a deeply religious person. From a purely formal point of view, he was a Protestant, but it's a simplification to assign his idea of Christianity to a single denomination. His Christianity was interdenominational, even if evangelical religiosity prevailed due to the powerful impact of the Protestant pastoral milieu he grew up in. But his Christian self-understanding, determined by sin and punishment in his youth, changed over the years and developed into a very different religiosity. If Froebel referred to exemplary models of human life, for example, he never referred to the church as the recognized authority for guidance, but directly to the life of Jesus. For Froebel, Jesus' life served as the model for one's actions, while the church wasn't a norm-giving institution for Froebel. On the contrary, he often expressed his discomfort with the official church.[107] That doesn't mean Froebel rejected religiosity, though. Like many others at that time, Froebel wanted to find 'true' Christianity, alternatives to the existing models – for him, the law of the sphere.

Froebel's religiosity is usually described as panentheism.[108] Froebel developed his concept before he started his correspondence with the philosopher Karl Christian Friedrich Krause, who coined the term panentheism in 1823. According to Krause, panentheism means that 'the One in itself and through itself also sees the All'.[109] While Froebel developed it independently, his friendship with Krause made the concept even more attractive. It's best understood as a complex product of elements of his Christianity in combination with ideas of contemporary philosophy such as (Absolute) Idealism, Panentheism, Romanticism, and the Enlightenment. There were other influences – above all, Pestalozzi's pedagogy, Arndt's national education, but also Schiller's and (somewhat weaker) Fichte's, Novalis', and Schelling's natural philosophy. Froebel combined those influences with natural-philosophical speculation in a very individual reprocessing.

Panentheism refers to the idea that unity and allness, the individual and the total, are connected and that God and the world are in an entangled relationship. God and the world are interrelated, with the world being in God and God being in the world. God is vivid in the sensual and in nature; the divine is the source of being and life. While pantheism asserts that everything is God, panentheism claims that God is greater than the universe; it's a universal spirit that is present everywhere and all the time but transcends all things created. Today that sounds esoteric.

For Froebel, humanity is tasked with understanding that God can be seen in everything and to live accordingly. Only the human being is called upon to be self-conscious and self-determining. Humans not only perceive their environment with their senses but can understand it through reason, and they can also understand the connections among all that exists. Only humans can realize what blindly happens in nature. The human being, Froebel's thinking goes, does not only live in the sphere but can also understand it. Humans must comprehend that they exist as a unity just as all being exists as a unity, and they also need to be conscious of this unity of all that exists. This way, any human being can form their inner by reflecting on their spherical essence and acting spherically.

Humans, however, are also tasked with living spherically by leading a conscious life. Only humans can grasp the structure of the external reality in its spherical essence and understand themselves as such spherical beings. By reflecting on themselves, humans understand themselves as self-aware beings and, at the same time, grasp the lawfulness of nature. In the whole of reality, in the cosmos, everything is related to everything, and every being (*Seiende*) unfolds themselves in this context. God does not work through revelations but – and this is Froebel's panentheistic position – indirectly through the divine lawfulness in things. God, however, does not merge into creation. For Froebel, God and creation aren't one. As a panentheist, Froebel assumed that God and creation are divorced but connected by the infinite, not exhausting radiation of God in creation, such as nature and spirit (the human being).

However, it is not enough to do so unconsciously. Instead, human beings need to live the spherical – to live life unification, a concept closely connected to the law of the sphere. While the spherical law is the law that exists in all things, life unification is the goal of the entire human life and education. To come true, every creature, as a child of God, strives to express the divine powers and internal laws in them externally; they want to make the inner outer. That is especially true for human beings. Moreover, humans first must develop an internal awareness of these regularities or structures. They need to act according to this awareness because then they can express their internal correlation externally. If the internal and external are combined, life unification is executed. As a creature born out of the unity (God) and destined to have self-awareness and rationality, the human being has the responsibility, or as Froebel puts it: the calling to reach life unification or, in other words, to gain an understanding of the regularities and their unity.

The Education of Man

In everything rests, works and rules an eternal law; it spoke and speaks itself in the outside, in nature, as in the inside, in the spirit, and in the both uniting (*Einenden*), in the life always equally clear and equally determined ... . This supreme (*allwaltende*) law underlays necessarily an all-acting (*allwirkende*), itself clear, living, itself knowing, therefore eternally existing unity ... . This unity is God.[110]

It is with these famous lines that Froebel begins his most fundamental work, *The Education of Man*. The translation is unfortunate; 'Education of Humankind' would be more suitable. It was published in 1826 as *Die Menschenerziehung, die Erziehungs-, Unterrichts- und Lehrkunst, angestrebt in der allgemeinen deutschen Erziehungsanstalt zu Keilhau. 1. Band. Bis Zum begonnenen Knabenalter* (*The Education of Man, the Art of Education, Instruction and Teaching, Aimed at in the General German Educational Institution at Keilhau. First Volume. Up to the Beginning of Boyhood*). A comprehensive and difficult reading of almost five hundred pages, Froebel had been working on it since 1823 after abandoning *The Striving of Humankind*. The title was deliberately chosen and meant to be programmatic as Froebel wanted to express more strongly the responsibility for humanity. At the same time, he edited the weekly magazine *Die erziehenden Familien* (*The Educating Families*), which included numerous essays he had written. The various publications allowed the public to inform itself about Froebel's sphere-philosophical and pedagogical ideas thoroughly – unfortunately, the public wasn't interested in what he had to say, though, and didn't buy the book.[111]

Figure 4.6 *The Education of Man.*
Bildarchiv Friedrich-Fröbel-Museum Bad Blankenburg (Picture Library Friedrich-Fröbel-Museum Bad Blankenburg)

Froebel explicitly dedicated *The Education of Man* to 'Him', probably meaning God, but perhaps also to the all-powerful, eternal law of nature, which then, however, must be equally divine. The book starts with an introduction (§§ 1–23) that elaborates on the philosophical foundation of Froebel's thinking, another variation of the spherical law (Part 1). The second part deals with the developmental stages of infants and young children (§§ 24–44), followed by the third part that describes boyhood (§§ 45–55). The rest of the book examines the 'main groups of subjects' in often tedious detail. Froebel had planned a second volume covering the pedagogy for further stages of human development – Keilhau had pupils aged seven to eighteen years; hence, this stage would have represented much of Keilhau's educational work. The second volume was never written, however.[112] One reason was probably the financial fiasco of *The Education of Man*; nevertheless, Froebel also lacked the scientific prerequisites to justify the connection between elementary and further specialized instruction didactically theoretically.

Since a multivolume edition was planned, Froebel presented the essential foundation of his pedagogy in detail and systematically in the first volume. Broader and more profoundly than before, he explored philosophical insights and included mathematical, scientific, and linguistic findings. The extensiveness gives *The Education of Man* a unique position in Froebel's oeuvre as it provides a comprehensive insight into the theoretical foundation, main goals, contents, means, and methods of his 'developing-educating humane edification' (*entwickelnd-erziehende Menschenbildung*). It's mainly a theory of school and a school's educational curriculum. The largest part describes the 'main groups of instruction subjects' (*Hauptgruppen der Unterrichtsgegenstände*) – religion, natural sciences and mathematics, language, and the arts – followed by sixteen 'educational and teaching means' and the presentation of seventeen courses.[113] Today, though, the introduction is the most valuable part. The first twenty-three paragraphs summarize the sphere reflections of the past fifteen years and represent the essence of Froebel's world view at the time.[114]

Froebel had hoped for a broad readership. However, he was soon disappointed. *The Education of Man* might be famous today, but it didn't attract much attention back then. It was hardly noticed and, financially, it was a disaster that added, in addition to the costs for the new buildings, to Keilhau's already dire financial situation.[115] The book was self-published, which was only possible because Wilhelmine's father had died in spring 1825 and the estate promised relief from many worries. However, the self-publication was a severe mistake as no one in Keilhau possessed the necessary skills of the book trade.[116] Furthermore, the complicated writing style, the many ambiguous expressions, and the cluttered and awkward style with endless repetitions made the book challenging to comprehend. It rather dulled than engaged its few readers. Ultimately, Keilhau gave away copies for free and begged people to read them.[117] The book simply wasn't of interest to his contemporaries; not many cared what the nobody in Keilhau had to say about education. Therefore, very few contemporary readers penetrate the depth of this unique work.

Putting Theory into Practice: The 'Path'

The ideas outlined in the writings were to be implemented in Keilhau's (educational) everyday life. Ideas and practice shaped each other; in Keilhau, Froebel had the chance to test his concept for the education of humankind.

Today, it's difficult to say what daily life in Keilhau looked like, as only limited descriptions exist. Julius Froebel and Christian Langethal, and to a certain degree also Bernhard Bähring, have shared their memories of Keilhau.[118] Their memories show an appreciation for the pedagogy, but also that they experienced the method, called the 'path' (*Gang*), as defective and hindering.

Keilhau's goal was to form independent, free-thinking, and self-active human beings. The ideas of the Wars of Liberation lived on in the seclusive valley; the 'spirit' of those years was 'incarnated in the institution,'[119] according to Barop. Contrary to contemporary elementary schools or gymnasiums, Keilhau stood for political freedom, civic democracy, and the nationalist idea, even during the Restoration era. Froebel's vision, according to Langethal,[120] was to educate originals and not copies, to educate people and not machines, not 'show horses' – children 'which one presents to attract the public's attention.'[121] Julius Froebel experienced it similarly. 'We should simply be educated "to be human beings", and from the knowledge of human nature it should follow what belongs to it. All-round development from the inner to the outer was the pedagogical slogan which I heard a hundred times from the mouth of my uncle and his disciples.'[122] That mind, spirit, and body were supposed to be developed harmoniously was something the children valued for the rest of their lives. Schooling – or, as Froebel preferred to call it, the 'educating teaching' – was supposed to be holistic, even if unique talents were supported. Cognitive ('thinking') and physical ('doing') activities were connected with the law of the sphere as the basis of schooling and boarding school life.

School days were quite long in Keilhau; even in winter, the community gathered at 6:30 a.m. Learning took place until 1 p.m., with half an hour for breakfast. From 2 to 4 p.m. and 5 to 7 p.m., pupils were again 'on duty'. In the mornings, the focus was on the 'head', while hands-on activities, calligraphy, drawing, music, or foreign language lessons dominated the afternoons. Wednesday and Saturday afternoons were free for independent activities and walks. The Sunday sermon was repeated in the Monday morning hour and applied by Froebel to Keilhau's daily life. The school day ended at 7 p.m. with religious singing, then the day-pupils such as the Bähring children walked home. After the evening meal, the children had some free time.

Later in life, the pupils called Keilhau 'praiseworthy'.[123] Nevertheless, they all experienced the actual teaching as flawed. Langethal wrote:

> I have now described Froebel as an educator, I confess that I share his principles, therefore I consider him to be one of the wisest pedagogues and only regret that I cannot say the same about his teaching. That Froebel was also a creative spirit in this cannot be denied, for it was precisely through this that he got into the wrong ways.[124]

Froebel must have insisted that all educational activities follow the 'path'. The general idea of the 'path' was to encourage discovery and creative solving, thinking comprehension, and application, with independent activities as the most important means of education. In principle, it was an innovative idea. But the insistence on the 'path' didn't work in the classroom. Still, Froebel was strict about keeping to the 'path', the slow and gradual build-up of individual topics, proceeding from the simple to the compound and always from what the children knew by sight. Too often, Froebel took the 'path' to an extreme. He didn't 'distinguish the different natures of the branches of knowledge, and therefore everything was lumped together'. More importantly, because his knowledge was insufficient, he 'lingered far too long on what he knew, extending it into the petty by unnecessary subdivision'.[125] Every subject – numbers, forms, tones, languages – started from the simplest form to more complex ones, and doing came before understanding.

While the boys detested the 'path', they valued Froebel as a teacher. Julius Froebel, who was critical of his uncle, praised the 'lively, invigorating' spirit of the school and Froebel's talent as an educator, which, in his words, was 'an extraordinary' one.[126] In the subjects in which Froebel was knowledgeable, the teaching was good, and 'one would have had to call it excellent if it had not been extended so far'.[127] Langethal was of a similar opinion, pointing out that 'no one else understood as well as he [Froebel] did how to exercise them with the right tact and to avoid extremes that could harm his work'.[128] However, Froebel often went too far or ignored his principles, and in the subjects 'in which Froebel understood nothing',[129] the lessons were useless.

Later, Froebel only taught a little directly. Instead, he 'floated above the whole'.[130] Other subjects such as languages and history were taught by Middendorff and Langethal and later by the newly hired teachers who possessed the needed expertise. Langethal was primarily responsible for many educational activities, even if Froebel and Middendorff continued to influence the lessons. However, everyone had to follow the 'path'. 'The idea of lawful development according to the "path" tyrannized us with the method relentlessly', wrote Julius Froebel. It was even worse when the older pupils had to give a lesson. While it was an innovative idea that might have worked in principle, the pupils who now had to teach often hadn't grasped the concept fully. Thus, the lesson was useless. Or, as Langethal puts it: 'If a student is to teach every morning what he learned the day before and has halfway grasped, the teaching must become bad.'[131] As a result, children didn't learn much, at least not facts and knowledge.

Langethal must have been the most capable teacher. Often, he had to make up for Froebel's shortcomings. 'Unfortunately, by then, a lot of time had been lost unnecessarily.'[132] While it wasn't a problem for the capable children who were able to make up for missed knowledge later – for example, Ferdinand was quite successful as a student in Jena[133] – for many, Froebel's teaching method was disadvantageous. It especially didn't work for many later pupils who had already struggled educationally before joining Keilhau, which is why they had come there in the first place. As a result, the 'public gradually came to believe that nothing could be learned in Keilhau.'[134] Only after Froebel had left and Barop was in charge did the teaching improve. Or, to use Langethal's words: 'One can see from all this that the Keilhau education of Froebel's time had its deep shadows, and to have cleared these is a glory for the new Keilhau.'[135]

However, until Barop took over, Keilhau's reputation suffered, and the growth was followed by an even more rapid and worrisome decline that would jeopardize Keilhau's future.

5

Keilhau's Decline and Froebel's Departure

One reason for Keilhau's new problems was that it had become too big. Initially, it was supposed to be a family-like institute for a maximum of twenty-four boys, a realistic size for the small estate. However, Froebel was never willing to sacrifice his lofty ideas for the sake of practicability: 'He still looked to the future with great hopes.' Christian Langethal summarized Froebel's mindset well. 'His imagination conjured up a cheerful picture of future years, and we know that no one else knew how to build magnificent pleasure palaces to dizzying heights like he did.'[1] Thus, Froebel constantly admitted new pupils, even when Keilhau couldn't accommodate them anymore. It wasn't about the money, which never interested Froebel. Instead, it was impracticality combined with pride. Now, with the success he had dreamed of for so long, Froebel wasn't willing to act responsibly. Instead of making decisions in Keilhau's best interest, he let the institute grow, and this led to practical problems such as unsatisfactory meals, which the children complained about to their parents.

Due to the new children, new buildings became necessary. In 1824, a new large hall and several attics above it had been built, a costly endeavour that Keilhau couldn't actually afford. What drove the costs through the roof, though, was Froebel's penchant for thoroughness. Everything, including the children's teaching and playing materials, had to be of the best quality. Initially, Froebel was able to appease the craftsmen. One popular story tells of how a locksmith, when asked by his lawyer to sue Froebel, replied that he would rather lose his hard-earned money than doubt the honour of Keilhau. Soon, however, many craftsmen became concerned that they would never see their money because everyone knew Froebel was living from hand to mouth.

That Froebel wasn't able to manage the school and finances properly, something he was never very interested in, became an issue. Froebel, the educator of humankind, didn't want to be burdened with running an institute effectively and efficiently. Despite the support of many – his brother and Middendorff sacrificed their inheritances, the countess gave a 'loan' of 1,000 thalers, and Wilhelmine received a considerable inheritance[2] – Keilhau was soon highly indebted and threatened with bankruptcy. Later, in challenging negotiations with creditors, Middendorff had to flatter them while Froebel escaped through the back door.[3] The financial worries led Froebel to become increasingly withdrawn and irritable.

The increasing number of students additionally led to educational problems. Now, with a diverse group of more than sixty children, it wasn't a united community anymore. New teachers needed to be hired, but they had to buy into Froebel's educational philosophy and indisputable leadership. Such teachers weren't easy to find, though. Soon, Froebel had to deal with employees who didn't care about Keilhau and its mission – a situation like in Yverdon twenty years previously. 'If Froebel had followed this original and very intelligently designed plan, or rather if he had been able to follow it', Christian Langethal described the misery, 'many a discrepancy would have been avoided later. His house would have been quite excellent and satisfied all demands.'[4]

A 'Demagogue's Nest'?

Keilhau's reputation was damaged further when it was suspected of being a refuge for demagogues. It wasn't only the old German dress and long hair that aroused suspicions, though, but also the fact that Middendorff's nephew Johannes Arnold Barop had joined the institute. The twenty-year-old student first visited Keilhau in 1823 as a friend rather than a teacher. As a fraternity member, Barop was considered suspicious within the political context of the Carlsbad Decrees and the persecution of demagogues (*Demagogenverfolgung*) that ensued. Secret police sat in on Schleiermacher's lectures, Wilhelm von Humboldt was removed from office, Jahn was arrested, and Arndt was forced to retire after his arrest – to name just a few prominent examples. Barop, who had been dubbed a 'prophet' by his fellow students in Halle, had become the subject of persecution. Suspected of demagogy in various writings, he was charged at the end of 1824 and sentenced to three months in prison, which he served in Wittenberg in 1825. Though his sentence was relatively lenient, the consequences for Keilhau were severe. Since Barop had been staying in Keilhau when his papers were seized, it was now portrayed as a hotbed of demagogy, both publicly and privately. Prussia and the Bundestag demanded Schwarzburg-Rudolstadt close the institute.

Ultimately, a commission led by superintendent Christian Zeh inspected the 'demagogue's nest'. He visited Keilhau on 23 November 1824 and 1 March 1825

Figure 5.1 Portrait of Johannes Arnold Barop, by August Lieber.

and published his official report in May 1825. In it, he praised the institute and expressed his approval of the 'fresh, vigorous, free and yet regulated spirit'. He described what he had witnessed in Keilhau as 'an intimately united family living in calm agreement', where all lived 'in the most cheerful activity', equal and free, 'like brothers of one father'.[5] Zeh's report was one of the best testimonies about Keilhau. Froebel, who had been deeply worried about the institute's future and even moodier than usual, was, of course, relieved.

Zeh's assessment that Keilhau was harmless and far from being a demagogue's stronghold was probably correct.[6] Wichard Lange later stated:

> It hardly needs to be assured at this point that there was not the slightest talk of political agitation in the institution … . The old freedom fighters, Froebel, Middendorff and Langethal … were naturally attached to our nation with great love and sought to educate German children to become Germans … . Of course, the shrewd pedagogues were as far removed from the pernicious endeavour to use education for political agitation as Sirius is from the earth.[7]

Interestingly, Julius Froebel saw things differently:

> In short, the school … was a hotbed of the revolutionary spirit of the time, and served the intentions of a party which, with all its great merits for our national development, always deserved the name of a sect … . But it is all the stranger that the German governments let us go unhindered. Probably there was no denunciator, and the Rudolstadt government, to which we were close enough, did not feel called upon to pursue high politics against us.[8]

Notwithstanding, Froebel was indeed a very unpolitical person. While he envisioned a different way of living, he was never a political activist and demagogue.

Thanks to Zeh's report, the government in Rudolstadt only forbade long hair and old German dress. The boys gladly complied; their appearance was, so they thought, of little consequence anyway.[9] Still, the persecution damaged Keilhau's reputation, and when the Prussian government published an order that pupils from 'revolutionary' schools wouldn't be allowed to enrol at Prussian universities, many frightened bourgeois parents unenrolled their children.[10]

Keilhau's reputation also wasn't helped by Barop returning to Keilhau in 1826 upon his release from prison. Barop's decision was a brave one, though, with severe consequences: his father, Johannes Herman Heinrich Barop, despised Frobel and blamed him for his brother-in-law, Middendorff, abandoning his parents to join Keilhau. Still, he let his son attend Middendorff's wedding as the family's representative, but threatened him with disinheritance if he stayed on afterwards. Convinced of Keilhau's pedagogical mission – and already in love with Emilie Froebel – the young Barop didn't care and officially joined Keilhau in 1827. Shortly after, Barop senior disinherited his son.

In the long term, Barop's arrival saved Keilhau. Without Barop, and this can't be stated clearly enough, the institute would have collapsed. Barop was a firm, purposeful personality with a manly and stately appearance. He was tall with full, dark hair and a long, full beard; indeed he looked like a revolutionary. When he did speak, which wasn't often, what he said was significant and apt. Compared to the handsome Barop, the lanky Froebel – with his protruding ears, low forehead, long and pointed nose, gaunt face, and sharp, haltering manner of speaking – never cut a good figure. And Barop, unlike Langethal and Middendorff, was willing to stand up to Froebel. He always maintained his independence, even if he accepted Froebel's educational principles. The two developed a collaborative but personally distant relationship, and disagreements between the two men were frequent. Interestingly, contrary to many other employees, Froebel was always able to reconcile with the much younger Barop to serve the common cause.

Keilhau's reputation suffered further due to a series of unfortunate incidents, which brought the institution into disrepute for negligence against the students in its care. One day, the dining room ceiling fell down and killed a pupil and a substitute teacher. In 1830, the music teacher Wilhelm Carl, who had joined Keilhau in 1825 aged twenty-one years, suffered a heart attack while bathing in the Saale. Carl had been a respected and well-beloved community member who 'lives and works in the institution's spirit and feels intimately connected with it.'[11] Many had seen Carl as the future husband of Christian's youngest daughter, Elise. Only the day before, he had written that it was 'so exhilarating to live amid a circle whose highest goal is the representation of a purely human life'.[12] Wilhelm Carl was the first to be buried in the institute's cemetery, with Froebel giving a warm eulogy.

The Undisputed Leader

While the external issues were a burden, the internal disputes were even more worrisome. Froebel was to blame for most of them. He had become increasingly irritable and now insisted on his role as the undisputed leader of the Keilhau community. There were also personal struggles, his 'inner demons', as some biographers have called them.

Froebel always saw himself as the ultimate authority. He hadn't even made a secret of it; already in 1817, when Langethal was contemplating joining Keilhau, Froebel declared that 'everything concerning education and instruction is determined solely and exclusively by me and takes place under my specific direction, where I cannot personally act directly'.[13] After Keilhau's successful establishment, Froebel stubbornly insisted on the correctness of the 'path' as the only way to teach, being 'deeply penetrated by the correctness of it and therefore unbending'.[14] He was neither open to justified criticism nor admitted any mistakes. No one was allowed to criticize Froebel, not even Langethal or Middendorff. If something went wrong, it was always the fault of the circumstances or others. 'The individualistic system of education', Julius Froebel wrote, 'which was calculated to establish spiritual and moral freedom, became pedagogical absolutism, which dared to assert its infallibility as boldly as the ecclesiastical infallibility of the Pope today'.[15] At least for Julius, his uncle had built an 'absolutism of the system'.[16] Froebel always had to have the final say, even if he lacked content knowledge. While Middendorff mostly blindly accepted everything that Froebel said, Langethal at least pointed out weaknesses and tried to correct them. However, he was never able to convince Froebel, and the lessons continued to be conducted miserably.

Froebel's leadership, as well as his erratic behaviour, had gone unchallenged in the community's early years. All members supported Froebel's vision wholeheartedly, and Froebel was allowed to act without restriction; his dominance was absolute. No member of the inner circle thought to seek a better paid position elsewhere. Whatever hardships they had to endure, they endured them. Everyone, including the women, enthusiastically believed in the educational mission.[17]

But with new teachers joining Keilhau, the situation changed. They were not wholly subservient and not used to Froebel's often irascible personality and harsh reactions. Froebel had always been prone to such outbursts, but during the years in Keilhau, his behaviour worsened, maybe because the constant financial worries had made him thin-skinned, and he had never experienced any objection. Notwithstanding, Froebel's erratic behaviour and treatment of his friends and co-workers disturbed many and drove away capable teachers, and ultimately some of the older pupils.

Again, Froebel had never been interested in equal partners and never even treated Middendorff and Langethal as such. What he wanted were teachers who obeyed and did what they were told. Christian Langethal wrote:

> Froebel was so imbued with the importance of his thoughts that he not only demanded literal execution of them, as far as he was able to control the matter himself, but he kept everything in his own hands as far as possible, and thereby extraordinarily restricted the effectiveness of his friends. A free response and now even independent action could so upset him that he did not speak for weeks, but for months, to the one who, in his opinion, had so transgressed against him.[18]

New teachers, and even his old friend and war comrade Bauer, were treated the same. After joining the community, Bauer soon angrily left Keilhau and later declared the former friend's entire demeanour hypocritical.[19] When someone passed on regards from Keilhau to Bauer in 1839, he replied dryly: 'After 12 (or 12½) years, the first friendly greeting again from Keilhau.'[20]

The new teachers weren't willing to accept Froebel's dominance silently, however, and especially Schönbein and the Swiss Karl Herzog maintained their critical independence. Internal disputes erupted in the second half of the 1820s, ironically somehow similar to Froebel's Yverdon experience. The new teachers were repelled, not to say shocked, when they experienced how Froebel dealt with his colleagues and friends. Even Middendorff and Langethal couldn't condone Froebel's behaviour anymore. 'The absolutism of the system was not only manifested in theory and method: it was also embodied in the person of Friedrich Froebel.'[21]

Julius Froebel has described the most infamous dispute in his memoirs. According to him, Langethal wanted to leave Keilhau for good, at which point Froebel confronted him in front of all the teachers and children.

> 'My former friend and co-worker, your teacher L . . wants to leave us' – he addressed us. 'He does not find in himself the strength of self-denial which should enable him to his profession' … . After more insulting accusations, Langethal defended himself. 'Not', he said, 'because I lack the strength of self-denial, but because you' – turning to my uncle – 'are not doing the work on which we have worked together out of love for humankind, but rather because self-love drives you, I want to leave you' … . 'You dare' – he [Froebel] said to him in the tone of a grand inquisitor – 'you dare to rebel against the duty which God has imposed on you! – Kiss the rod that punishes you, and do not presume a judgment that you are not qualified for.'[22]

Langethal then burst into tears. The teachers and pupils who witnessed the scene were outraged and disgusted by how Froebel treated the beloved Langethal. But his words had the intended effect. Langethal, still under Froebel's spell, stayed.

Today, it isn't easy to characterize Froebel's personality and role as Keilhau's leader. While some criticized him sharply, others remained loyal to him. Biographers have often described Froebel as a charismatic leader; a prominent example is Liebschner's biography from 1992 in which he quotes Julius Froebel as follows: 'Friedrich Froebel was one of the most remarkable men of his time. The head, with its parted hair falling down to his shoulders, appeared priest-like … . His gift as an educator was extraordinary, and in other times among other men, he might have become the founder of a religious order.'[23] However, Liebschner's quote is misleading. He doesn't quote Julius Froebel correctly; the accurate and complete quote is as follows:

> Friedrich Froebel was one of the strangest people of his time. His outer appearance was peculiar, although in it the general type of the more important representatives of an intellectual trend of that time in the German national life could not be misjudged. There is a bust of him, after which a photograph is excepted, and among a hundred intelligent people who get to see this or that one, there will not be one who does not want to ask who the man is or was who looked like that. The head with the parted hair falling to the shoulders had something priestly. The profile was very regular, almost antique, the expression sharp and puritanical. When I saw him for the first time in my childhood, he seemed different from all other people, and in the institution, he was regarded almost as a superior being. His talent for the educational profession was extraordinary, and at another time, among other people, he might have become a founder of a religion … . For his intimate friends and co-workers, he was the master on whose mouth they, his disciples, hung and whose sayings were gospel for them.[24]

While Julius, who left Keilhau in dispute, always acknowledged Froebel's pedagogical genius, he saw Froebel's character flaws, and many have described Froebel similarly. Froebel must have been a complicated character with often irascible and unacceptable behaviour. Thus, to think of Froebel as a charismatic leader seems to be a retrospective myth. It's safe to assume that he wasn't a charming personality; even his loyal supporters never described him as such. Froebel was impulsive, especially in his relationships with his closest employees. He could lose his temper quickly, which irritated many observers. In the end, many – not to say almost all the employees – distanced themselves from Froebel, and many left in dispute. Only Middendorff, and to a certain degree Barop, remained true to him until the very end. While he must have had immense power over people through his personality and ideas, he wasn't a beloved community leader.

Due to Froebel's behaviour, many well-educated and promising new teachers left Keilhau immediately or after only a short time. Others even went so far as to accuse Froebel of only being interested in becoming famous. The most outspoken critic was Dr Carl Herzog. Herzog didn't hold back with his criticism and sneeringly declared that many of the craftsmen were waiting for their money and that the unification and peace of mind preached by Froebel didn't exist in Keilhau. When his rants became public, Keilhau's reputation suffered even more.

Consequently, the institute started to fall apart. When Michaelis, who had briefly taught mathematics in Keilhau, left, Froebel's nephews Julius, Karl, and Theodor followed soon after. Julius, who had witnessed the conflict with Langethal, was repelled by the behaviour of his once-beloved uncle. 'The sectarian spirit and the grandmaster position, which my uncle had brought to light on this occasion, repelled me to the point of reluctance.'[25]

In his memoirs, Julius Frobel felt forced to explain his behaviour. He wasn't only disgusted by how his uncle treated his associates, but especially how he treated his mother. Julius blamed Froebel for his mother's dire economic situation. After selling the estate to Froebel, Christiane rented a farmhouse in Volkstädt near Rudolstadt. The purchase money, however, had remained with Froebel, who kept his nephews in the institution free of charge in exchange. They had agreed that Froebel would pay back the money, but he only did so little by little and often after long delays. Thus, Christiane couldn't start a new economic enterprise; even worse, she could hardly meet the necessities of life. 'During a hard winter, at 20 degrees of cold, I met my mother during a visit lying down with a heavy fever without money and without fuel, while Friedrich Froebel with hard words refused me the payment, for which I asked him for her and to which he was obliged.'[26] As usual, Froebel felt no sacrifice was too great to maintain his cause. It's clear why Julius felt Froebel was exploiting his mother.

Until this point, the now nineteen-year-old boy had been torn by his feelings for his mother and his beloved uncle. Now, things changed drastically. 'Now I began to hate the man, and it was natural that I could not stay in Keilhau.'[27] As the oldest of the brothers, Julius felt responsible for the family and wanted to leave to support his mother, which he did in 1825. Michaelis, who was now working for the *Cottha'sche Buchhandlung* publishing house, offered Julius a position as assistant after Julius contacted him on the advice of Schönbein and Herzog. Julius accepted and left Keilhau. Froebel's alleged reaction was short and dry: 'So go in God's name.'[28]

Froebel never forgave his nephew(s) for leaving Keilhau. Especially Julius was regarded as a renegade and disowned. When Froebel received letters from Julius, he sent them back unopened. Froebel allegedly told Karl and Theodor that he would put their letters on the fire unread. When the three contacted Christian Froebel in 1838 because they wanted to reconcile, Froebel replied coldly and let them know that it had been their fault and that they needed to apologize for what had happened in the past. 'This is the second thing you must acknowledge if you want to give yourself up on the hope of regaining clarification and unification of your family relationships. If you cannot, then burn this letter before you get unnecessarily excited; for we must now descend further and further into the particular and individual.'[29] Only later did Froebel became milder towards his nephews. Still, it would take until 1847 before Julius received some warm words from his uncle, and the relationship with Karl, who later married one of Froebel's students and lived in Hamburg at the same time as his uncle, remained complicated.

Froebel's 'Inner Demons': Albertine and Emilie Froebel

Froebel became increasingly challenging to handle. Especially the years from 1829 to 1831 were overshadowed by what some biographers have called his 'inner demons':[30] the struggle to understand himself and the complicated relationships with his nieces, especially Emilie, who was about to marry Barop. Froebel's actions led to a deep rift within the Keilhau community.

Biographers have alluded to Froebel's complicated relationships with his nieces, indicating that they had been odd and inappropriate. However, today it isn't at all clear what happened, why they were inappropriate, and how and why Froebel's behaviour irritated many in Keilhau. It's possible that previous biographers had access to sources that are today lost or could still rely on hearsay. These days, however, sources are rare and don't give a clear picture. One can only find vague remarks, especially in the letter to the women in Keilhau. Furthermore, Froebel's letters to Emilie and Barop also give an indication of his feelings. But we don't know how the nieces felt about their uncle's behaviour. Thus, one should be careful when trying to reconstruct what happened.

Nevertheless, after he departed from Keilhau, Froebel felt urged, again and again, to justify his past behaviour and how he had treated the community members. Furthermore, both Albertine and Emilie were very distant from the once-beloved uncle in later years, but it's likely that this was more due to Froebel's constant financial demands and their fear that their husbands would follow Froebel into his next adventure. They probably also never forgave their uncle that their husbands were away from Keilhau for 1½ or four years, respectively. In the following, we carefully try to reconstruct what happened and how it impacted the Keilhau community.

When Christian's family joined Keilhau, Emilie was not quite sixteen and Albertine was eighteen. The youngest daughter, Elise, was only six years and, interestingly, Froebel never showed much interest in her as a child. The relationship with Albertine, however, must have always been close. According to

Gumlich,[31] Froebel adored her passionately. He had twice asked for Albertine to come to Keilhau to keep house, but Caroline Froebel had always refused to send her. Only after Froebel's marriage was Albertine allowed to come.

When Christian's family moved to Keilhau, something afflicted the relationship with Wilhelmine. It's not clear what happened, however. When Albertine arrived, Froebel must have embraced her passionately and inappropriately; at least, that's how Wilhelmine perceived it. 'Albertine came, and at the same moment as I saw her enter our staircase, the full living memory of the whole peaceful and domestic life of Osterode came before, or rather into my soul, seized my mind as I had lived it before unconsciously and without reflection, so unconsciously and without reflection now.' Froebel describes his memory as follows in the letter to the women in Keilhau:

> Thus I saw and received, as it were, here in Albertine her entire family, at least or actually the entire life of her family, of which she was also a living member, in one *person*, in *her* person and thus the expression of my reception, which seemed and was so natural to me there, I would like to say so necessary, as it is clear to me here and also seems necessary.[32]

It all sounds relatively harmless. However, it had a lasting impact on the community. Even eleven years later, Froebel was urged to justify his actions and reveal 'the highest, the deepest, innermost truth still hidden to me'.[33] There's not much more that we know. While it might have been weird that Froebel embarrassed Albertine instead of Caroline as the embodiment of Osterode's exemplary peaceful, domestic life, his later justification doesn't make much sense. It also doesn't explain why the memory tormented Froebel, Wilhelmine, and the community for so long. There must have been more to it. In the letter to the women in Keilhau, after a lengthy digression, Froebel continued to justify the pain and emptiness that had come from the incident by explaining that it had originated from 'my confusion, by not being able to give a clear account of it and by misunderstandings in several directions'.[34] This is one of Froebel's favourite rationales. Whenever someone close to him felt hurt by his behaviour, he claimed it to be a misinterpretation of his noble intentions. He never took ownership of his actions and their effect on other people, however. 'For where I wanted to give you dear Albertine signs of closeness, you found those of distance; where I wanted to give you those of sympathy, you read those of indifference; where I wanted to give you very dear Albertine proofs of the most intimate care of your innermost life, you felt rough disregard.'[35] It's another one of his typical arguments. It had been he, not Albertine, who had suffered and sacrificed.

Wilhelmine, and at least this we know, was hurt by her husband's actions. One reason might be that she had never experienced such passion from her husband. But it's possible that she, who would never be able to give him such passion or children, felt neglected and at the same time guilty for not giving Froebel what he longed for.[36]

Biographers have furthermore alluded that Froebel had erotic feelings for Albertine. If true, Froebel was always able to repress his feelings, and when Albertine and Middendorff came closer, it became easier. Froebel had always thought of the two as a couple, a united family. There isn't any evidence that he didn't support their love and relationship, even if it might have hurt him. He also fully supported the relationship between Langethal and Ernestine, Wilhelmine's foster daughter, whom Froebel, as he wrote twenty-five years later to Langethal, always saw as a daughter. That the four young people had become so close pleased Froebel and found his approval. It was what he had envisioned: a united life, united families, a real community living a spherical life.

On 16 September 1825, on Christian and Caroline's silver wedding anniversary, both couples celebrated their engagements. One year later, on Ascension Day 1826, the pastor Bähring married the two couples. That the marriages took place within the small Keilhau community was precisely what Froebel wanted. It showed how close the community was, but also how separated from the outside world. Still, united families were established through the marriages, which seemed essential for the community's continued existence. Living up to his ideal of united families was critical for Froebel. 'We are now together two to four times a week in the evenings, that's to say, my wife, I, Middendorff, Elise, Emilie; Mrs. Langethal, Mr. Carl Johann and the young girl who is with us, Luise Beyer from Jena.'[37] They often discussed books, even if it were mainly Froebel, Middendorff, and Wilhelmine who did the talking while the others listened quietly. It was nevertheless seen as worthwhile, as 'the whole is nevertheless a great exchange of the inner life and much that is beautiful for mind and spirit has been spoken.'[38] Froebel's position within the extended family might have been extremely dominant. However, he still longed to live the idea of a united family living.

Following her marriage, Albertine became increasingly distant from her uncle. Only two letters to her have survived; the one from 25 December 1831[39] was his attempt to reconcile with her. It's unknown if she ever answered, but it doesn't seem likely. Later, when Froebel lived in Blankenburg and Keilhau, they saw each other often and Albertine supported her uncle, though often reluctantly. They were no longer close.

Figure 5.2 Wilhelm and Albertine Middendorff.

After 'losing' Albertine to Middendorff, Froebel intensified his relationship with Emilie, rendering the relationship with her even more complicated. Biographers have noted that, in his way, Froebel must have loved and desired his niece. Again, sources are scarce.

In 1817, Emilie had stayed with her mother for fourteen days as a guest in Keilhau, a time that Froebel always cherished. When she moved to Keilhau, Emilie was not yet sixteen years, and Froebel soon enjoyed her companionship. Already in 1817, he wrote to her:

> If every friendly conversation that I have had with you since my last visit to your dear parents had become a letter to you, I almost believe that you would already have received so many of them from me that they could make up a whole book, so much and often have I thought of you and chatted with you.[40]

While in Keilhau, Froebel sent her little notes on her birthday on 11 July; in 1829, he devoted a poem to her. While his feelings for her might have been passionate and erotic, he needed her more as a conversation partner or, better still, as someone who listened to his never-ending monologues. As already mentioned,

Froebel became very withdrawn in the late 1820s. And while he was often quiet and lost in thought when he was with Wilhelmine or his associates, he opened up around Emilie. Around her, Froebel felt able to communicate everything that moved him and express his thoughts and feelings, more to clarify them for himself than to share them. 'Emilie, Emilie! You see how true my mind always was, how clearly it felt: didn't I always feel compelled to tell you everything and everything, when a thought that was important to both of us and so to mankind arose in my mind, when an eternally true feeling permeated my mind?'[41] And the very childish Emilie listened to him devoutly.[42] It must have been unsettling for the members of Keilhau to see how much time Froebel spent with the young woman, time he didn't spend with his wife.

It must have overwhelmed Emilie, too, who probably neither understood what her uncle wanted to tell her nor knew how she should react appropriately. An example of Froebel's boundless need for communication is the letter he wrote on 23 April 1825. He wrote from Berlin, where he stayed with Wilhelmine, explaining to Emilie how malign and degenerate Berlin is and that it can't be Keilhau's goal to educate children to return to such a life.[43] One wonders today what the young woman made of such words. And Froebel knew that he was overwhelming his niece by assailing her with his thoughts and feelings that were hard even for him to express clearly: 'Do not let the thought of answering me scare you I will gladly refrain from answering if you have only you have not made a frowning face while reading the letter.'[44]

Notwithstanding, Froebel needed Emilie for confession. 'She was a joyful child. I saw in her a joyful mind, and so I liked to share with her memories from my childhood and youth.' And he also needed her to understand himself. 'Whatever Emilie endured for my sake during this time and practiced the high art of self-conquest, if I perhaps thought less of her than of myself in these communications in relation to understanding – I found myself.' 'I found the right, so necessary self-respect.'[45] But seeing Emilie so often also meant growing estrangement from Wilhelmine. While he felt misunderstood and alone with his inner struggles, he increasingly withdrew from his wife and the community, and his behaviour at the same time became more irascible. Even for his friends, he was often unbearable, and the pupils suffered.[46] According to Halfter, 'the demon was above Keilhau's leader and told him to disregard all the mines laid in his being.'[47]

Again, one should be careful when making assumptions about the relationship. We don't know how Emilie felt and what she thought of her uncle's behaviour. Emilie had, however, fallen in love with Barop. The two met for the first time in

1823 and became closer after Barop's return in 1826. In 1827, Barop expressed his courtship of Emilie, so Christian asked him if he would stay in Keilhau. 'The idea we live by seems to be timely and important', Barop answered. 'And I have no doubt that people will be found who, if the idea is correctly executed, will trust us as we trust the invisible.'[48]

Froebel took the message with mixed feelings. On the one hand, he knew the capable Barop could save Keilhau from its decline. On the other hand, the marriage meant losing his most intimate listener. Froebel reacted by separating his life and mind from Emilie's. 'Since the decision was made that the two would marry – have I ever actually seen and spoken to you since that time?'[49] Still, he gave the couple his blessing and actively supported the blossoming relationship, wishing them nothing but the best. As with Albertine, Froebel sublimated his feelings by consolidating the relationship through marriage, thus making the niece taboo for himself.[50] However, in a letter to Barop on 11 May 1828, he implicitly declared how much Emilie meant to him. It was an inner struggle, and the separation showed him just how much he needed Emilie and what she meant to him. Her loss precipitated a crisis for him.

Another Disaster: Helba

After 1826, parents began to unenroll their children from Keilhau, as if from 'a headlong plague. It was as if everything about the institution was suddenly considered to be a sham and bad.'[51] In 1829, only five pupils lived in the large house, and Keilhau was on the brink of closing its doors for good.

To save Keilhau and its educational vision, Froebel looked for new opportunities and sources of funding. When the Duke of Sachsen-Meiningen showed an interest in sponsoring a new educational institute by providing the Helba estate, Froebel was excited. He saw it as the chance to save Keilhau not only as an institute but also as an idea. Froebel threw himself into work and began drafting an extensive plan for a comprehensive educational reform, a model for a unified educational system. The idea wasn't new; Froebel had written a draft in 1827 and now shared it with Barop on 18 February 1829. It was an ambitious and comprehensive plan. The institute would admit children from the age of three, thus including early childhood education for the first time. In association with Keilhau, the institute would have led to vocational training or a university entrance qualification. Froebel had already printed the announcing advertisement when people in the duke's circle began to slander Froebel. Soon,

Figure 5.3 Portrait of Friedrich Wilhelm August Froebel.

the duke became doubtful and forbade Froebel from publishing anything about Helba without special permission. Froebel was once again ridiculed. His reaction was the usual one when faced with opposition or mistrust: the offended Froebel immediately ended the negotiations.

It was another disaster that left its mark on Froebel, who felt misunderstood and alone, disconnected from Keilhau and was deeply frustrated. His lofty plans were crumbling before his eyes. The institute was collapsing, and copies of *The Education of Man* were piling up in Keilhau. No one was interested in his pedagogical concept outside of Keilhau. Not to speak of his personal crisis. He had failed as a human being; he was a weak and ambivalent man driven by his desires; and, due to his deeds, the spherical life in a united family was falling apart. At the end of the 1820s, Froebel was a tired and broken man.

In 1830, Barop assumed responsibility for Keilhau's administration. He immediately contacted the creditors to get a clear picture and demonstrate the willingness to square debts. The creditors, who had trusted Langethal the most, were relieved when they realized Barop would now be in charge. Soon after, new applications came. Under Barop's leadership, but without the man who had founded the institute, Keilhau began to grow again. As Christian Langethal puts it, Froebel's departure saved the institute in a certain sense.[52]

When the christening of the youngest member of the community – the son of Albertine and Wilhelm Middendorff, Wilhelm Jr – took place on 30 January 1831, Froebel turned the event into a celebration of unification. Since Barop was in Berlin to settle the affairs of his deceased father, Froebel assumed the role of the bride's suitor and solemnly requested her parents' consent, despite his inner struggles and feelings for Emilie. Probably not on this day but soon after, Froebel decided to leave Keilhau.

Froebel left Keilhau on 9 May 1831. Biographers have often claimed that Froebel's departure came suddenly to escape the wedding festivities. While it's not entirely untrue, the reality was probably more complicated, even if the marriage can be seen as the final blow. Two days later, Froebel arrived in Frankfurt to meet old acquaintances. Most importantly, though, he wanted to see Caroline von Holzhausen again. 'What is', Froebel asked himself, 'the power that draws me to this woman again and again, that forces me to not throw away the relationship unrecognized but to let it clarify itself in an illuminated way?'[53]

6

The Swiss Years

One Last Time: Caroline von Holzhausen

It didn't come as a complete surprise that Froebel wanted to see Caroline again. His departure also wasn't wholly hurried; rather, it had been imminent. Barop, encouraged by Froebel, had visited the von Holzhausens in March, which led to the revival of the correspondence between Caroline and Froebel. Today, three letters exist, written between 25 March and 15 April 1831, two of them long and detailed. In these letters, Froebel gave an account of Keilhau and justified his life and work there. In addition, he carefully addressed the religious tensions that had led to their previous alienation, claiming to be misunderstood, using his usual argumentation. Froebel hoped to gain his soulmate's approval for his achievements over the last years. While he never announced it officially, it was clear that Froebel wanted to see Caroline again – and so did she. A letter fragment exists in which Caroline expresses her hope to see him again one day.[1]

Froebel arrived in Frankfurt on 11 May and stayed until 14 July 1831. He didn't visit the von Holzhausens immediately, though, despite having been invited by Georg and Adolph. Instead, he first met old friends such as Susanne von Heyden and made new acquaintances, among them Xaver Schnyder von Wartensee (1786–1868), a well-liked musician and composer. Schnyder had stayed with Pestalozzi in Yverdon in 1816.

On 13 May, Caroline invited Froebel to the family's city apartment. Froebel accepted, and four days later, he moved into *Auf der* Öde. In the weeks that followed, Caroline, still the bustling lady of the world, passed Froebel around the Frankfurt salons. The strange, priestly looking Froebel with his long hair parted in the middle and his wooden, non-committal manner was a curiosity. However, the soirees mainly went well, even if Froebel was still socially awkward. The soirees allowed him to interest people in his pedagogical work, even if only few had heard of Keilhau or *The Education of Man*, as the disappointed Froebel wrote to Wilhelmine. Soon, Froebel started to give what he called 'lectures'.

Froebel had come to Frankfurt to open new professional opportunities. However, to see Caroline again was equally important. And while the relationship was warm and amiable, the previous intimacy didn't return. Caroline wasn't willing to buy into Froebel's claim to possess the ultimate truth. Whenever they discussed Froebel's spherical philosophy, educational approach, and the united living in Keilhau, Froebel insisted on its rightness, but Caroline quickly lost interest.

> Mrs. v. Holzhausen has already left the room twice in the evening and almost immediately during the conversation and without saying good night … but the victory of truth must finally begin somewhere, at least it must be fought for with dignity outside the four walls. Once I had to say to Mrs. von H., where the whole family was present: in the past she had been able to intimidate me by the way she asserted herself, but now the time was over, because after twenty years of validation I knew clearly the truth of my willing.[2]

It was clear that the relationship had changed and would never be as intimate as it once had been, and maybe now Froebel realized that the 'spiritual marriage' had been only a figment of his imagination. Finally, he was able to let Caroline go.

Seeing the woman he had desired and idolized for over twenty years had a cathartic effect on Froebel. It helped him realize how much Keilhau, and especially Wilhelmine, meant to him. 'Beloved wife', he wrote, 'you write to me that you have recognized your place and position; yes, your place and position is at my side and your place in my heart. Believe me, I not only know, no, my mind feels deeply what conjugal love, what spousal love is.'[3] While in Frankfurt, Froebel wrote at least thirteen letters to the Keilhau community, many addressed to his 'dearly beloved and dear wife', and his words show his struggle to find inner peace and, at the same time, continue to be a part of Keilhau. But it was also clear that they were drifting apart, which hurt and worried Froebel: 'For there is only one Keilhau spirit and only one Keilhau life, we are all foolish and every individual who … is dissatisfied with Keilhau despite all the hardships and pressure and even despite all misunderstandings and disturbances and pain, should realize this the whole as well as every individual vividly.'[4]

Initially, Froebel had promised to return for Emilie's wedding on around 15 June;[5] however, this never happened. There were practical reasons for him not wanting to come back. The institute didn't provide enough working opportunities for everyone anymore, which was why Helba had been so attractive as it would have enabled Froebel to stay close to Keilhau while being separated spatially. This might have helped everyone to overcome the tensions and find their ways of life. After the Helba disaster, such a future had become impossible. Living close to the newly married couple wasn't an option for Froebel either.[6]

Froebel knew that he was to blame. To justify his overly dominant role and departure, which he claimed to be his suffering and sacrifices, he explained it as necessary for the greater good:

> Now I move away … and the whole remains behind … and now I realize, if only this, the so vividly felt as clearly recognized and most firmly held unification or rather unity [*Einung*] of the whole, which is not at all capable of disturbing and clouding, the result of my present journey would be and is nevertheless already unspeakable much, indeed the highest thing that I could only foresee and expect of it.[7]

Yes, he might have hurt people, but it had only been for their own good. Moreover, wasn't he the one who was making the real sacrifice?

While in Frankfurt, a new and rather attractive option arose: Switzerland. Froebel first hinted at this option in his letter dated 28 May. He had grown closer to Xaver Schnyder, who had become a champion of Froebel. Schnyder was fascinated by Froebel's ideas and wanted to start an educational institute with Froebel in charge in his Wartensee Castle besides Lake Sempach. However, Froebel was undecided. Other future plans were Gotha to visit his nieces in Döllberg, which wasn't far from Keilhau, living from giving lectures in Frankfurt, or returning to Keilhau, at least for the wedding.[8]

Such plans, though, were short-lived. On 17 June 1831, he informed Wilhelmine that he had accepted Schnyder's offer. Keilhau would always 'remain to be my closer home and my closer fatherland (i.e., Germany), for which and to which my mind has always longed and I will always protect and cultivate it as the heart of my life under all circumstances,'[9] and every community member was welcome to join him – but he would go to Switzerland.

The back and forth shows Froebel's inner struggles. He likely wanted to test the community to see if he was still the leader. Maybe he even hoped they would ask him to reject the offer and return to Keilhau. If so, he was soon to be deeply disappointed. Keilhau reacted rather coldly, which hurt Froebel. 'For remember, neither from you, my Wilhelmine, nor from any of the beloved Keilhauer, have I heard even one word of the thoughts and views which especially my latter communications to you have awakened in you.'[10]

For the moment, Froebel really was on his own.

'Now My Tears Can Flow Silently' – Emilie's Marriage

A few days earlier, Froebel had learned from Emilie and Barop that their marriage would, as he had initially suggested, take place on 11 July 1831. Without knowing if the community leader and uncle would attend, Keilhau had decided to go ahead with the nuptials. Froebel had mainly ignored the topic and never indicated whether he would come or not. The couple didn't want to wait any longer; maybe they hoped the irascible uncle wouldn't come, but it is equally likely that they tried to force his return. Barop's ambiguous words hint at the former, though: 'How you want to be here on the feast, the 11th of the lily month, you know – and how it is best. I may wish for nothing but only insight into what should be. Every pain dissolve in higher joy; that I believe, that I hope, that I know certainly.'[11] While he wasn't uninvited, it hinted at what would be best for everyone. After all, Froebel would have had enough time to return in time. However, now he declared it to be impossible, even if he was torn: 'With what feelings I write this letter, who can describe them, [but] he who feels them, whose heart they flow through alternately and almost simultaneously.'[12] Froebel likely referred not only to leaving Wilhelmine behind but also saying goodbye to Keilhau and 'losing' Emilie.

Even without him attending, Froebel's actions around the wedding drove a deep wedge between him and the community, which upset many of them for the rest of their lives. Initially, Froebel had given the couple his warm blessing on 3 July. On 11 July, though, knowing he would be absent, he wrote three relatively short letters to Emilie, Barop, and the whole community. Only now, knowing that his words would arrive after the wedding, he told Emilie the truth:

> I must believe and fear that my body in these days can't meet the demands of the spirit, of the soul, and how sorry, how deeply sorry I would have been if the slightest, even just a barely noticeable hint of cloudiness had come into your celebration; I, no I wouldn't have done anything for it; but now everything is different and better: – now my tears can flow silently and in such quantity. I do not need to give an account to myself and others: why? – because I can, I don't know why? Now it doesn't disturb and cloud the celebration of your unification of soul and life that I am making known to you and to you these expressions of my innermost soul life, for in peace and clarity your soul and life covenant is now closed when these lines find you.[13]

Barop received similar words: 'Let me be silent Barop and say nothing more, let my tears flow silently Barop of which I do not know and cannot tell myself why they flow you Barop whom I love you dearly and forever, who I love your Emilie, dearly and forever, who I love you forever and who will give you God.'[14]

It's impossible to say today what drove Froebel to write these words. But Froebel knew what effect they would have. It was common in Keilhau to share letters, so he could assume that Wilhelmine – who was already wracked with guilt because she was neither the soulmate nor the mother Froebel had always longed for – would read his words to Emilie. Words that Wilhelmine wouldn't take lightly. Such considerations, though, were subordinate. The only things that mattered to Froebel were his emotions and pain; as usual, it was all about him. 'Renunciation and abandonment are my fate; I was born to lead by the most destructive examples in it.' Giving Emilie to the man she loved was nothing but 'renunciation and abandonment' for Froebel. Not being with them, so he wrote to the community, was hurting him, but his hope was that they would understand his absence was the 'greatest proof of silent renunciation and quiet deprivation.'[15] Being absent and giving away Emilie was nothing but another sacrifice for Keilhau's greater good.

At least he wished Emilie the best: 'Now farewell, O farewell well! Peace of mind Heavenly joys to you, to you and to your Barop. It is possible that we will see each other again in four weeks, or maybe only in four months, who may determine it? But until when I return, keep me an open sincere heart, is it possible a faithful trusting heart.'

Froebel must have known that his words would come back to him. For now, though, he had said his goodbyes to Keilhau. Leaving for Switzerland was the end of an era, but also a new beginning.

A New Life: Wartensee

Froebel's decision to move to Switzerland seems random. What if he hadn't met Schnyder? Nevertheless, Switzerland was an attractive option. It was the origin of Pestalozzi, Froebel's father-figure in everything related to education, who had died in 1827. Maybe even more critical, Switzerland was more free-minded and liberal than Germany. The French July Revolution of 1830 had led to the fall of the aristocratic and obscurantist governments in almost all cantons, and Froebel hoped to find political freedom and support, which he couldn't expect anywhere in Germany.

Froebel and Schnyder travelled together and arrived at Wartensee Castle at Lake Sempach on 20 July 1831. Schnyder left again for Frankfurt the next day, so

Froebel was alone in what he would call his 'Wartenburg'. The little castle on the lake's south shore was luxurious and lovely. From the boarded 'monastic parlour', Froebel could see the summit of Mount Pilatus, and the sun often shone on the stained glass. The castle had a lovely flower garden and chapel, and Froebel was delighted that he was allowed to use the library and the expensive silverware. It was an unfamiliar luxury.

The founding of the institute went quickly. On 12 August 1831, the canton's education council and small council announced the approval of the private educational institution in Wartensee.[16] However, the institute couldn't open immediately, which gave Froebel the time to reflect on his life and Keilhau. As expected, Emilie had shared his wedding letter with Wilhelmine, and Wilhelmine felt guilty, but this wasn't the only issue. As Wilhelmine told her husband, new tensions had arisen in the aftermath of his letter, whose words had disturbed herself but probably also Emilie's parents and the newlywed couple.

Froebel didn't chide Emilie for sharing the letter. Instead, Froebel felt the need to explain himself. He now wanted to enlighten all the women in Keilhau about his innermost feelings, to tell them 'the story of my heart, of my mind'[17] in absolute truth so that he would no longer be misunderstood. That had been his goal for a long time, Froebel told Wilhelmine in a separate letter. Sitting alone in the 'monastic parlour' of the magnificent estate, with the lake and mountains in front of him, Froebel wrote a hundred-page confessional letter, today referred to as the 'letter to the women in Keilhau'. Froebel intentionally addressed all women – Wilhelmine and Emilie, Elise and Albertine, Caroline and Ernestine – because, for him, the families formed a whole, and they all had lived and suffered for his educational idea. Froebel began writing his confession on 18 August 1831, and it took him three months to finish, working on it day and night. When not writing, he would read the letters from Keilhau's children, which expressed how deeply they loved him and hoped he would return. Their words touched him deeply, even if it would take until December before he replied to many with caring, understanding, and warm letters.[18] For the moment, only the women mattered.

The letter is a monstrously long document of life confession, but also justification. In retrospect, Froebel reflected on his childhood and youth, intimate moments such as his relationship with Caroline von Holzhausen, his erotic feelings for Albertine and Emilie, and his relationship with womankind. At the same time, it was a strong creed to the philosophy of the sphere, arguing that his life is exemplary and that the spherical law can be seen in him. While the letter is honest, open, and blunt, it still needs to be taken with a grain of salt. It was his attempt to justify his behaviour and life, and refute the (often unspoken) accusations in order to calm down the community and reconcile.

The long letter, a mix of autobiographical reflection and anthropological and educational remarks, was a forerunner of things to come. While in Switzerland, Froebel didn't publish much; the only official publication was *Die Grundzüge der Menschenerziehung* (*The Outlines of Human Education*) (1833), which had already been written in October 1830. It was another programme of national education and a call for national unification, which made it impossible to publish in Germany during the Restoration.[19] Instead, his letters became his new favourite means of developing and sharing ideas. Over the next five years, Froebel wrote almost two hundred, often very extensive, letters. Apart from the letter to the women, the sixty-page letter to the confirmands from April 1832, in which he focused on his religious self-discovery, stands out. It often took Froebel weeks to draft and write such letters. The letters weren't used for communication only; instead, he used them to develop his anthropology, philosophy, and pedagogy through autobiographical reflections, always emphasizing the universal truth of the spherical law. Froebel often justified his life as exemplary and an illustration of the spherical law or even humanity in general. While he had begun with such an approach in the letters to Krause and the Duke of Meiningen, in Switzerland it became common. There were different reasons for the never-ending stream of opaque words and thoughts. Froebel was lonely; after fifteen years within the close circle of the Keilhau community, he was now alone with his emotions and thoughts. Furthermore, he had lost what he had always envisioned, the united family living. Worse still, Keilhau was turning its back on him, and he must have been afraid of no longer being the community's leader. Thus, his letters were probably his attempt to maintain control over Keilhau from afar. Especially in the first months, Froebel was harsh and unyielding. The constantly recurring sermons must have annoyed Keilhau, mainly because large parts were *au fond* incomprehensible. While the community was fighting for Keilhau's survival daily, Froebel was creating worlds made of thought and words. It's unlikely that anyone, apart from Middendorff, Langethal, and Barop, took the time to read them, let alone understand them.

'A Miracle-Working Pedagogical Christ': Attacks on Froebel

The growing alienation from Keilhau wasn't the only stress of the first months in Switzerland.

Even before the new educational institute opened, Froebel was criticized heavily. On 1 October 1831, the *Appenzeller Zeitung,* a crucial liberal paper, published an anonymous attack with the headline *Einige Worte über die Wartenseer Erziehungsanstalt und den Stifter derselben Friedrich (August Wilhelm) Froebel aus Keilhau bei Rudolstadt in Thüringen (A Few Words about the Wartenseer Educational Institution and Its Founder Friedrich (August Wilhelm) Froebel from Keilhau Near Rudolstadt in Thuringia).* The author called Froebel a 'pedagogical adventurer' with a 'pitchman hut' who would announce 'with eloquent bombast a source of healing for all those in need of education'; a man without a 'profound plastic education (*blastische Bildung*)' who had 'absorbed Pestalozzi-Fichte's ideas about human and national education without digestion'; 'a miracle-working pedagogical Christ' who has united 'as much pride and vanity as ignorance and bias'[20] in himself and whose previous endeavours had been a financial disaster.

The malicious, deliberately hurtful criticism deeply wounded Froebel's self-esteem as a reform educator. Froebel, alone in the foreign country and without Keilhau's support, was hurt. That an insider must have written the attack only made things worst. Later, it was revealed that Karl Herzog, the Swiss history teacher who had stayed in Keilhau from 1825 until his departure after long quarrels in 1828, was the author. Despite the pain, Froebel was still optimistic: 'You will see from this, beloved', he wrote to Keilhau, 'that the Appenzeller or whoever else the journeyman is and where he lives, has not yet given me a mortal blow, which is what he actually wanted, that it was not a blow to eternal sleep, but that it was, which must have been necessary, an alarm clock to life.'[21]

Initially, Froebel didn't plan to defend himself publicly. The attack was pathetic and self-refuting; while his cause was good, true, and just, his work would speak for itself, so why defend it? However, Schnyder, who suspected Niederer, Krüsi, or Herzog of being the anonymous author, thought differently:

> You owe it to your honour, to the honour of your family, to your institution in Keilhau, you owe it to me, you owe it to our government, you owe it to all your friends, not to rest, not to rest, until you have documentarily disproved the mendaciousness of this article … . You are not only being attacked scientifically, but also civically and morally. You must not remain silent about this.[22]

But Froebel was reluctant, as the long letter to Schnyder from 6 to 11 November 1831 shows, in which he discusses the pros and cons of such a response. Interestingly, though, Froebel had already written the extended essay titled *Echo d.i. Widerhall einiger Worte über die Wartenseer Erziehugsanstalt (Echo d.i. Repercussion of Some Words about the Wartenseer Educational Institution)* between 15 and 23 October 1831. One of Froebel's most peculiar works, the essay is his attempt to refute each accusation in a tone that Froebel must have thought ironic, polemical, and humorous, even if some serious thoughts – for example, on the role of the educator – were included. For once, Froebel isn't trapped in his jargon. The central part, written as a Bildungsroman about himself as the 'stupid village Peter from the mountain', refuted the accusation of lacking 'profound plastic education' by demonstrating the opposite sarcastically. However, the piece was too long to be published in a journal, and there were no means for self-publication. Thus, 'Echo' was never published, apart from the last part in which Froebel demanded the author reveal his name. That no one read it was probably for the better. His lukewarm response wouldn't have helped much and ultimately only led to a disgruntled Schnyder.[23]

For Froebel, however, a public defence now seemed unnecessary. Only in February 1832, the *Neue Aargauer Zeitung* published a defence written by Langethal, Middendorff, and Barop that included export reports and testimonials.

The institute in Wartensee finally opened in November.[24] It was never a success, though, and only existed for a short time. Its pedagogical structure was similar to Keilhau's concept, with general and holistic education as the goal. It went beyond this, though, by including explicit curriculum differentiation to prepare the pupils for simple bourgeois trade(s), higher business life, or the arts and sciences (university maturity). The curriculum was further supplemented by modern languages (French, English, Italian), which made sense because Froebel wanted the institute to be a boarding school for German, French, English, and Italian children. It never happened, though, as only children from the surrounding area attended, and Wartensee remained a traditional day school. Only twelve boys and girls attended at the beginning.

'I Am to Be Lonely, Must Live Alone': Ongoing Tensions with Keilhau

'Two months ago today, you wrote and sent the last letters to me. Please consider this!'[25] These were Froebel's opening words to Keilhau on 4 November 1831. His frustration is typical of the first months in Switzerland. While Froebel needed solitude for self-reflection and self-analysis, the spatial and especially spiritual separation from Keilhau hurt him. Froebel missed Keilhau. What he feared most, though, was losing his influence. For many years, he had been the community's undisputed leader, but now Keilhau was drifting apart and making decisions that might have been best for Keilhau, but not the ones he wished for.

In this sense, the constant and often lengthy letters shouldn't only be seen as continuous reflections on his self and his relationship with Keilhau, even if they served this purpose. 'I am again in harmony with life because I always become richer through the same in me because I get through me or receive from the outside, therefore it is now also quite the same to me to be quiet and alone creating or in life and acting together',[26] he wrote to Elise Froebel, now one of his favourite correspondence partners. But such moments of happiness were short-lived, and afterward, Froebel was desperate and tried to maintain influence. While he was no longer officially in charge of Keilhau, Froebel continued to see himself as its 'father', including the right to demand financial and personal support. After all, wasn't he the one who possessed the ultimate truth, had shared it, and made Keilhau's united life possible? Wasn't it he who had sacrificed and suffered? Loyalty to him should be a given. But Keilhau lacked the financial resources to support Froebel in a way he felt appropriate, which increasingly frustrated him. The more he felt forsaken, the harsher his reactions. When his nephew Ferdinand, after completing his studies, joined him as an assistant teacher in November 1831, it wasn't enough. He wanted Elise, Christian's youngest, unmarried daughter, to come to keep house. The previous housekeeper had just quit because she couldn't stand it any longer with the eccentric.

The tensions intensified over the summer of 1832. Between 2 July and 10 August, Froebel wrote almost daily, typically addressing the community as a whole, as he saw Keilhau (including himself) as united and less as individuals. Froebel often addressed the 'non-understanding and misunderstanding (*Nicht- und Mißverstandenwerden*) of my letters'[27] and his actions, especially during his last months in Keilhau. Froebel now justified his departure as a necessary 'voluntary removal'[28] to enable each member to develop freely spiritually. He again declared that he only acted this way for the good of the community, not his own. Again and again, he claimed he was the one suffering. 'I am to be lonely, must live alone',[29] and he had made this sacrifice so that the community could understand life unification and live it. Keilhau grew tired of the never-ending tirades, however, and perceived his words as harsh and inordinate. The tensions only increased. Froebel, for his part, was relentless. While he sometimes realized he had gone too far, he never apologized and instead continued to justify his accusations as necessary for Keilhau's further development.[30]

To retain his influence, Froebel bombarded the community with his truths. Over many pages, he shared his insights with Keilhau, long and often incoherent, difficult-to-understand passages consisting of anthropological and educational thoughts, the law, and what it means to live as united families as well as Keilhau's unity. With this unceasing flood of words, Froebel wanted to convince Keilhau not only of the correctness of his ideas but also to justify his behaviour. We don't know if and how much Keilhau cared.

One shouldn't be overly judgmental, though. Froebel indeed wanted the best for Keilhau's future.[31] 'What is Wartensee supposed to be as an educational institution in relation to Keilhau? – Is Wartensee supposed to be a transplanted Keilhau, or a daughter, a further development of Keilhau?'[32] Froebel saw Wartensee as 'a real further development of Keilhau',[33] a part of the idea of Keilhau as a whole. In this sense, he felt Wartensee would benefit the youngest members of the community – Ferdinand, Wilhelm, and Elise – as it would enable them to find their path and way of living. It was for thIs reason, and not because of selfishness, that he wanted them to join him. 'These three should now become the three actual founders of the true foundation stones of the expanded work.'[34]

Even if Froebel's intentions were noble, Keilhau perceived it differently and considered his constant demands impossible. Above all, Froebel wanted two things: female support[35] and money, despite Keilhau's evident struggle for existence. Keilhau, on the other side, was reluctant to provide any resources, even bedding, for Froebel's uncertain endeavour, fearing that it would be lost forever without any benefit. And sending Elise? Not even Wilhelmine wanted to go to Switzerland, Middendorff wrote to Schnyder, so they would certainly not send young Elise there alone.[36] Still, Keilhau offered him an olive branch: Barop and Elise would come if they could come up with the travel costs.[37]

The proposal didn't satisfy Froebel. On the contrary, his tone became harsher and unyielding. In a letter from 25 July 1832, he attacked Langethal and Middendorff while defending his actions. 'Above, you complain or have complained there that no help came to you from me, that I always pointed you to yourself by force and that this took away your courage.' He accused Langethal, who had dared to criticize and contradict him: 'Here you say: according to my nature I cannot understand anything of which I do not find the truth in myself. Now where was the hostility of me, since I acted with you in the spirit of your own nature? Don't you find a contradiction here?'[38] The next day, his words to Middendorff were friendlier, but he still demanded loyalty: 'Up to this point we certainly go together – I do not doubt that. Now, however, we have arrived at the point from which our ways of looking at things and of representing them may, at least in terms of clarity and decisiveness, separate into two definite paths.'[39] Froebel was in a blind rage with everyone. He acknowledged that 'the entry and the history of the entry of the Osterode, the brother's family into the educational circle and their unification with the educational circle is the main reason for the effectiveness of the given spirit of our educational life as well as the foundation and cornerstone of the new to be established building of life'.[40] However, he now felt that his brother wasn't fully supporting the once common mission anymore. Everyone could read the personal reckonings as the letter was addressed to the community as a whole.

For Froebel, the condescending tone served the greater good. Treating the community in a disrespectful – maybe even punishing – way was necessary:

> Now, see here, is a main point of all complaining about me. But I always spoke to you: You have now once said we want to be knowledgeable, now I cannot treat you differently, take back the word, and immediately another way of treatment occurs from my side. Did I ever speak differently? …. . Should I now treat you as men-to-be less manly than the little boy? – You are not so small in my opinion, I could not think so small and little of you![41]

This was the overriding message of his letters in his first year in Switzerland. He had only acted in the community's best interest, for the greater good, and it was he who had made sacrifices.

Only once during the summer months of 1832 did Froebel cheer up. Schnyder had pledged to continue to support Wartensee financially so that Wartensee could exist until Easter 1833 – or at least this was Froebel's impression. Maybe Keilhau and Wartensee even would become a joint endeavour.

> Keilhau as the parent company of Wartensee enters into direct economic connection with Schnyder as the subsidiary company of Wartensee giving land and house. To support Wartensee economically and domestically becomes a joint affair of Schnyder and Keilhau … . Thus, Wartensee gets a genuine root in Keilhau and Keilhau receives and gets in Wartensee a blessed further development.[42]

For Froebel, it was a perfect solution. He would no longer be responsible for the institute's organization; rather, it would be Keilhau's and, especially, Barop's responsibility. And he could instead focus on the educational work.

The second, maybe even more important, reason for his good mood was Keilhau's promise to send Elise to Wartensee, accompanied by Barop.

Elise has decided to come here; they have decided to let her come here; I cannot find it anything other than right and good, I would like to say as salutary and necessary, we would have to want to give up our chosen life purpose and profession at least as a common one. You will accompany her here; I do not know how to arrange it any better.[43]

Suddenly, the otherwise so serious Froebel became preoccupied with even the most trivial of matters: 'If something is sent here, please enclose my red leather suspenders, they are necessary here.'[44]

But the cheerfulness was only short-lived. Early in September, Froebel announced that he would return 'for the promotion of the common work in Keilhau'[45] after Wartensee's closure on 28 September. Schnyder had refused to provide further funds, and without Schnyder's money, there was no future. Froebel felt betrayed and no longer obliged to stay: 'It looks and smells to me like Duke's politics: only sought division and discord is already won. This policy is worn out; against me, this knife is too blunt.'[46] Schnyder's betrayal hurt him. 'They don't believe you – nobody believes you! Because no one even believes, because no one loves, no one is faithful, no one united.'[47] Froebel only wanted to go home: 'I think it is best we return home.'[48] However, he needed 100 thalers from Keilhau for the journey as he was too old to walk.

What hurt him more than Schnyder's alleged betrayal was Keilhau's reaction: 'I felt and knew for a long time that Keilhau', he wrote to Wilhelmine on 16 October 1832, 'or whatever else you might call it in my present life and circumstances, would sink me or walk out on me.'[49] In his eyes, Keilhau, the 'friends and those who called themselves so',[50] had betrayed him.

Why the frustration and harsh words? When Barop arrived, he had indeed given Froebel 100 thalers; however, they weren't from Keilhau, but rather from Wilhelmine's mother. For Froebel, Keilhau had betrayed him again. The justified demands necessary for his 'conduct of life', 'protection of life', and 'care of life' were not fulfilled 'and therefore does not in the least diminish the demands I have made on you in relation to Wartensee.'[51]

On 19 October 1832, Froebel wrote a short letter to the Keilhau *Gemeinsamkeit* (community), including everyone, even the youngest children, teachers, and students. Interestingly, he mentioned Emilie as last, maybe because she was the only one who had sacrificed something: her husband. It was nothing but a harsh accusation and reckoning. Keilhau, Froebel insisted, must support him whatever its financial hardships. Froebel made clear that his demands were justified: 'Yes, I can and may, should and must, want to act and act like this.'[52] Wasn't it he who had lost his mother so early, suffered so much, and done everything possible for

Keilhau and every individual? From now on, 'it will depend on you whether you want to cultivate the achieved expansion and unification as a common entity or not'.[53]

This letter constituted the lowest point in Froebel's relationship with Keilhau, even if others would follow. Today, it's hard to understand Froebel's harsh reaction, which damaged the fragile relationship with Keilhau even further. The feelings of loneliness, loss, and disappointment probably overcame him. Interestingly, Froebel didn't mention that Elise had stayed in Keilhau. It's unclear what happened, though her parents, who weren't supportive of Froebel's Swiss endeavour anyway, probably hadn't allowed her to go. Still, it is interesting that Froebel failed entirely to mention what must have been a big disappointment.

Keilhau wasn't amused either. Wilhelmine reacted surprisingly harshly:[54]

> You can't want to be unfair, dear. When did Keilhau let you sink or sit? And not rather strived to support you through every sacrifice? How could you, in that everything here lives only for it, only anticipate the opposite of it, or foreknow, was not everyone ready to everything possible? not everyone, whom you demanded, ready to hurry to you, whom it was only possible?[55]

Wilhelmine insisted that sending Barop and the money was a sacrifice.

Froebel had enough of Wartensee. The next time he wrote to Wilhelmine, he was already in Frankfurt. Ferdinand and Barop, however, stayed to ensure the institute's future. For Barop, it was a sacrifice. Not only he abandoned the slowly reviving institute, but Emilie was also pregnant with their first child. Notwithstanding, he had travelled to Wartensee – in his own words – on foot with only ten thalers in his pocket and nothing but an old summer coat and a shabby tailcoat on his body.[56] Barop felt obliged to help Froebel as much as he could, so he stayed to restore order to Froebel's failed business once again. Emilie, Albertine, and their parents probably weren't amused, and had they known Barop wouldn't be back until Christmas 1833, then they would have been even angrier. By the time Barop returned, his son could already walk and speak.

The reunification with Wilhelmine

Froebel arrived back in Keilhau in November 1832. While the future in Switzerland was uncertain, a new project was at least already emerging: shortly before his departure, Froebel, Barop, and Ferdinand had met at an inn some of the progressive and wealthy citizens of Willisau, a small Lucerne town. As usual, the three were discussing education, hence the citizens, dissatisfied with their children's education, introduced themselves. A few days later, they visited Froebel and made him an offer. If he wanted, Froebel could open a school in Willisau. Froebel, who was hesitant, left the negotiations to Barop.

Froebel was relieved to be back in Keilhau and especially to see Wilhelmine. But the visit was overshadowed by a new tragedy. Wilhelm, Froebel's nephew and one of the first students in Griesheim, died on 30 November 1832, after a series of unfortunate events. It was a shock both for Froebel, who had placed great hopes in Wilhelm and seen him as a leader of the Swiss daughter institute, and for the community as a whole. Wilhelm had been a talented artist, admired gymnast, and popular sub-teacher in the handicrafts. Earlier in the year, Wilhelm had fallen through the ice while skating on the frozen pond in Watzdorf, but managed to save himself. A few weeks later, he had fallen through a trapdoor left open onto the hard threshing floor, but again miraculously survived. Then, he suddenly collapsed during a lesson due to a haemorrhage and died before his pupils' eyes.

Froebel, who had been close to his nephew, never discussed Wilhelm's passing in his letters. It was his usual approach to death. Their son's death was also a blow to Christian and Caroline, who had already been critical of Froebel's Swiss adventures because they felt they had lost Ferdinand. Now, they were even less inclined to allow Elise to go away. To make matters worse, Barop announced that he wouldn't return until Froebel went back to Switzerland. To be fair, Froebel never demanded that Barop stay; he instead made it clear that this was alone Barop's decision.[57]

While in Keilhau, Froebel visited the countess to discuss his debts. It was a successful meeting as the countess declared that she had never wanted the money back. In addition, he taught a little and tried to recruit teachers and pupils to join him in Switzerland. One new teacher was the Krause student Adolph Frankenberg, who would later open one of the first kindergartens in Dresden. The other two were the music teachers Gnüge and Langguth.[58] Froebel even asked Emilie, who had given birth to her son *Johannes* Wilhelm Karl Gottfried on 27 January 1833, if she could consider living with Barop in Switzerland. We don't know for sure, but it's unlikely that Emilie showed any enthusiasm.[59]

A topic of ongoing tension was Elise's future, as Froebel explained to Barop on 9 January 1833:

> Almost on all sides, relations or internal relationships would have been violated
> if one had wanted to implement or rather enforce the idea of Elisen's transfer

to Switzerland now … . In addition, I would now have led Elisen herself into a relationship in which she could only have maintained herself by referring back to me. To the already double burden would now also have come that I would have had to ask Elisen also in her outer, perhaps even inner circumstances … do not forget and remember 1832 is not 1833 and even less 1833 is what 1831 was in which I expressed my wish and demand.[60]

As so often, Froebel's words are ambiguous. Still, it shows that his previous actions were still on many people's minds.

Froebel tried to reconcile with the community while in Keilhau. But it was complicated, and Froebel must have felt that he was no longer welcome and more of a temporary guest. At least Wilhelmine finally agreed to accompany him, and in her case, it was indeed a sacrifice. Wilhelmine was unwell and travelling to Switzerland, and the prospect of running the house in Willisau was daunting. Wilhelmine also didn't want to leave Keilhau, especially the children, who were dear to her heart, yet still, she followed her husband.

While away, Froebel stayed in touch with Barop to discuss life unification and advise him in the negotiations. Froebel didn't want to look like an imposter again[61] and insisted on an official invitation and an appropriate salary. Keilhau, or at least the men, was supportive. 'Willisau or Switzerland is now, as Langethal's letter clearly shows you, the watchword even in the Keilhau men's council and the care for preserving this new vessel for the Keilhau tree of life, the subject of this consultation.'[62] Unlike the men who saw Willisau as a chance for Keilhau's survival, Froebel saw it as Keilhau's natural extension.

Finally, the negotiations were concluded. Before leaving, Froebel and Wilhelmine visited Berlin from 12 February until 12 March to say goodbye to Wilhelmine's mother. Interestingly, Johannes Barop was baptized while the two were absent, despite Wilhelmine being the godmother.[63] It might have been a coincidence, or maybe it meant more. Emilie, however, and the hope of re-establishing the old familiarity was still on Froebel's mind. Writing to her from Berlin, Froebel addressed her as 'mother'. He hoped the letter would 'be the forerunner and introduction to a series of letters that I will certainly write often on my new journeys through life, even if only in thoughts of you'.[64] It's unknown whether Emilie replied, though unlikely, as she blamed her uncle for her husband's absence (as letters between Wilhelmine and Keilhau show)[65] and would never forgive him. Emilie was also no longer interested in her uncle's advice, which was often inappropriate; Froebel criticized her in April, for example, that she was still only nursing her newborn and not giving him solids.

'Chase the wolves out to the land': The attacks continue in Willisau

Froebel and Wilhelmine – joined by the new teachers Gnüge and Langguth, the helpers Ludowika and Luise Herrmann, and a few pupils – arrived in Willisau on 29 April 1833.[66] On 2 May, the new school then opened. A combination of a boarding school and day school with a curriculum similar to Wartensee, Willisau's citizens and children gave an enthusiastic welcome. Willisau seemed a far more favourable place: the population was larger than Wartensee and its citizens fairly wealthy.

Willisau was located close to the ultramontane district of Entlebuch, however, and when the news of a 'heretic school' spread, many people there were unsettled. The clerics began stirring up the Catholic population before the school had even opened. This agitation should be viewed within the context of the *Kulturkampf* (culture war):[67] in around 1830, clashes between Catholics and Protestants permeated every aspect of public life. To support their people, the churches had become more involved in charity work, social work, and education, demanding loyalty in return. Especially Catholics showed their allegiance, as they felt being under constant threat from the state, liberalism, and the increasingly dominant Protestantism. With its elements drawn from Enlightenment, Protestantism was seen as different, more rational, and more 'German' than international Catholicism. It didn't matter that both churches were conservative forces at their core; a 'we-versus-them' mentality prevailed.

By presenting himself as a representative of an enlightened version of Protestantism with interdenominational tolerance, Froebel only made himself seem more suspicious. Protestants like Froebel were not welcome in the Catholic canton. Hence, when the school finally opened, protests erupted. The clergy and Catholic majority in Willisau considered Froebel a heretic who wanted to 'steal' Catholic children. Journals published negative articles about the alleged 'dangerous' institute and attacked Froebel with insults. 'However, the rage-breathing priests now rose up against us with truly diabolical force', Barop described the situation. 'We were afraid for our lives and were warned many times by merciful souls when we were going for a lonely walk.'[68] During a church celebration that Froebel and his associates attended, a Capuchin monk fanatically accused the citizens of Willisau of tolerating heretics in their midst. After describing the hellish punishments that awaited them, the monk incited the citizens to chase the heretics from their country: 'Put an end to the misery and no longer tolerate the wretched in your midst. Chase the wolves out to the land, in honour of God, to the devil's displeasure!'[69] While nothing happened that day, Froebel and everyone else feared for their lives.

To find support, Barop was dispatched to the canton's government for official protection. The government recommended a public evaluation to convince the public. This took place in autumn 1833 and proved very favourably. The government praised the institute and ordered the inflammatory Capuchins to leave the canton.

Nevertheless, the verbal attacks never ended, which burdened Froebel. Once again, he felt misunderstood and not valued. Increasingly, he now mentioned that his idea of a humane education had no future in the German-speaking world.

The attacks on the institute and Wilhelmine's ongoing illness overshadowed the first months. They made it necessary for Barop, who had planned to leave after Frankenberg's arrival in spring/summer 1833, to stay.[70] The institute was thriving, but the constant public quarrels wore Froebel out. 'For this reason, I have now, with certainty and clarity, completely given up the profession of educator in and of itself, the work purely as an educator, in the now common sense of the word. With the disintegration of Willisau, I will never again undertake the execution of a purely educational institution as such.'[71] Froebel was fed up with being a schoolteacher and an educator in the traditional sense.

Still, he stayed and started the second school term in October. Around this time, the Protestant canton of Berne contacted him with the offer to train future teachers. Representatives from Berne, who had attended the public evaluation, were impressed by Froebel's educational work. Froebel met with government councillor Schnyder, and during the conversation, the idea of an institution for the education of the poor came up. Froebel was excited. Unlike the canton of Lucerne, Berne wanted him! On 1 November 1833, Froebel finally received a request to submit his concept for an educational institution for the poor.

The sudden appreciation gave Froebel confidence. The relationship with Keilhau had improved, or at least Froebel was calmer. The letters were now amiable, mostly discussing practical questions. It probably helped that Wilhelmine was at his side, she also corresponded with her sister-in-law and others in Keilhau, and her letters were more friendly. In addition, Frankenberg had shown himself to be a capable confidant. Only Wilhelmine's illness worried Froebel. The house in Willisau was large and full of people, and running the house was a burden for the weak Wilhelmine, mainly because their helper, Luise Herrmann, was incapable. 'Oh it is not good to be sick',[72] the exhausted

Wilhelmine revealed to her sister-in-law Caroline. Wilhelmine also missed Keilhau sorely, especially the children. She regularly wrote to them, especially Christian Friedrich Clemens, her 'dearly beloved son'.[73] Notwithstanding, Froebel felt Willisau was on its way to becoming a community like Keilhau. Over Christmas and New Year 1833/4, Froebel wrote a long letter in which he described Willisau's idyl, the idyllic calmness of these days, the music and religious festivities, and playing and losing chess against Frankenberg. Nevertheless, his thoughts were still and would always be with Keilhau. Without question, the letters show how much he cared for Keilhau and its future. At the same time, he hoped Keilhau wouldn't forget him. 'Perhaps some of you had the thought today: what might your uncle and great-uncle have thought and said to himself during these days of birthday celebrations and especially today?'[74]

On other days, the frustration came up again. It was a constant back and forth; Froebel was proud of what they had created in Willisau, but at the same time missed Keilhau. While he was happy they had become more independent and lived their individual lives in unity, he felt the loss. Emigration to America came up as a possible new path, and with it the idea of a chain of institutes around the world. If the Germans didn't want him, the new world would embrace him with open arms.

Barop goes and Langethal comes

At the turn of the year, Rudolph 'Titus' Pfeifer arrived in Willisau. Titus had first been a pupil and then a teacher in Keilhau. Froebel valued him and was saddened when he died only six years later.[75] Titus' arrival enabled Barop to finally return to Keilhau; he left Willisau on 17 December 1833 without getting paid.

While Froebel was happy that Barop was back with his family, it made him worry about Willisau's future. No one could replace Barop as the institute's organizer and discussion partner. In the months that followed, Froebel tried to persuade Barop to come back,[76] but the Barops weren't interested. Eventually, Froebel invited Langethal: 'I wish you would visit me during the Easter holidays here in Willisau, I would have a lot to talk to you about.'[77] The Langethals had just endured a stillbirth for the second time.[78] The letter is a rare document of Froebel mentioning death; he hadn't even offered his sympathies to the Middendorffs when Albertine had given birth to a stillborn child.[79] It's possible that the stillbirth made the Langethals more open to the idea of leaving Keilhau with its dark memories behind.

Worries about Keilhau's future and survival were constant during spring 1834. Still, Froebel hoped Keilhau would send Barop – or at least Langethal – or, better still, join him in his next adventure: emigration to America. Froebel now claimed he had given up hope for his vision of developing-educating education in the old continent. Instead, America became his dream: 'But these two stages will hardly be given to us and even to our next descendants by the bound western continent of the old world; it seems to be reserved for the overseas free North America to hand over these and the following stages of human development to us for completion.'[80] The plan was to emigrate in spring 1835 or spring 1836.

While dreaming of the distant future, Froebel prepared for the upcoming one in Berne. On 17 February 1834, he was asked to come to Münchenbuchsee to select four young seminarists to be trained in Willisau for 1½ years.[81] During the trip, Froebel also visited Burgdorf, where a new orphanage would soon open, and submitted his draft *Entwurf zu einer volkstümlichen Erziehungsunternehmung geknüpft an das neue Waisenhaus zu Burgdorf, im Kanton Bern in der Schweiz* (*Draft for a Popular Educational Enterprise Linked to the New Orphanage at Burgdorf, in the Canton of Bern in Switzerland*). The draft is interesting as Froebel merged many of his previous educational ideas with a precursor of what would come later.

However, organizing the everyday educational life in Willisau and planning for the future took its toll on Froebel. He was tired and overwhelmed:

> In all these relations I now wish very much that you Langethal, like Barop 1½ years ago, would be sent here from Keilhau as an envoy for some time, and especially for the cultivation of the close, the immediate, the Willisau life, all those who are here, who surround me here now lack the view, the experience the strength.[82]

When it became clear that Langethal would come without Ernestine, Froebel only recommended dryly: 'You express my conviction from the depths of my soul for you, Langethal, and for your Ernestine, it is good if each of you lives his life completely for himself for a few weeks, and even if it really is a few months (more would not be possible under the present circumstances).'[83] It's once again a staggering lack of empathy.

As Langethal arrived alone on 29 March 1834, the incapable Luise Hermann had to be kept on until Frankenberg's sister Luise arrived to take over. Altogether, twenty-four people were crammed into the castle – teachers, pupils, and the teachers from Berne; Willisau was full of life – and growing. While Luise Frankenberg proved of little help to the household, she did become another loyal member of the community, which was developing to Froebel's taste: 'Yes, I would almost like to say that I have not been so well since my first founding work in Griesheim, i.e., I have not had such a calm overall feeling in me as I had the day before yesterday'.[84]

There were setbacks, though. The music teacher Gnüge was dismissed in May, and Langguth wanted to follow him, declaring to Froebel that 'it was no longer bearable with me, he had tried hard to bear me and my actions, but it was absolutely impossible for him'.[85] It was clear that Langguth would never be part of the community. Instead, Froebel wanted Keilhau's music teacher, Bromel, to come to Willisau.[86] When Luise Hermann finally left, Froebel was relieved but also worried because it meant more work for the sickly Wilhelmine.

A New Chance: Burgdorf

During the first months of 1834, Froebel began to warm up to a future in Burgdorf. When he received the offer to establish an educational institution for the poor attached to the orphanage and lead training courses for elementary teachers in April 1834, Froebel accepted happily. Langethal and Ferdinand would run Willisau, with Langethal as 'the real leader of the whole under my superintendence as Keilhau'.[87] With Wilhelmine and the support of a female helper, he would live in Burgdorf. Froebel now emphasized that his aim had always been to create new educational institutes as new opportunities for the Keilhau community, which would one day be independent of him. 'As I made Keilhau independent in the past and handed it over to its management; as I now intend to make Willisau independent and hand it over to its special management, so it would also be my most serious endeavour to make Burgdorf independent in itself and hand it over to its special management'.[88]

For himself, he now envisioned being independent 'because the plan remains firmly in me to gain a corresponding space and appropriate conditions where I can devote myself quite independently free and not disturbed or inhibited in any way, to the clear living (*Darlebung*) of the basic feelings of my mind and the basic thoughts of my spirit'.[89] Unfortunately, he told Keilhau that this might mean Barop would be in charge of Burgdorf. Keilhau reacted coldly and unfriendly, which forced Froebel to clarify that 'Barop's family life, like any real family life, is dear to me, indeed sacred'[90] and that 'it never occurs to me to harm Keilhau through regulations from here'.[91] It was the same story all over again: Froebel felt misunderstood and only had the best for everyone in mind.

Over the summer, Froebel gave a three-month refresher course for experienced and prospective primary school teachers. Initially, only forty teachers were supposed to attend; in the end, the number rose to sixty. Froebel was assisted by the pastors Bitzius and Steinhäuslin and the helper Mr Müller, but was responsible for most of the training. His workload was thirty hours per week, while his three co-workers taught only twenty hours.[92] They all lived together in the old Zähringer castle in Burgdorf.

Apart from infrequent visits from Langethal and Wilhelmine, Froebel was mainly alone in Burgdorf. He was happy with the course and described in many letters to Keilhau the beauty of nature and the surrounding mountains, maybe to convince at least some of them to join him.[93] Still, the looming final exam of the refresher course on 11 September and another evaluation of Willisau worried Froebel.[94] There was also another offensive article by Fellenberg, and the constant attacks wearied Froebel. Money was always an issue, especially because *The Education of Man* was selling so poorly, and he didn't want to squander the remainder of his funds. 'Froebel seems to me somewhat irritable at present, so that it is necessary to deal with him silkily',[95] Bitzius wrote to government councillor Schnyder.

Both evaluations went well, however, even if opinions differed. 'My known fate meets me also here, I am lifted up to heaven and pushed down to hell',[96] he let Keilhau know drily. Pastor Bitzius saw it similarly:

> The most peculiar judgments are made about our exam. The department is, as it seemed to me, very well pleased and that is the main thing; the audience was also largely edified. Only a few pedagogues made commotion and said all sorts of things that basically mean the least to us, which sounds strange because one would think that their judgment would be the most competent.[97]

The participants' feedback was also positive, even if they recognized Froebel's peculiarities.

> By the way, I am far from worshipping Froebel. He has his quaint peculiarities, a significant one-sidedness, but no more and no less than any pedagogue who has worked in his field for twenty years. It is these whimsical idiosyncrasies, however, that often tempt him to gimmickry, that most quickly attract attention and produce in soI… the judgment that he is a pitchman.[98]

Nevertheless, they appreciated his teaching and enthusiasm.

> As far as Mr Froebel was concerned, we could see very well that he lacked neither knowledge nor goodwill to solve his high task and to become useful to us. His

lectures were serious, tireless and friendly. Already in the manner of them one has certainly learned a lot … . Also highly instructive for us was the course for young children, in which we were certainly shown quite clearly in the few hours that we could spend on it, how even in young children, all the soul forces can be exercised and strengthened evenly. I have seen a beneficial light over many dark things and I have expanded my knowledge.[99]

As this statement shows, the education of young children was already on Froebel's mind in 1834.

While the evaluation of Willisau angered Froebel – he mainly blamed teachers such as Langguth and their inner disputes for the difficulties[100] – at least the Bernese government was satisfied. For his services in Burgdorf, he received 400 francs, and five more seminarists were sent to Willisau. Berne also offered him another refresher course for the following year. The Willisau seminarists also appreciated Froebel's work:

Froebel was a teacher like few others. His main endeavour was always to stimulate and develop. Everywhere he knew how to use the immediate environment with great skill; play, number, nature and language offered him rich means to this end. His clear, childlike mind, his lively conception of things and his exceedingly vivid presentation made him dear to children. With little children he was in his element; he was a friend of children (*Kinderfreund*).[101]

Not without reason, Halfter has called the summer in Burgdorf the 'peak of his life as an educational artist'.[102] When everything was over, Froebel and Wilhelmine went on a little tour through Switzerland, almost like a holiday, as Wilhelmine explained to her 'foster son' Christian Friedrich Clemens in October 1834.[103]

However, the most important result of the summer months was the offer to take charge of Burgdorf's orphanage. Already in July 1834, Froebel informed Keilhau that he had accepted the offer for both the orphanage and the refresher course, and that there still was the possibility of an educational poorhouse.[104] While the yearly salary was only 600 francs, room and board were free, and he would receive funds for a female educational helper and a household helper. Froebel was satisfied by the offer, but the negotiations took longer than anticipated, mainly because a letter got lost in the post, and both sides spent almost six weeks waiting for a response. In November, he signed the one-year contract in anticipation of moving to Burgdorf by the end of December,[105] but the orphanage only actually opened on 1 April 1835 in the end.[106] The delay didn't anger Froebel as it gave him more time to establish Willisau, work with Ferdinand, organize the move, and find suitable helpers. The last months in

Figure 6.1 Friedrich Froebel.

Willisau were pleasant. Wilhelmine described how they experienced the Swiss carnival in February 1835, with its gruesome masks and the wild goings-on. In general, however, life in Willisau must have been 'monotonous'; according to Wilhelmine, it was shaped by the daily routines and work.[107]

Although it still wasn't clear whether the poorhouse would open, Froebel wanted the Langethals to join them in Burgdorf as Ernestine's company and help was beneficial to Wilhelmine and he also wanted to keep Langethal close. Ultimately, the Langethals and Wilhelmine moved to Burgdorf on 14 April 1835, where they found seven 'daughters' and the cook and the maid in the orphanage waiting for them.[108] Froebel followed on 21 April but immediately returned to Willisau, where he stayed until the end of May. Upon his return, he began with the second refreshing course. It was a busy time, and Froebel, optimistic about what would come next, didn't write many letters in the weeks that followed. For once, he seemed satisfied with his life.

Time and Time Again: Quarrels with Keilhau

The move to Burgdorf again raised the question of who would oversee Willisau, however. While the still-young Ferdinand, together with Adolph Frankenberg, was seen as a capable school leader, no one thought Luise Frankenberg could run a household. New people were needed, ideally ones Froebel could trust.

Barop was his top choice. Already in July 1834, Froebel had asked him 'whether you cherish the thought of returning to Switzerland with your family one day or another'.[109] Over the next months, he would regularly follow up on the idea[110] until it became clear that neither Barop and Emilie nor the community were interested. 'My heart lifts high, my chest breathes more freely at the thought that Barop could become free in Keilhau. Keilhau does not have to go under because of this.'[111] It never happened, though.

Finally, he asked Middendorff. The idea was for Middendorff and Christian Friedrich, Wilhelmine's foster son, with whom she was very close, to come over Easter 1835 for no longer than six weeks.[112] Keilhau wasn't very enthusiastic when it learned of this new plan.

Then there was Elise. In November 1834, Froebel began pushing Keilhau to send her. His goal, Froebel now argued, had always been to offer 'the siblings-three (*Geschwisterndrey*) – Ferdinand, Wilhelm, and Elise – a safe sphere of activity according to the chosen educating-teaching life-long profession (*Lebensberufe*)'.[113] Now, Elise was needed to help her brother run the Willisau household. Froebel probably knew very well that neither Elise's parents nor Albertine and Emilie were keen on sending Elise to her uncle – 'Before you dismiss the proposal, hear me out.'[114] He also didn't hide the challenges: 'I do not want to deny it at all, indeed I want to admit it with certainty that Elise is put to the test of fire by the relationship proposed here; but we all have to be baptized with fire or purified by fire one day.'[115] Nevertheless, he felt it was the best for Elise but also Keilhau, Willisau, and Burgdorf – so the 'great whole-total'.[116]

Interestingly, he invited his brother Christian to bring Elise to Switzerland to see for himself. He also wanted Christian to decide if Elise should stay in Willisau or join him in Burgdorf so that the Langethals could return to Willisau. His words once again hint at his brother's alienation and that something disturbing had happened at the end of Froebel's time in Keilhau. It furthermore shows that Froebel didn't want to make decisions anymore. Or, at least, he didn't want to be blamed for these. In the months that followed, Froebel constantly emphasized that he no longer wished to mandate what should happen and what was best for the community. It was Keilhau's decision. 'Now think about the whole thing, I want to leave it completely in your hands; I want to personally step back entirely.'[117]

It's an interesting change, which shows the ongoing struggles in the relationship with Keilhau. Froebel might have realized that voicing his wishes too loudly was counterproductive. Still, it is also possible that he finally realized that his constant demands were contrary to his vision of a united family living. Either way, he became more empathetic towards Keilhau's needs.

> Each one of you and your family weighs the same to me and counts the same to me …; so if it is the case that Keilhau cannot exist without him [Barop] in the first place, or secondly that you wish to work together in Keilhau as a united family, then from now on every thought of Barop coming to Switzerland is silent.[118]

What mattered was the whole-total: 'Keilhau is important – Willisau is important – Burgdorf is important.'[119]

Still, the uncertain future and Froebel's never-ending stream of new ideas burdened the relationship with Keilhau, mainly because the unresolved questions dragged on.[120] As he had written in July 1834 to Middendorff: 'I appear outwardly as the cause of this sorrow, burden, and evil; so it is my task to take this sorrow, burden, and evil away from you again.'[121] Keilhau's silence hurt Froebel, and in the months that followed, he often complained that he hadn't received a single letter in such a long time, ultimately wondering if his letters had been lost in the post.[122] He was desperate to hear from Keilhau. There were probably simple reasons for the silence. Work and life in Keilhau were hard. Christian was losing his eyesight, livings needed to be secured, there were newborns, and the families had other things to worry about.

Especially Emilie's silence hurt Froebel. He longed to revive their previous closeness, not in its old form, of course, but in a new form of united living. However, his actions at the time of their marriage and how the whole community had perceived it made it impossible, and Emilie never accepted her uncle's offer of reconciliation. In June 1834, while alone in Burgdorf, Froebel wrote her a long letter. It was his reply to the birthday wishes she had sent him – the only note, it seems, in a long time. Froebel needed two weeks to finish the letter in which he, as in the past, wanted to express his inner feelings to his niece 'because I suspected, believed and hoped to be fully understood by you, not misunderstood in nothing at all'.[123] He was lonely, he confessed, and still hoped she and her husband would join him. Still, it seemed to be the 'fate of my life, that I must live my highest I must tell myself purest, most soulful life mostly alone'.[124] He longed for her understanding and support. 'I have gladly and openly, trustingly and purely shared my life and whatever moved my mind with yours, your childlike mind; few know my innermost life and nature like you do'.[125] He once more felt misunderstood. But he also urged Emilie to avoid the mistakes his parents had made:

> Emilie! You are the mother of a child, of a son; you will become the mother of several, God's blessing rests on you. I have communicated to you the gained life goal of a much-misjudged child, boy, youth and man, so that you may not misjudge the life of your child and boy, God Grant! once a youth and man.[126]

What he really wanted, however, was to be close to them and live a united life. 'On the eve of your celebration of life, I close this letter. How glad I am that I know I think and feel the same with you and you today, I think and feel the same happiness, the same praise, the same thanks and – the same love'.[127] While writing the letter, Froebel learned that Emilie was pregnant again. The news excited him and he began to obsessively write about family life, the education of young children, and what it meant to be a united family. Sparked by such thoughts, the desire for closeness only grew, once more longing for what he had been missing since childhood.

The letter was a new offer of reconciliation. That Emilie didn't embrace it disappointed Froebel deeply. 'I hope Emilie! You would and will forgive my longing for just one word from you, if you would only think for a moment into my entire situation',[128] he wrote two months later. 'I then feel such a pain of life inside, such emptiness of life, pressure of life and darkness of life outside of me, that I would like to escape from life right away'.[129] To be alone and far from his beloved Keilhau community and neglected by them hurt Froebel the most. Whenever Froebel received a word from Emilie, he rejoiced. 'My mind was so absorbed in these days of Christmas celebration and when I received your dear letter that after I had read it, I could not find coherent words to describe what had been going on in my soul during the reading of it, and yet it was so much, so lively, such an intimately coherent whole.'[130] The fear of being ignored and no longer admired and needed by Keilhau can be gleaned in many of his letters from that time. Froebel wanted to be close to Emilie and Barop, to be loved by them, to live in life unification – but he must have known that it would never happen.

Constantly summoning Elise and the fact that his letters were shared with the entire Keilhau community tarnished Froebel's relationships, especially with Christian and Caroline. Though the letters invariably remain vague and only contain insinuations, one cannot help but feel the mistrust that must have been felt (at least by Christian). In an unusual move, Froebel even addressed his brother directly in one letter: 'Recognize your position, my dear brother, with your faithful wife, that you stand with her in a circle of people trusting you; I also trust you, my brother! But also convince yourself that I want your entire well-being as a great whole-total (*Gesammtganzes*) in the present and developing to perfection in the future.'[131] Elise was certainly a much-discussed topic, and Froebel accused his brother of not supporting her in becoming what she was supposed to be, namely an 'educator of human beings, creator of nascent humanity'.[132] In Froebel's eyes, his brother had never fully supported their joint mission of human education – a ridiculous statement in light of Christian's achievements and sacrifices.

Over the weeks that followed, Froebel repeatedly tried to convince Keilhau that his intentions were noble, that he was misunderstood, that they needed to trust him, and that he only wanted to strengthen the community. Otherwise, the mistrust would destroy Keilhau. 'I beg you, raise, strengthen each other's trust in me, and beware of weakening or even destroying each other, or in a few years, before we know it, the whole thing will be on the brink of destruction.'[133] Being misunderstood and making sacrifices for the greater good again became a constant theme. 'To make personal perfection not an end in itself, but a means for the perfection and elevation of the whole as a whole, that is one of the things I call the present martyrdom, because by it I have to relinquish in myself and for myself at the moment, that's to say for my present human life, many levels of higher spiritual, inner formation.'[134] The allegations, as Froebel constantly explained, were nothing but misunderstandings. 'I know I am often not understood and my goal has so often not been achieved.'[135] He only wanted to help everyone understand the unity of his and their life, the truth of his thinking, and the unity of humanity and the whole. The only things missing were the words to express his truth.

My Barop and all of you, my beloved and faithful, there are great life- and world-encompassing thoughts which move my heart deeply; I have often tried, I would like to say in a hundred and a hundred incomplete forms, to suggest them to you, but you must forgive me – for the best thing about me is and always will be that I am taken calmly just what and how I am – if I dare again and again to suggest this thought to you in incompleteness.[136]

Only for this reason he was insisting on the unity of the community, of the families, of the 'links of the closest circle of Keilhau commonality (*Gemeinsamheit*); the 'three families united by mind, spirit and life – FröbelMiddendorffBarop'.[137] Keilhau – including Willisau and Burgdorf – must be united and live as united, educating families, because not as individuals but as united families would they be able to solve their mission in life.[138] Unceasingly, he reminded Keilhau of the importance of a united living.

Finally, Keilhau conceded they would send both Elise and Middendorff. Froebel was relieved: 'I am especially pleased that a man from your midst is introducing her into the circle here, a man who, like all of you, is equally close to her as a soul friend – Middendorff.'[139] However, until it actually happened in June 1835, Froebel remained worried and constantly asked about their departure.[140] When they finally had arrived, he informed Keilhau cheerfully that a 'dozen happy people'[141] are sitting together and celebrating Pentecost with a simple lunch and 'clear, sparkling wine'.[142] For once, Froebel was happy.

Today, it's almost impossible to reconstruct what happened within the Keilhau community, how different members felt about specific events, and what they meant to the community as a whole. Letters have been lost and especially insights into Froebel's counterparts' feelings and thoughts are lacking. Still, it's safe to assume that the first months of 1835 were happier ones for Froebel, also prompted by the birth of Emilie's second child. The child and its role in the complicated relationship is yet another mystery, however. Online genealogies claim that Friederike Martha Gertrud Barop was born on 22 October 1834;[143] however, this is not true. The correspondence in November and December 1834 doesn't mention the birth, and on 3 January 1835, Froebel asked: 'When is our E.B. expecting her Christmas?' – probably referring to the newborn. On 22 January, Froebel received the news that a little girl had been born.[144] So, Emilie's daughter must have been born in the first weeks of January, rendering the Froebel researcher Erika Hoffmann's statement – that Emilie's second child was born on 12 February 1835 – impossible. In a letter to Barop on 7 February 1835,[145] Froebel expressed his pride in being named one of the godparents. He immediately shared his thoughts on a suitable name, and his excitement is tangible; maybe Froebel hoped they would grow closer again.

> Finally and lastly, since I wish that you may know me in my innermost being, – it has truly pleased me that you Barop and Emilie close your life letter to me with the words 'Yours', not to appropriate something for me but so that we may always be together. Being and you, you and being may be; therefore also yours and your Friedrich Fröbel.[146]

Inspired by the newborn and the 'blissful mother of pure strong Johannes and little angel-clear Maria',[147] Froebel reflected once more on his life and Keilhau's future. This time, the focus was on young children, their education, and the children's future. The next generation, Froebel's vision unfolds, would be the saviours not only of Keilhau but also of humankind.

Therefore, it is noticeable that Froebel soon became very quiet about his godchild. He didn't mention her name in later letters to her parents while still addressing Johannes. Online genealogies state that Friederike Martha Gertrud Barop died in October 1835.[148] According to Erika Hoffman, though, her name was Johanna Christiane Marie *Gertrud*,[149] and other online genealogies mention a Johanna Christiana Friederike Marie Gertrud Barop, born on 22 October 1835, who would live until 18 July 1892.

The child's name was indeed Gertrud. 'Why did you name the dear little girl Gertrud!!!?' Wilhelmine wrote to Caroline Froebel. 'Marie, Marie, may she be called after Fröbel's and my wish … . When I spoke of the little daughter, I always called her little Marie. That was again one more lesson against pertness! But why did also Froebel's letter have to come so late?'[150]

Gertrud is surrounded by further mystery. In two letter fragments from December 1835,[151] Froebel reflected on questions of death – a topic he usually avoided – trying to give sense and meaning to death, pointing out how strange it is that birth and death happen on the same day (Barop's birthday was November 29), mentioning his mother, the early deaths of beloved ones, as well as 'stillbirths of our dear Unnamed Nameless little one'. He further wrote that Albertine gave birth and lost 'heaven near angels', that Elise lost her friend (probably referring to Wilhelm Carl), and that Emilie 'gave God both what each of them lost'. Again, he is ambiguous, but something tragic must have occurred. It seems most likely that Emilie had a stillbirth in November 1835, which might also explain why Elise travelled back to Keilhau at around this time.[152]

One daughter survived, however. When Emilie gave birth again on 1 December 1836 – Froebel was staying in Keilhau at the time – Froebel mentioned that Johannes had expressed his wish to his mother the day before to have two sisters. Froebel's statement, 'May God now also preserve the new life as this request and hope lies in the boy's simple childlike wish',[153] shows that they were worried the newborn might not survive. The five Barop daughters[154] that Henriette Schrader-Breymann mentioned when visiting Keilhau in 1848 also indicates that Gertrud was alive.

Supposing this was the case, and it seems to be, it's noteworthy that Froebel didn't have a close relationship with his godchild, despite all the initial excitement. He sent her a play song for her father's birthday in November 1835 but didn't mention her again thereafter. Only one more letter from May 1849 still exists, noting her confirmation. While there was no need to write letters for many years as Froebel was living nearby, it is suspicious and speaks for the increasing alienation from Emilie and her family. Already in June 1835, a disappointed Froebel complained to Barop: 'No one, neither Elise nor Middendorff, has brought me a greeting from your dear wife, have they or has she forgotten me so completely; I do not want to ask.'[155] The old intimacy would never be re-established.

Finally: Middendorff and Elise Froebel Come to Willisau

Emilie wasn't the only issue that afflicted Froebel's relationship with Keilhau. The decision to send Elise to Switzerland to oversee Middendorff's household in Willisau was a thorn in her parents' side – 'when I knew you yourself were in a life crisis because of Elisen's journey', Wilhelmine wrote to Caroline in July 1835. When Elise arrived, Froebel's excitement about Emilie's newborn had already subsided. Instead, he now turned to Elise to share his emotions. Biographers have again indicated that Froebel developed romantic feelings for one of his nieces. Since his move to Switzerland, Elise had been one of his favourite correspondents.[156] Already in 1831, he had told her that her letter was 'one of the loveliest flowers in the sensuous (*sinning*) cross of so kindly blossoming as invigoratingly fragrant letters'.[157] Elise, who was only seventeen then, was overwhelmed by her uncle's complex remarks on united families and life. She probably didn't understand much of what Froebel said. As far as we know, she responded to Froebel's deep and often incomprehensible thoughts only with short letters, which Froebel nevertheless valued.[158] As usual, a listener to his monologues was what he needed. Elise, who was unique to him, as Froebel told her with flowery words, became the confidante to whom he could express his feelings and thoughts, what he had sacrificed, and how much he still had to suffer. 'I am alone, I am lonely with my life, with my mind and with my ideals', he had confessed to her in 1832, 'with a soul full of life and longing for life I am alone in life! What may be the meaning of this, what is the meaning of this?'[159] Similar to Emilie, Froebel was hoping to unite souls with Elise. The modest Elise, however, with her rather childish mind, was never very responsive to her uncle's complicated feelings. Still, when Keilhau finally agreed to send Elise to Switzerland, Froebel asked her to take along 'the various life messages I gave you and the words to which I attached them, to develop life blossoms and life fruits from them'.[160] For Froebel, these letters must have been significant, but they are lost today.[161]

Elise and Middendorff left for Willisau after only ten days. Seeing and immediately 'losing' Elise overwhelmed Froebel emotionally: 'Nothing could I say to you when I left you and you yesterday, nothing could I say but to press you to my heart, your heart to mine; what is left to say when silent speech speaks more than all words taken together?'[162] Over the following weeks, Froebel regularly wrote Elise flowery letters which expressed his longing. 'I have thought much of yours and ours this week, much thought of your life and ours.'[163] The sight of another great comet in October 1835 completely overwhelmed him. Froebel had hoped to watch the phenomenon at her side, and when this didn't happen, 'immediately at the sight and recognition of the comet, a really deep longing for you seized me'.[164] Changes and an 'evolution of life'[165] were necessary and forthcoming – 'unfortunately, now I can only hint you the fact, soon in writing or once under favourable living conditions verbally more'.[166] We don't know if he ever did, though.

The correspondence between Froebel and Elise continued until the end of the year. Froebel shared little poems with her; the style and words show his inner turbulence. Nevertheless, the desire ceased at the turn of the year. It would take more than one year for him to write to her again, this time in a joint letter to Elise, Ferdinand, and Middendorff. His feelings and the inner turbulence seemed to have come to an end.

In retrospect, it's easy to condemn Froebel's behaviour during the Swiss years. His relationships with his nieces seem inappropriate, and the constant demands and recruitment attempts, the increasingly unwanted suggestions and interferences, and the intrusive comments show him as very selfish and lacking empathy. However, at the same time, he was deeply interested in the community's well-being and future, and one should by all means take his words seriously. Froebel wanted to create new working and living opportunities for the younger members of the Keilhau community. He also wanted Keilhau to flourish. But the demanding selfishness, the disrespect for the lives of his friends and associates, their families, and children, can't be denied. His constant remarks about united families and the goal of life unification show a striking dissonance between the abstract concept and lived reality. Without the personal sacrifices of the ones close to him, Keilhau's 'further development' would never have been possible. Thus, it's easy to understand Keilhau's anger, especially Albertine's and Emilie's. Their husbands sacrificed years for what they perceived as their impractical uncle's daydreams. That Middendorff stayed in Willisau for almost four years because he felt responsible for what his 'master' had started certainly didn't help. Since Albertine refused to leave Keilhau, the family was separated for four years. It's no surprise that Albertine later reacted very coldly towards her uncle.[167]

A New Idea: The Education of Young Children

Workwise, the time in Burgdorf was one of the pinnacles of Froebel's life. Three educational institutions were working in his spirit: Keilhau was growing under Barop's leadership; Willisau – despite further hostility – was led by Middendorff and Ferdinand; and Froebel oversaw the comprehensive educational institute in Burgdorf, which wasn't really an orphanage as the pupils' parents were actually still alive but simply neglected their children.[168] Since the educational poorhouse was still an option, Froebel drafted an extensive plan which included an institute for young children. It was a new idea: a play and activity institute for young children – a kindergarten in all but name. The plan, however, was never realized.

That Froebel began to think more about young children and their education was caused by Emilie's pregnancy and Keilhau's offspring growing older. But Froebel also began to observe young children's play in the orphanage more carefully. Already in 1834, he shared with Keilhau: 'Here in the institution is now a very dear six-year-old boy Raimonde – a little Italian.'[169] The boy created geometrical shapes and everyday objects with blocks, probably an early inspiration for the later gifts.

As usual, Froebel felt the urge to share his new insights with Keilhau. Some of the letters written in 1834/5 include extensive remarks about the nature and education of young children and the first ideas about the gifts.[170] However, the uncle's advice was no longer wanted. Albertine and Emilie mostly ignored it; later, they never used the gifts and occupations. Apart from Allwine, none of the community's female members showed an interest in Froebel's later kindergarten work.

With the new thinking, the spherical law was modified slightly, even if the foundations remained remarkably consistent. The term 'life unification' became more prominent due to the constant self-reflection and the problematic relationship with Keilhau. Froebel didn't see such unification as perfect harmony; tension was actually necessary. Froebel understood life unification as the conscious realization of one's life situation, the harmonization of one's inner life, and life unification in concrete action. Thereby, he presented his life as exemplary of such life unification. National unification was another concept still on his mind. But he also started to think about terms that later became prominent; one example is 'premonition' (*Ahnung*).[171]

To achieve the goal of life unification, Froebel announced at the beginning of 1836 that future endeavours should focus on young children as well as the education of their parents. He further advised Keilhau not to go beyond the education of fourteen-year-old children. This age group, Froebel now claimed, is the most crucial period for humane education. And he already had a plan what to do: to support perception and learning, he wanted to create plays for young children in a sequential, structured order as a 'means of self-occupation and self-instruction'.[172] Play pedagogy, gifts, and occupations – it all took shape in his head during these last months in Switzerland.[173]

The Personal Crisis at the End of 1835

However, Froebel's new ideas and plans must be seen in the context of his deep frustration at the end of 1835. Froebel was utterly disillusioned. The public still didn't value his work, and Froebel must have known that his educational method would never be implemented in public schools in German-speaking states, including Switzerland. Grand Councillor Stähli, one of Froebel's most influential supporters, had just died, and it was clear that public support would only decline.[174] The constant struggles and the never-ending attacks, especially by Fellenberg, were tiring. 'The struggle and war within my life and work has begun anew.'[175] But Froebel was unwilling to fight back publicly. He felt misunderstood, convinced that the Swiss had a 'hatred for the Germans'.[176] Switzerland seemed less and less of an option. 'What do we actually want to gain? – What can we gain by the captivating pressure that lies at first on the world of the German tongue (Switzerland completely included), what can we gain there?'[177]

In this sense, Froebel's new devotion to early childhood education can be seen as a last hope. According to Froebel's new argumentation, a real developing-educating education of humankind needs to start earlier – this was also a convenient explanation of the current failure. Only united and educating families can achieve real education of humankind. 'Life must be grasped as a great whole and solved and carried out with firmness and perseverance according to a great, clearly defined plan, first as a personal task, then as a family task, then as a tribal and ancestral (*Geschlecht*) task, and finally as a task of the people and of humanity.'[178] For this reason, the focus needs to be on families. As usual, in Froebel's world view, everything was connected and made sense.

For his part, though, Froebel envisioned nothing but independence – independence from the daily troubles of running an educational institute and independence from the responsibility for Keilhau as a whole. To achieve it, he wanted to transfer the management of the Willisau institute to 'Keilhau as the mother institute'[179] after his departure. He wanted freedom for himself, but also for the community members. To Langethal, he announced that 'from now on, I will absolutely no longer start any enterprise, I will not enter into any activity … . My decision is quite irrevocable in me that from now on I want to belong only to the clear basic idea of my life, to its clear development, simple exposition, and perfect execution of the same, to live only to it.'[180] Froebel was tired of his life as a school leader and of his responsibility for others who didn't even value his sacrifice – 'As I am free in myself, I also want to be free externally in my life.'[181]

At the end of 1835, the personal and professional turmoil became too much. Froebel plunged into a personal crisis that manifested as a mix of depression, constant restlessness, and utopian thinking.[182] Inspired by Adolph Frankenberg's brothers, who had emigrated to America, Froebel dreamed of a new beginning in the new world.[183] And if no one joined him, he told Barop, he would go by himself. But it was only words. Froebel probably hoped Keilhau, or at least some members, would join him, even if he must have known that the plan would be met with hostility. Once again, he felt the need to explain himself. The result was another treatise: *Erneuerung des Lebens fordert das neue Jahr 1836* (*Renewal of Life Demands the New Year 1836*).[184]

Froebel had felt that change was coming for a long time. 'I have lived a very strange time in the last few weeks', he wrote to Barop in November 1835, 'in my and therefore in our or if you prefer in our and therefore in my life a great change is preparing itself deeply silently and almost unnoticeably … I, have no choice.'[185] The move to Columbus, Ohio, where the Frankenbergs were living now, became

Friedrich Fröbel (geb. 21. April 1782, gest. 21. Juni 1852).

Figure 6.2 Friedrich Froebel, photo of a wood engraving from 1872.

a constant topic. Froebel, who had always had a foible for symbols and numbers, was somehow convinced that 1836 would bring meaningful change. 'For a long time, I saw and see the year 1836 coming full of expectation.'[186]

The treatise was circulated in handwriting only among his closest associates; it only became known to a broader public through the Lange edition of 1862/3. This was for the better, though, as Froebel's relatives considered the treatise problematic. Most probably shook their heads when they read it, if they did at all. Froebel had written it on New Year's Eve in 1835, and it's indeed a strange piece of writing. Over sixty printed pages long, it gives the impression of being written in a fever. It's a rambling, sometimes highly prophetic, poetic, foreboding, occasionally philosophical, socialistic, but always patriotic statement. It also includes new thinking about the family, a forerunner of later thoughts. However, it reads as if Froebel had barely been able to contain the profusion of thought. It was bold, revolutionary, and accusatory but at the same time an admonishing call for rootedness and order. In a certain way, it was the peak of Froebel's mix of unjustified optimism and deep despair. What was needed and what he wanted, Froebel made that clear in the conclusion, was to emigrate to America. In Germany, Froebel explained, it was impossible for the individual, the family, and the people to live a humane life, to live in life unification. It would only be possible in unspoiled America, where they would find suitable soil for realizing the ideal of a community of life unification and where they all could start anew.[187]

We don't know how Keilhau reacted. The silence, however, speaks volumes. No one in Keilhau wanted to get involved with Froebel's newest fantasy.

Leaving Switzerland for Good

When 1836, the proclaimed year of change, started, Froebel felt he was no longer wanted and increasingly superfluous in Switzerland. He wasn't interested in the orphanage anymore, and Willisau, where Ferdinand had established himself as a capable leader and Middendorff was still in charge, was doing well without him. Against Keilhau's wishes, the two had decided to stay.[188] However, such decisions weren't his anymore – and Froebel emphasized this constantly now. 'Once again I repeat what I already expressed to you in my most recent letter: – life, life's destinies now lie entirely in your, in Keilhau's hand, only you can determine.'[189]

Froebel, though, wanted to leave Switzerland, and in February 1836, he announced his return.[190] It was the best for Wilhelmine, his 'dear wife'. Despite her frail health, the loyal Wilhelmine, who had always sacrificed her needs for her husband's cause, was at the end of her tether. She had cooked and managed the large amount of laundry alone, knitted and gardened, and always sought to mediate, care, and preserve. Now, she was critically ill. Wilhelmine longed to see Keilhau, the children, and her beloved dying mother. The doctors also hoped the Thuringian air might improve her health. And Froebel, who had always worried about Wilhelmine's health and cared for her in his peculiar way, wanted to fulfil her wish.

However, Wilhelmine's mother died on 5 March 1836, before they even left. Froebel withheld this fact from Wilhelmine, frightened by how she would take the news.[191] He only dared to tell her twenty-four hours later. Wilhelmine was devastated for many days.[192]

Soon after, on 1 May, the couple left Burgdorf, 'where my life and work, as I felt especially in the weeks and days of separation, took deep and healthy roots that will last'.[193] Froebel was proud of his achievements in Switzerland, but knew he wouldn't return. And neither was a return to Keilhau an option. It was time to start anew, in a new place and field of activity. It may have happened by chance, but the Swiss years helped Froebel find his true calling, which would determine the rest of his life – the education of young children, and women as their educators.

Part 3

The Playing Froebel

7

The Kindergarten Years

Homecoming

Froebel and Wilhelmine left Burgdorf on 31 May 1836. Middendorff and Ernestine accompanied Wilhelmine to Herzogenbuchsee, where they met Froebel and Langethal, who had hiked there together. The goodbye wasn't easy; a letter written by Wilhelmine to Albertine in July 1836 hints that Ernestine might have been pregnant again. If true, the Langethals must have suffered another miscarriage or child death.[1] However, the one who suffered the most was Middendorff, who hadn't seen his family for almost a year. 'I stood', Middendorff later told his son-in-law Wichard Lange, 'as if in a campaign at a dangerous post; I could not and was not allowed to retreat. The hostile Catholic clerics were advancing violently; how could I, out of love for my own, flee from their crude artillery!' Middendorff felt responsible for what his master had started, and it would be more than two years before he returned to Keilhau. 'I hardly understand myself how it was possible.'[2]

The strenuous two-week journey to Berlin in an uncomfortable stagecoach exhausted the weak Wilhelmine. But she endured it bravely, as the concerned Froebel wrote to Langethal on 13 June. Two days later, the couple arrived in Berlin, staying with Wilhelmine's aunt for three months to take care of inheritance matters and sell the house. It gave Froebel a modest fortune, making the production of the envisioned play materials possible.

Wilhelmine didn't like it in Berlin, where she felt like 'a fish on the dry land',[3] and she became even weaker. Froebel, though, used the stay to visit several day nurseries, educational institutions for children aged three to six that had started to spread in the German states in the 1820s. He wasn't impressed, and the treatment of the young children and the lack of play and occupation materials even appalled him. It wasn't what he had in mind for the education of young children.[4] In the end, they were both glad when they left for Keilhau, where they arrived on 21 September.

A New Home: Blankenburg

Wilhelmine was glad to see their family and especially the children again. The following months in Keilhau were relatively uneventful. Emilie gave birth to a daughter without complication on 30 November,[5] and they celebrated Christmas together; Froebel used the inheritance to reimburse expenses that Barop had covered for him. Nevertheless, it had always been clear that Keilhau wouldn't be a long-term solution, as it would only have led to new tensions. Froebel was therefore actively looking for a new domicile, and the couple ultimately opted for Blankenburg in the romantic valley of the River Schwarza. On 16 January 1837, they moved into a former powder mill. Blankenburg was a good choice, the doctors had recommended its healthy air, and Keilhau was only one hour away, which made regular visits easy. Barop and later Middendorff came often, and Keilhau supported the Froebels with food or other necessary items. Still, the relationship wasn't as warm as before. The stiff letter Froebel sent to Barop on the day before Christmas 1837 speaks volumes, even if they all spend Christmas together in Keilhau.

Froebel used Wilhelmine's inheritance to quickly establish the *Autodidaktische Anstalt* (*Autodidactic Institution*), which opened in March 1837. It wasn't a kindergarten in today's sense, but a production and shipping business for the play materials he referred to as gifts. Since Froebel had developed the materials in Switzerland, it was possible to start with the production of the first gifts immediately. First came the coloured balls, and bowls and cubes arranged in cubic boxes, followed by laying boards and boxes with peas and sticks for construction work, coloured papers for braiding and folding, cutting out, and interlocking. Over the months that followed, Froebel developed verses and songs to accompany the materials and modified the play pedagogy accordingly.

Since the materials were supposed to look and feel good, each gift was made of excellent materials by a specially hired cabinetmaker and other employees, and each cube was made according to unique measurements. Each cloth ball was made in exact roundness, and all materials were packed beautifully and carefully with accuracy. That costed money that neither Froebel nor Keilhau had. Since he initially provided the items mainly for free for demonstration purposes and sold hardly anything, the new enterprise swallowed up large sums. New debts were amassing, which worried Keilhau. Barop warned Froebel, but as usual, Froebel didn't care about the commercial side of the business.

Froebel began to advocate tirelessly for his new idea, modifying it and always coming up with new plans. In August 1837, he renamed the Autodidactic Institute *Anstalt zur Pflege des Beschäftigungstriebes der Kindheit und Jugend* (*Institute for the Nurture of the Activity Drive in Childhood and Youth*). It remained a distribution and production facility, though. To get people involved and train them according to his idea, Froebel wanted to connect the institute with what he referred to as the *Bildungsanstalt für Kinderführer* (*Educational Institute for Children Guides*), an idea he first mentioned in March 1838. At this time, he still had young men, and not women, in mind. To make his ideas more popular and find influential supporters, he and Barop presented the first two gifts to the territorial princess in the same month. Froebel also began to publish a weekly journal, the *Sonntagsblatt für Gleichgesinnte* (*Sunday Paper for Like-Minded People*), with the motto 'Kommt, last uns unsern Kindern leben', usually translated as: 'Come, let us live with our children.'[6] Froebel wrote most of the articles, but the journal was only published in 1838 with thirty-one and in 1840 with twenty-one issues. While the pieces were relatively independent due to their chronological origin and detailed elaboration, his thoughts were embedded in his world view and idea of developing-educating human edification.[7] In addition, he published pamphlets to explain the meaning and use of the gifts. The most important pamphlets accompanied the ball (1838), the second gift (1838), and the third gift (1844 and 1851). In all these writings, Froebel elaborated on his play pedagogy, which would become the core of his later kindergarten pedagogy. He also continued to share his thoughts through letters; one example is the letter to Langethal from December 1837, in which Froebel developed the idea of the self-teaching mathematical cube.

It was undoubtedly a busy and productive time.

A First Success: Meeting the Queen in Dresden

Unfortunately, few were interested in Froebel's new idea. To make the idea more popular, Froebel went on a promotional trip first to Dresden and then Leipzig from December 1838 until February 1939. The trip had been prepared by Frankenberg, who had visited Dresden prior to this with some pupils. They had demonstrated the gifts, and Dresden's influential circles had shown interest.

Froebel hoped Dresden would become the centre of the new movement. But the trip was overshadowed by Wilhelmine's illness. Wilhelmine was critically ill but still wanted him to go; all that mattered to her was his educational work. 'But my life and my desires are quite subordinate to the furtherance of your uncle's basic idea and the next wishes for the same', she had already told Emilie on 15 July 1836, 'what less could I do now that my forces have dried up – than to offer at least my good will for it?'[8] While away, Froebel wrote his wife affectionate letters. 'How fervently my heart longs for you; I have never felt this longing in my life as I do now.'[9] Froebel missed her, especially over Christmas. 'It seems strange to me at this moment that, just as I had to pay for the foundation of my present work here by depriving myself of Christmas, so I had pay for my work in Switzerland by depriving myself of the wedding of Barop and Emilien.'[10] Once more, it was he who had to make sacrifices.

Froebel was accompanied by Frankenberg, a few Keilhau pupils, and Middendorff, who had just returned to Keilhau after Willisau's closure. Albertine was probably not amused that her husband was already following Froebel again. Still, Froebel asked for Middendorff because he was the most capable of convincing audiences of the value of the materials and plays.[11] The first presentations to parents went well, and there was talk of a new institute for young children. The highlight came on 7 January 1839, however, when Froebel gave a presentation in the natural history lecture hall of the Zwinger in Dresden before an audience of about five hundred people, including the queen of Saxony. 'As I learned later, one or two of the 200 seats were still left and probably about 300 tickets had been issued for the standing room. Privy Councillor Reichenbach had told me beforehand: "You have a select audience, that's to say very educated people among the listeners."' This is how Froebel described the day to Wilhelmine. Froebel had been late; the lecture notes had only been prepared with Middendorff's help at the very last minute; and Froebel arrived at almost the same time as the queen. Still, he managed to receive a formal introduction. The lecture was supposed to last for an hour as most of the attendees wanted to visit the theatre in the evening, but Froebel went way over the time. In the end, even when Middendorff tried to stop him, he spoke for almost two hours. According to Froebel, the queen listened 'very attentively and with the expression of sympathy, yes, probably also of joyful satisfaction'.[12] The citizens of Dresden were surprised to see her stagecoach still waiting one-and-a-half hours after the presentation had ended; the queen had even wanted to see the materials.

The queen's interest helped Froebel's cause tremendously. Soon, three or four families established a play circle. 'I have the firm conviction that a new daughter activity will be formed here in Dresden, namely already with the beginning of spring with a larger extension, although only in the area of the preschool children's years, that's to say up to the completed sixth year (as it should be called in the circular).' The plan was for Frankenberg to be responsible for establishing the institute on Froebel's behalf, while Froebel would move on to Leipzig to give more presentations. To get to Leipzig, Froebel took a steam car for the first time.[13]

Wilhelmine's Death

Soon after arriving in Leipzig, Froebel learned Wilhelmine was on her deathbed. Until this point, Wilhelmine had insisted on not disturbing her husband with news about her declining health. Froebel immediately returned home. 'My poor, sick wife is always equally weak and I am daily, especially when the evening hours come, in danger of her imminent loss,'[14] he wrote on 4 May. When their loyal helper, Louise, suddenly passed away on 1 May, Froebel didn't dare to tell her. Froebel was utterly overwhelmed, and in his helplessness, he asked Barop and Middendorff for support. 'I am mentally and physically tired and depressed, so I feel like my poor wife: I only want to sleep all the time.'[15] Finally, on 13 May, Wilhelmine's suffering ended. 'Monday, 13 May, Mrs. Froebel, like a light gently extinguished, fell asleep to a higher awakening ... . When I think of the woman, my heart immediately becomes full. I have met many and noble women, but still she stands out for me,'[16] Middendorff, who had been at her side in her final moments, wrote to their friend Leonhardi.

Wilhelmine's death shattered Froebel. While she had never been a spiritual partner, she had always been caring and loyal and, convinced of her husband's genius, supported him wholeheartedly, sacrificing her life for his. Now, Wilhelmine was gone. The only thing close to family was Keilhau, but Froebel had realized long ago that the community would go their own way. Ferdinand would stay in Willisau, as he had explained to Wilhelmine in one of his last letters, 'Langethal will not leave Burgdorf and the canton of Berne', 'Barop will not want to leave Keilhau', and even Middendorff won't follow him anymore as 'his wife, as I am told, is anchored in Keilhau'.[17] Froebel was alone.

After Wilhelmine's death, Froebel raised his deceased wife to the status of a saint. 'No wife could have been so sweet and good to her husband as Frau Froebel was to hers.'[18] He didn't allow anyone to touch her belongings, and when Karoline Revonanz, one of his early students, picked a sprig of ivy from her grave to plant it in a pot for his pleasure, Froebel was furious. 'He knew no bounds at all in his destructive rage.'[19]

But for now, Froebel was devastated. He delayed his latest plans and stopped publishing the *Sonntagsblatt* because, as he explained in the preface to No. 6 of the second volume in 1840, 'only with the greatest effort and manhood could he rise again into himself'.[20] Otherwise, Froebel only spoke about Wilhelmine once in a letter to the 'Muhme Schmidt' from 19 September 1943. Talking about death and loss and public grievance wasn't for Froebel.

The Invention of Kindergarten

After Wilhelmine's death, Froebel threw himself into his work – as he had done in the past during personal crises. He wasn't responsible for anyone but himself and the kindergarten idea anymore (and maybe the Keilhau community), and he spent even more energy on promoting his newest idea. Since the presentations in Dresden had gone so well, Froebel considered opening an institute there. However, when the city of Blankenburg made him an honorary citizen on his birthday and offered to make the *Haus über dem Keller* (*House above the Cellar*) available to him for free, he opted for Blankenburg. In June 1839, Froebel opened the *Spiel- und Beschäftigungsanstalt* (*Play and Activity Institute*). Froebel, often supported by Middendorff, used the place to demonstrate the gifts and train play guides. Around fifty children from different social circles came almost daily for a few hours, which gave the course participants the chance to try out the play materials to acquire skills in directing the children's play. While it wasn't a kindergarten, it was more than just a gift production site. Shortly after, a similar institute opened in Rudolstadt.

What was still missing was a proper name for his idea. Finally, in spring 1840, Froebel came upon it. While hiking with Middendorff and Barop from Keilhau to Blankenburg, as the often told story goes, Froebel suddenly stopped when looking at the greening valley below them and shouted joyfully: 'Eureka! Kindergarten is the name of the institution.' Later, Froebel described the name-finding as a revelation: 'If I should actually say how I came to it', he wrote to his second wife Luise, 'I do not know how to say it myself; enough the name came out of the soul as if in an instant, so that the name itself first alienated me, then delighted me, as it also very soon received the sympathy of all simple, unbiased people to whom it was pronounced.'[21] It was probably his attempt to give the kindergarten movement a fitting story. Already in April 1839, Froebel

Figure 7.1 View of the Garden of Children, lithography by A. Schmiedeknecht, around 1840.
Bildarchiv Friedrich-Fröbel-Museum Bad Blankenburg (Picture Library Friedrich-Fröbel-Museum Bad Blankenburg).

had used 'kindergarten' in a letter, a term he had read in Schefer's *Laienbrevier*[22] in April 1837.

While Froebel invented kindergarten, he wasn't the first to come up with the idea of extra-familial early childhood education.[23] Around 1840, several hundred such institutions existed in the German states. There was a wide variety; one can find a confusing array of names. The most common ones were *Kleinkinderbewahranstalten*, which literally translates to 'safe-keeping institutes for infants' but is generally translated as 'day nurseries', and *Kleinkinderschulen*, or 'infant schools'. These names didn't actually mean much: institutions with the same name could be very different, and those with different names similar. Their number had mushroomed since the 1830s, though, mainly in response to the alleged societal and especially the moral crisis among the lower class: due to the growing industrialization and pauperism that forced mothers and older children to seek work outside of the home; the image of the private, patriarchal nuclear family as the new universal norm; and because the Prussian school reforms excluded young children from primary school, children from working-class families were perceived as neglected. Indeed, for many of the bourgeoisie, the image of children living in haphazardly constructed, unsanitary quarters became synonymous with the life of lower-class children. They saw these children – who were neglected physically and mentally but, above all, morally and growing up entirely free of care or on the streets – as a threat, not to the children themselves or their families, though, but rather to the existing social order. Various measures to suppress unrest and stabilize the current social order were thus established – and this included early childhood institutions. The primary, albeit not the sole, function of day nurseries as envisioned by one of the most prominent supporters, Johann Georg Wirth, was to prevent children's neglect by emphasizing moral-religious education and teaching a little reading, writing, and arithmetic. Unlike the day nurseries, the Christian infant schools popularized in Germany by Theodor Fliedner were denominational and mainly Protestant. The children were meant to learn something at these strictly structured, discipline-based, and school-like establishments with a very strong religious emphasis. Neither type of establishment was interested in helping lower-class children improve their living conditions through general education, though. Rather, they were merely a means to maintain the existing social order.

What Froebel wanted to achieve with kindergarten had almost nothing in common with such institutes. His dreams went way beyond this.

On 28 June 1840, the term 'kindergarten' became official. In the weeks before, Froebel had thought deeply about the meaning and purpose of kindergarten, or better put, the *Allgemeine Deutsche Kindergarten*, or *General German Kindergarten*, as he called it. The result was the *Entwurf eines Planes zur Begründung und Ausführung eins Kinder-Gartens (Plan for the Establishment and Execution of a Kindergarten)*.[24] Over the years, Froebel would continuously redefine his kindergarten idea.[25]

Initially, Froebel understood kindergarten as an umbrella term. He wanted to establish a 'child care, play and activity institute', a 'real kindergarten', or 'kindergartens in the narrow sense', combined with an *Anstalt zur Bildung von Kinderpflegerinnen und Erziehern*, or *Institute for the Education of Childcare Workers and Educators*. But Froebel wanted to achieve more than opening a single kindergarten. He planned to spread play institutes all over the German states, in every city and village, for all classes. Such kindergartens would help familiarize families and women with the concept of *Spielpflege* (play care).

The opening of the General German Kindergarten was celebrated on 28 June 1840, the day of the 400th anniversary of the printing press. In the previous weeks, Froebel had written to various acquaintances, influential figures, the editorial teams of multiple newspapers, the princess of Schwarzburg-Rudolstadt, and even the king and queen of Saxony to advertise his newest idea and the plan to sell shares. The goal was to sell ten thousand shares worth ten thalers each and thus acquire 100,000 thalers.[26] With this capital, he wanted to construct a large seminar building to train children's guides in connection with a 'real kindergarten' and to found women's associations to support the cause. Ideally, the capital would have also been used to establish more 'kindergartens in the narrower sense' all over Germany.

The endeavour was a spectacular failure. Three years later, only 155 of the planned ten thousand shares had been sold, and of these, only thirty-seven had been paid in cash. Prussia didn't allow subscriptions because Froebel had forgotten to apply for permission,[27] but there wasn't any interest anyway. As a 'worthless pile of paper', Osann's laconically remarked, 'the shares ... rotted in an attic of the kindergarten premise in Blankenburg'.[28] And the little he did earn with the shares, Froebel spent on clothes and handkerchiefs for the children.[29]

Langethal's 'Betrayal'

One person who hadn't been at the opening of the General German Kindergarten despite Froebel having invited him warmly was Langethal. After Froebel had left Switzerland, the two had continued with an intense, initially amicable correspondence. But rifts had developed, especially because Langethal was no longer willing to mince his words. 'I therefore confess to you quite openly that if the most recent letter had not thawed the ice again, you would hardly have received another letter from me this year and hardly one at the beginning and in the first month of the new year',[30] Froebel wrote at the end of 1839, mentioning the 'congealing and devastating' effect of Langethal's previous letter. But Froebel didn't give up hope that Langethal – besides Barop, his most effective associate – would return. 'With your return to Germany and your reunion with me and us here in Blankenburg, our entire life must receive the clearest possible design, the most lively and vital link-building (*Gliedbau*) possible, and in short, the purest possible completion in every respect.'[31] Froebel fought for his old friend. 'Our common relation to each other and our standing to time and to certain spatial and living conditions is not an ordinary one; let us recognize it in its significance, let us observe and cultivate it in this', he tried to invoke the old unity. 'Individually, we all go down against what we should and can do, despite all the individual good we do; united, we can become benefactors of humanity, first of all of our people.'[32]

Interestingly, the two even kept Barop – who was seriously ill by then – in the dark about their conversation.[33] Especially in the first months of 1840,[34] Froebel courted Langethal, also to force a decision. Surprisingly, Langethal suddenly told Froebel that the canton of Berne wanted Froebel and Middendorff to come back[35] – one doesn't want to imagine how Albertine and the rest of the community reacted when they heard the news, if they ever did. Froebel wanted to meet with Langethal, Middendorff, and Barop in Frankfurt at the end of April 1840 to discuss this option and the future and to clarify what role the 'manly Langethal'[36] could play within the Keilhau community. '– What do you actually want? – Or in other words: – What do you demand? – Again different and yet the same. What do you say? – What do you teach, what do you instruct about? – In one word: – What do you reveal that is new, unprecedented in the relationship?'[37] But the meeting never happened. After stepping down from his position in Burgdorf so that Ferdinand Froebel could take over, Langethal founded an independent institute, a higher school for young ladies with Gustav Fröhlich, in Berne in 1841.[38] The decision meant he bid farewell to Keilhau as an (educational) idea. Langethal, who had been loyal and at Froebel's side for almost twenty-five years and who was, besides Middendorff, Froebel's closest associate and maybe one of his very few friends, no longer wanted to be a part of the community.

Langethal's decision hurt Froebel deeply. While the correspondence continued for a while, the tone became colder. Langethal must have criticized and attacked Froebel once more in January 1841. This time, Froebel reacted kindly:

> See, you are again quite wrong when you write in your most recent letter of 22/I: – 'Are you angry with me, considering possible dark sides of my life?' – I can say quite sincerely that I am not angry with anyone and do not rest on their dark sides … . How would I now even come to be angry with you and to rest on your dark sides, yes, I must tell you with the greatest sincerity that I do not know them at all, that I would first have to seek them out if I wanted to rest on them.[39]

It must have been clear to everyone that the friendship had come to an end. While Froebel toyed with the idea of visiting Langethal in his last letter in January 1842, this never happened. The two had nothing more to say to each other.

Froebel never forgave Langethal. In his eyes, Langethal had betrayed him and the greater cause. 'You see I do not think bad, not bleak, not impure of him; but an egoist he is like this',[40] Froebel wrote to Middendorff at the end of his life. Whenever the topic of Langethal came up, Froebel reacted resentfully and harshly. If you weren't with Froebel, you were against him. Only Langethal was to blame, of course. 'I don't want to write down what echoes in my soul!' he wrote to Middendorff after rereading the letters Langethal had sent to him during his time in Blankenburg. 'But I, I did not evoke it in the same!'[41]

The two never saw each other again. Only after Froebel's death did Langethal return to Keilhau, where he lived from 1862 until his death on 29 July 1879.

Froebel's Pedagogy of Kindergarten and Play

Over the years that followed, Froebel would constantly modify his pedagogy of kindergarten and play, even if major elements stayed remarkably consistent. Froebel changed or emphasized certain aspects based on his audience. The numerous essays and letters of this period, especially the ones to Nanette Pivany and Theresa Brunzvik, and the correspondence with Muhme Schmidt give insights into Froebel's complex pedagogical thinking and its development.[42] They are all rich sources to understand his developing idea. The letter to Max Leidesdorf from 23 March 1846 is also of interest as it contains concise and comprehensible remarks on the spherical law and its connection to kindergarten pedagogy. Many letters didn't serve as correspondence; they were essays on his developing kindergarten pedagogy. Writing these letters helped Froebel redefine the concepts, even if he probably overwhelmed his correspondence partners with the complex and difficult-to-understand writings.

Froebel saw kindergarten as a necessary piece of his concept of humane education with the goal of life unification. As with everything in his thinking, kindergarten was connected with the spherical law; he envisioned kindergarten as a place to understand or, at least, sense the law and to live a corresponding life. The early years, so Froebel had started to emphasize in the last months in Switzerland, are critical for a child's development, and children thus need conscious education. The best place for such a conscious education of young children is kindergarten, which must support and supplement – but not replace – family education. Only when what usually happens unconsciously becomes the subject of reflection can life unification be achieved. Hence, the primary goal of kindergarten is the 'education of the human being to be a human being'.[43] *All* children need humane education, though, not only those from upper-class families.

For Froebel, such humane education needed to be general and holistic. Kindergarten must support and nurture children in their holistic development so that all children can develop all their strengths. It's the responsibility of kindergarten to stimulate, awaken, and foster all abilities, strengths, and possibilities of each individual child. Kindergarten's goal must be the unification of body, mind, and soul. Only in this way can an individual achieve wholeness.

These short and simplified remarks show that the kindergarten concept was embedded in the law of the sphere with the goal of life unification. Everything else would have been a surprise and made no sense in Froebel's thinking. Education in kindergarten needs to be holistic because unity (among humans, nature, and God) and wholeness (thinking, feeling, and doing) are closely connected, and life unification can't be achieved without them. This must, of course, be the ultimate goal of kindergarten: 'The child will be educated in kindergarten as life-unified; the name kinder*garten* guarantees that this also happens as nature-unified'.[44] Kindergarten must achieve unification with nature, society, and God, or at least work towards achieving this.

However, such a unification with society, nature, and God can't succeed without appropriate activities and support: education. While a child wants to express the internal regularities that are within them – the spherical law – and thus feel the urge to be active, to create something, to be self-active, they also need conscious guidance. This is an aspect of Froebel's pedagogy that is often forgotten, but Froebel was clear about it. While a child possesses what Froebel later liked to call 'premonition' (*Ahnung*), more of a feeling of the possibility of life unification, this premonition must become consciousness, insight, and reflection. A child cannot achieve this alone, though; according to Froebel's thinking, they have a 'need for help' (*Hülfsbedürftigkeit*) – in the form of education. In their helplessness, they need support and stimulus from an adult. While children have an activity drive (*Tätigkeitstrieb*) and want to be self-active and express their inner self, they need to be nurtured and educated. Froebel's pedagogy of kindergarten and play was never about absolutely free or random play; he always emphasized didactic elements.

To help children become conscious of the spherical law inside them and live a unified life, Froebel developed the three main kindergarten areas of activity: garden care, movement games, and the 'whole of gifts and occupations' (*Ganze der Spiel- und Beschäftigungsgaben*); he always used the term 'whole' rather than 'system'. In kindergarten, children should practise and thus live life unification, and even if Froebel saw the movement games and garden care as essential, the most important area was definitely the whole of gifts and occupations.[45]

They consisted of four different groups: figure shapes (gifts 1–6: ball; bowl, cylinder, cube; building sets), flat-surface shapes (wood or cardboard pieces in five shapes), line shapes (sticks, rings, slats, jointed slats, and interlacing), and point shapes (peas, small rocks), whereby gifts 3–6, the building sets, were the ones used the most in the kindergarten years. Each child should have their own sets and play with these individually, based on their stage of development.

What the children were supposed to do with these gifts was to play, and even if his concept of play varied throughout years, Froebel had a clear understanding of what it meant. For him, play – and not school instruction – must be a young child's main activity. Play, and not instruction, is the suitable way for a child to learn at this age. Young children's learning takes place during and through play, play that is enriching and educational. Play is therefore – and such an idea was uncommon at the time – not a didactic tool to instil desired behaviour or values, not a motivational tool for supervision, or solely for recreational purposes. It's not a pastime, never just a frivolity or devoid of learning but 'rather a continuous learning, but one at, around and in life itself'.[46] Play is learning.

Such play needs to support the development of skills and abilities that enable a child to understand the regularities of reality, the spherical law. While children possess the fundamental ability for the premonition of regularities in the world, they need a suitable environment and the play materials: the 'whole of gifts and occupations'. For Froebel, the gifts were never simply educational, hands-on play materials; they were an image of reality, and playing with them enables a child to sense (at this age, not consciously understand) the structure of reality and, at the same time, be a part of it: the law of the sphere. Through play, a child can penetrate reality constructively; thus, its regularities and structures become transparent.

Ultimately, kindergarten and its play pedagogy served the same goal as all of Froebel's educational endeavours, namely humane education, experiencing and understanding the law of the sphere, and thus becoming conscious of and living life unification. Only in the context of his episteme did kindergarten make sense for Froebel.

Living for Kindergarten

Over the years that followed, Froebel devoted himself entirely to his kindergarten idea. Until 1844, he lived in Blankenburg and made only one long trip to Hildburghausen in November and December of 1841. Of course, he visited Keilhau frequently.

Despite his immense workload, Froebel managed to have a lively social life. A letter[47] written to his niece Amalie 'Malchen' Müller, the daughter of his late sister Juliane, and especially Ida Seele's reminiscences give vivid insights into Froebel's personal life of the time.[48] Especially Seele's memories are of interest, as it is one of the rare sources that offers a detailed outside perspective of Froebel's personal life. Malchen had run his household after Wilhelmine's death, and Seele, one of Froebel's first students and later the first kindergartner in Blankenburg, had lived with Froebel in Keilhau and Blankenburg between 1843 and 1844.

Froebel continued to live in the powder mill, where the owner Ms Wolfram and Auguste ran his household. Ms Wolfram must have been warm and caring; Seele was fond of her. He also used the service of a washerwoman. Guests must have been frequent, and some stayed longer, as did Seele and the other pupils who shared a small chamber with only one window in the mill. In the letter to Malchen, Froebel mentions a Miss Köhler, who had lived with him for 1½ months; Menger and Stephani; and Unger. Unger was working on the illustrations for Froebel's latest endeavour, and he frequently came for coffee or buttered bread. Middendorff came every Tuesday and Friday for the gift presentations and stayed overnight – 'he then lives here like me and also sleeps here with me.'[49] The two were still very close, but Middendorff's frequent visits meant he was often away from Keilhau, which probably upset Albertine and Emilie.

Life in Blankenburg was relatively simple. Froebel ate breakfast and supper at home, mostly milk and black bread, probably because he had lost almost all his rotten teeth in the 1840s. 'How often I found him standing in front of his kitchen cupboard, holding a piece of bread in his hand and eating an apple, because his bad teeth didn't allow him to bite.'[50] According to Seele, Froebel rarely ate or drank anything on his long and strenuous hikes, which still gave him pleasure. For lunch, Froebel had a table at Ms Weitzel's house, 'fairly, but proportionately too expensive; however, since it isn't a dining house, what can I do.'[51] His guilty pleasure, so it seems, was cake, maybe because he could enjoy it without teeth. Emilie's standard phrase was: 'The uncle is coming today too, isn't he? There is fresh cake.'[52] Since lunch was too expensive for the pupils, Ms Wolfram prepared a modest meal, including coffee made of roasted beets, potatoes, and meat only on Sundays. Froebel thought the food as too simple. Over lunch, Unger, Stolze, Schwarzkopf, and Mehltau often accompanied Froebel. Schwarzkopf was Froebel's manager, and Mehltau his travelling salesman. Froebel also paid a Mr Straubel to pack the play materials. It meant expenses, and as the lunch table was costly, Froebel was always in financial difficulties.[53]

Presentation still mattered to him, too. One story goes that Froebel was ashamed of how inaccurately Karoline Revonanz, one of his students, had prepared the buttered rolls for tea for a foreign lady from Warsaw looking for a kindergartener for her young daughter. Wilhelmine and the women in Keilhau had been masters in the art of preparing buttered rolls.[54] On such occasions, Froebel lost his temper.

From January until the end of April 1843, Froebel lived in Keilhau, probably because he lacked the financial means to get through the cold winter. However, he also hoped 'to achieve my next purpose all the better through the cohabitation of even more educating people'.[55] And it was indeed in Keilhau that he started training kindergartners.

On 8 March 1843, Ida Seele, 'a dear young girl from Nordhausen (the name really describes her)',[56] arrived in Keilhau. The friendly Elise greeted her and she later met Barop – 'tall, stately, black-eyed, with black hair and a serious face' – and then the 'agile, incredibly lively, extremely friendly and trusting'[57] Froebel entered the parlour. The first impression wasn't good; Barop and Froebel unsettled the young woman so much that she wanted to pack her bags immediately. Only when she met Middendorff did Seele change her mind. Middendorff, together with Elise, became her favourite, and she soon felt at home in Keilhau.

Seele wasn't Froebel's only pupil. Christian Stolze and Christiane Samsche (later Erdmann) were in Keilhau as well, and a short while later, Karoline Revovanz and Agnes Lommatzsch joined. Allwine Middendorff and Luise Frankenberg participated in the lessons, too. Froebel taught the theoretical lessons, but Barop, the music teacher Kohl, the painter Unger, or Middendorff also gave lessons. On Sunday evenings, meetings with singing occurred in the big hall, or Froebel gave lectures on the materials and play care.

Seele has also described that Middendorff had to direct the play hours. Froebel must have been inept in leading the children's games because he was absorbed in his games like a child. The same happened in the kindergarten – another reason why Middendorff had to come so often. When Middendorff led the activities, Froebel acted more as an observer, but remained the all-dominating power. Once he stormed out of his room and criticized Middendorff so much in front of the children and the students 'that we were really scared and silently called this behaviour a pedagogical mistake'. The only one who kept his cool was Middendorff. 'Yes, yes, the master's eye sees all, and we will gladly obey the master.'[58] The similarities to the incident with Langethal in Keilhau years ago are striking. Some things would never change.

Keilhau also had a kindergarten now, attended by eight to twelve children, of which none paid any fees. The same was true in Blankenburg.[59] There, the kindergarten was quite some distance from the powder mill, and Seele and the others had to make the arduous walk a few times every day. When Seele first visited the kindergarten, everything was dusty, but they cleaned and made it welcoming. While the parents and children were thankful for the kindergarten, Froebel didn't receive much support from Blankenburg apart from the room.[60] Thus, there was no money, and Froebel couldn't heat the room in winter. They had to close it, and the children often came to the powder mill instead.

In the kindergarten, the children mainly built with blocks and other materials. Froebel was in his element, as can be seen from Seele's description: 'Froebel stood at the exit of the hall, shook hands with each child, wiped with his beautiful white handkerchief once more over the face of the first, over the mouth of the second and over the eyes of the third, looked after them with touching, one might say motherly tenderness – and then it was over.'[61]

There was also a kindergarten in Rudolstadt led by Mr Menger, a young teacher. In the beginning, they all went there once a week; later, Seele went to Rudolstadt and Keilhau on her own. Froebel was busy writing letters, finishing the new book, writing the building and ball songs, and finalizing his educational system. Since he constantly gave lectures and discussed his ideas with Barop and Middendorff, he had no time for the kindergarten. Seele was fully responsible, and the kindergarten closed for good when she left.[62]

Froebel expected a lot from his students. After only three months, he told Seele: 'For now, I must confess, I was deceived in you; you didn't fulfil my hopes of being able to use you as a director of a kindergarten.'[63] Seele burst into tears. Only later, when he observed Seele playing with a young child, did Froebel change his opinion, claiming: 'Yes, you are born to be a kindergartner.'[64] During the training, Froebel was often very critical. For example, he accused Seele of being stubborn. The young woman worked so hard until late in the night till she became ill. When Froebel learned of this, he was shocked.

Froebel might have been harsh, but for good reason. He only recommended kindergartners he fully believed in; thus, they had to prove that they understood his idea. His feedback might have been harsh, but it was always honest. However, Froebel could also be warm and caring. Seele – who was young at the time; she was sixteen, even if Froebel always introduced her as fourteen – became very close to Froebel and the whole Keilhau community. On her seventeenth birthday, after she and the other students returned from a riflemen's festival, a table laden with birthday gifts and seventeen roses, a poem by Middendorff, and a mug from Froebel with the engraved words 'Peace, Joy, You' was waiting for her. The evening ended with a dance, with Middendorff, Barop, and Froebel joining. The otherwise so serious and strict Froebel could enjoy life.

Keilhau touchingly cared for Seele. When she needed new clothes, the women tailored new ones, or Allwina shared hers. 'Such kindness and goodness of heart could probably only be found among the women of Keilhau.'[65] Later, on her last visit before leaving for Darmstadt, the women tailored more clothes, and Froebel promised to pay for them. 'Whether it will also happen, I also don't know,'[66] so goes Seele's commentary.

Listening to Seele's description, it becomes clear why Keilhau was a special place, even if Albertine let her know she had only seen the nice sides because she had been treated like a guest and that life could be very harsh in Keilhau. Life in Keilhau was sociable and not completely cut off from the world. They were well connected and well liked by Keilhau's citizens, attending festivals or concerts, or enjoying nature on hikes. The same was true for life in Blankenburg. Froebel was far from being solitary.

Still, Froebel mainly lived for his new idea. When absorbed in thought, he could forget everything around him and to whom he was talking. Once when on their way to Rudolstadt, Froebel lost his students who were unfamiliar with the area. Later that day, he insisted they walk home in the rain, even though they had been offered a carriage. When they arrived at the mill, even Froebel was exhausted. Still, when Ms Wolfram wanted to wake him up – Froebel was usually awake early – the bed was empty. Froebel had walked to Keilhau in the night because he wanted to share a thought and was afraid he would forget it by the morning. Froebel was restless, obsessed with his idea.

The relationship with Keilhau in these years was warm, but tensions were palpable. According to Seele, Froebel and his now blind brother Christian were highly respected, and everyone followed their words. In Blankenburg, however, he was solely in charge and only what 'Froebel had said was true'.[67] In Keilhau, Froebel was more of a guest, and especially the women were wary. 'Until there is a decisive change in the present position of Keilhau women, I think it would be best to let Luise Frankenberg go to Rothenburg,'[68] Froebel wrote to Middendorff. Froebel still became sulky quickly. When he learned that Keilhau wouldn't accept an invitation, he told Middendorff: 'Then it is also the last time that I will ever invite someone from Keilhau here again … . What does a little rain do; but do it as you will.'[69]

It's safe to assume that the families in Keilhau were wary of Froebel's next endeavours, but also had their problems. With Christian – the aged patriarch of this community – being blind, Keilhau had lost its most efficient worker. Caroline Froebel was also getting older, and Albertine's and Emilie's children were growing up. Life in Keilhau wasn't easy; financial worries were ever-present, and their uncle squandered money that none of them had.

Still, visits were frequent. According to Seele, they were allowed to come to Keilhau every Sunday, every holiday, and every family celebration. Froebel went often, and Barop, Middendorff, Kohl, Luise Frankenberg, and especially Allwina frequently came to Blankenburg. The ones who didn't come were Albertine and Emilie. At least Elise often joined them on the frequent hikes. But it wasn't too bad. Once, when they went to Keilhau from Rudolstadt by mistake, the community welcomed them warmly and invited them for dinner. And if no one from Keilhau came, others visited the kindergarten. It was a busy time for Froebel, who was satisfied with his new work and far from growing lonely.

Mother-Play and Nursery Songs

While the letters and essays were crucial, Froebel's main work of the time was *Mother-Play and Nursery Songs: Poetry, Music and Pictures for the Noble Culture of Child Life, with Notes to Mothers*, an educationally interpreted collection of popular rhymes and songs for children. Froebel saw it as a direct continuation to Pestalozzi's *Book of Mothers*. He had started collecting songs in 1841 when he observed a young farmer's wife directing her child to wave to chickens and pigeons in the yard. 'Wave to the chicken – wave to the pigeon!' was the first play song that Froebel wrote down. Later, he picked up ideas from young mothers, often within the Keilhau community. Seele has called it a real collaboration; she and Allwine Middendorff helped create it, especially with the songs, and so did Middendorff.[70]

In 1844, after an extensive and time-consuming preparation, *Mother-Play and Nursery Songs* was published, again presenting Froebel's motto on the title page: 'Come let us live with our children.' The book differs in its design from Froebel's other writings. It consists of seven nursery and fifty play songs, forty-four of which were set to music by Robert Kohl. The songs were published as full-page prints with etchings by Friedrich Unger, including verses depicting mothers and playing children, along with explanations and song texts with notes. While brilliant in their conception, the songs were often only mediocre in execution, partially due to flat rhyme structures.

Friedrich Fröbel auf dem Wege nach Keilhau
nach einer Tuschzeichnung von Alb. Schmiedeknecht

Figure 7.2 On the way to Keilhau.

Bildarchiv Friedrich-Fröbel-Museum Bad Blankenburg (Picture Library Friedrich-Fröbel-Museum Bad Blankenburg)

Nevertheless, the book is more than just a collection of songs. Froebel described the developmental peculiarities of infants and young children; it's a testimony to his advanced understanding of young children. The early years, Froebel's argument goes, are essential, and the education of young children must start by giving attention to the body and then proceeding to the next environment. He also emphasized that emotional attention is essential for the infant's development. It's a remarkable concept of early infant education, a guide to support children in exploring the world holding their mother's hand to live a spherical life and develop life unification.

The only problem was that it didn't sell well, if at all. Since the production had been costly, it only increased the debts and financial hardships.[71]

A Journeyman for Kindergarten

Although now over sixty years old, in 1844 Froebel changed his lifestyle drastically once more: he became a kind of business traveller. Over the years that followed, he often went on long, arduous journeys to arouse interest in the General German Kindergarten, initiating new kindergartens' openings and finding influential supporters. Since the powder mill was no longer needed and had been a financial burden anyway, Froebel gave it up. In the summer of 1846, he auctioned all the dispensable furnishings to get at least some money. Froebel had no home and no possessions, only his idea. When not travelling, he lived in Keilhau to give educational courses for kindergartners.

The first journey in 1844 took Froebel to the south of Germany. Middendorff had prepared the trip by visiting Frankfurt, Homburg, Offenbach, Heidelberg, Worms, Mainz, and other cities. Middendorff had stayed in Darmstadt and met with influential figures of the local early childhood education scene.[72] Froebel, however, first went to Frankfurt. He was in touch with Schnyder again, who now lived in Frankfort, though he was away when Froebel arrived. Frankfort wasn't a success, and Froebel couldn't arouse much interest in kindergarten. We don't know if he visited Caroline von Holzhausen or contacted her, but it doesn't seem so. Afterward, Froebel visited Heidelberg, Darmstadt, Cologne, Stuttgart, Osthofen, and Ingelheim before returning to Frankfurt.

Such travels became frequent in the years that followed. In November 1845, Froebel travelled to Annaburg near Torgau to stay with the pastor Wöpke for a few weeks; Annaburg was planning to open a kindergarten. He also visited Wittenberg over Christmas and stayed in Magdeburg with the pastor Uhlich, another supporter. Then he went on a short journey through Vogtland in Saxonia before returning to Keilhau in November 1846. In the summer of 1847, Froebel went on a longer trip, this time to Marienberg in the Ore Mountains, Halle, Quetz, Magdeburg, Brunswick, Hanover, Bremen, Eisenach, and Gotha, before returning to Keilhau on 9 September 1847. In May 1848, Froebel again travelled through Saxony, visiting Leipzig, Oschatz, Dresden, Bischofswerda, and Bautzen, trying to make contact with local primary school teachers.

The goal was always the same: give lectures and presentations, meet with influential people to create networks, and initiate kindergarten openings. Froebel was often successful, but not always. He found many supporters with whom he stayed in touch if they were supportive and helpful. Over the years, a vast network developed.

However, due to Froebel's complicated personality and his unyielding insistence on the correctness of the kindergarten idea, many promising connections never blossomed. Especially if people dared to come up with their ideas or modifications of the kindergarten idea, Froebel broke off contact. Froebel wasn't interested in collaboration. A prominent example of this pattern is Johannes Fölsing in Darmstadt.[73] Middendorff had met Fölsing before, and the two had liked each other. Froebel stayed at Fölsing's house for half a year while in Darmstadt; he gave lectures and presentations that convinced the local infant school board of Froebel's concept. They wanted one of Froebel's students as a teacher and bought his materials worth 200 thalers. It was a promising start. But the board didn't want to adopt the name kindergarten, which led to the first arguments, even if they agreed on the term *Kinderführer* (child leader). Froebel also used the term *Spielführer* (play leader). Finally, Ida Seele was sent to Darmstadt to work in the infant school.

Seele has described these first weeks and months vividly. Since Froebel had negotiated that Seele only needed to start in September but was already paid from August, the two travelled to Darmstadt via Frankfurt. In Darmstadt, Froebel once again stayed with Fölsing's family, attended the baptism of Fölsing's child, and gave a copy of *Mother-Play and Nursery Songs* as a gift. He also visited the infant school daily. Seele portrayed a socially active Froebel who enjoyed going to the theatre and attending events. Once, because the street was overcrowded, he must have jumped from stone heap to stone heap, endangering them both. Later the same day, he got lost in the crowd, returning home late at night. He was restless, open to everything, and always curious – 'but we loudly and quietly admired Froebel's tireless endurance, strength and freshness in his sixty-first year!'[74]

However, disagreements between Fölsing and Froebel about appropriate early childhood education soon arose. While they said goodbye on friendly terms, Froebel never returned to Darmstadt, and Middendorff only came after Froebel's death. Later, Froebel spoke ill of Fölsing, and a public dispute arose between Fölsing and Wichard Lange. While such tensions were not solely Froebel's fault, such behaviour was typical. Froebel sought support and only stayed in touch with people if they were helpful. However, if people dared to disagree or weren't supportive, Froebel broke off contact. Whoever wasn't for him was against him.

The same was true of his students. The correspondence with Seele, who had felt 'as if my father had died for the second time'[75] when Froebel left, continued for a while. As so often, his letters served as instruction and professional development, but Froebel also used such correspondences to demonstrate his power. When he wasn't satisfied with her, Seele wrote, he didn't write for a long time. 'That statement of yours, that you were mistaken about me, hurt me deeply in my soul.'[76] Froebel also wanted to wield influence, and in Seele's case, he wanted her to come to Hamburg to take over the responsibility for a citizen kindergarten in 1850.[77] When she refused, Froebel reacted angrily and broke off the correspondence. 'I never saw him again,'[78] the disappointed Seele stated.

A Man on a Mission

Seele described 'Froebel's pure love for the children, his tireless sacrifice, his great frugality and unpretentiousness'[79] as his dominant traits. His lifestyle became increasingly nomadic and chaotic: there was always a new idea, nothing was ever thought through, and everything was constantly changing. Convinced of his concept, Froebel's expectations for the General German Kindergarten were high, unrealistic even. He expected nothing less than the moral rebirth of the people, the rebirth of Germany, and a new 'springtime of humanity'.[80] Despite his age and busy life, he was never tired of promoting his idea in writing, speech, and deed. 'Froebel was so firmly convinced of his mission, of the importance and truth of his way of education, of his principles, that he thought day and night about it.'[81] He was always working, often until late at night, and never rested. But he seemed peculiar to many, with his craggy and rugged face, toothless mouth, prominent nose, energetic chin, and obsessive nature. To be convinced, one had to hear him speak. Benfey saw Froebel's oratorical talent as his 'sparkling, inspiring gift' and the 'most important trait in his character'.[82] For it was then that Froebel came across as the man on a mission that he was.

In the eyes of his supporters, Froebel was like a saint. Seele described how they listened to one of Froebel's lectures during sunrise on a Keilhau mountain, which reminded her of the Sermon on the Mount. While she couldn't remember Froebel's words, she felt they all went back down the mountain as better, purified human beings and that Froebel was more and more venerable.[83] Deinhard, who visited Froebel in Blankenburg, described him as someone who would 'pour out his heart and his mind, as it were, to everyone who met him and showed any interest in his thoughts; indeed, he literally hunted down people to scatter his ideas, as it were, as seeds in receptive minds, and he often gave himself up to too great hopes of the lasting effects of his talks'.[84] While Froebel's words were often unclear, he saw Froebel as 'an unusual phenomenon'.

For his critics, though, he came across as a fanatical preacher or a naïve and idealistic dreamer. Many contemporaries didn't take him seriously; after all, eccentrics like him were no rarity. Rudolf Benfey, who later became an influential supporter of the kindergarten idea, remembered how he first heard of Froebel during a train journey in 1844. A fellow passenger told him of an event in Darmstadt where a 'strange man' named Fröbler or Fröhlich had lectured, a 'wonder-worker who makes learning extremely easy for children'. Another passenger, however, mocked the unknown man as one of the many educational charlatans. When Benfey discussed it with a teacher a few days later, he was told that it was all a 'pedagogical hoax' and that Froebel was keeping the children busy with useless trifles.[85]

Such criticism, hostility, and slander, of which there was no shortage in the 1840s, hurt Froebel deeply. Criticism was something he still couldn't handle. Usually, though, he didn't consider it necessary to answer his opponents publicly and instead liked to draw his supporters' attention to praise and statements of agreement. But deviating from his point of view was out of the question – and everyone in Froebel's circle knew this.

New Tensions with Keilhau

Froebel frequently wrote to Barop and Middendorff while away. The correspondence shows the tensions, especially in November and December 1844. As so often, money was the issue. The business in Blankenburg was a significant financial burden due to the publication of *Mother-Play and Nursery Songs*, and its poor sales had added to the costs. Debts were high and creditors were demanding payment, threatening to take legal action. If he ever wanted to return to Keilhau,

Barop told Froebel sharply, he needed to be careful with his financial ventures. Barop, who felt responsible for Keilhau and the families who had to live off the educational enterprise, was no longer willing to spend unlimited sums on Froebel's costly endeavours. Froebel was resentful towards Barop but also his brother Christian because they were no longer willing to sacrifice Keilhau in order to support his new ideas.[86] At the same time, he had to beg for money.[87] 'Barop, Barop … . You all have – you have me and everything in your hand. You should now make the demand of the 600–800 Rhenish thaler possible through your circumstances so that I do not have to give others the profit and glory of my life's work.'[88]

Apart from the money issue, Froebel felt misunderstood and insufficiently supported. As in the past, he saw the unity of the whole in danger. 'Barop! Let me speak to you as a friend, as a brother, as a father', he wrote in August 1844,

> the present moment of life is important, is important beyond all description, it will never return to this extent, in this coherence, even unison. Do not let yourself be deceived by the desire for decay and perhaps again the real decay of my outer life, let us be clear, alert, prudent, courageous, strong and persevering in ourselves: it is the renewed time of a new beginning of fruit.[89]

Froebel feared Keilhau would abandon him completely, an accusation that Barop and Middendorff strongly denied.[90] Matters worsened when Froebel heard a rumour while in Frankfurt in December that Keilhau, and in particular Barop and Middendorff, had 'completely separated from my personal educational aspirations'.[91] Froebel was shocked. At the time, he was glum anyway because he had met with indifference, not to say hostility, in Frankfurt.[92] Froebel felt isolated, once again betrayed. 'Feeling and seeing myself abandoned by everything on earth, I reached into my own self, holding on within myself to the spirit and life that had so far nurtured, carried and protected me, to the spirit which I must recognize as divine spirit.'[93]

Still, Keilhau was the only home he had. But Barop was now in charge, and Froebel was merely a tolerated guest. The women looked critically on everything he did because he was responsible for the ongoing outflow of money, and Albertine and Emilie always had to fear that their husbands would follow Froebel on his next adventure. Middendorff must have indeed expressed his willingness to support Froebel wholeheartedly, whatever the costs, but Albertine had strictly forbidden it. She was also worried that her husband, who often suffered painful headaches, would overwork himself. Thus, Middendorff was always torn and suffered from the constant quarrels, even if Barop tried to mediate between the sides.[94] Still, apart from Middendorff and his daughter Allwine, no one showed

Figure 7.3 Johannes Arnold Barop.
Bildarchiv Friedrich-Fröbel-Museum Bad Blankenburg (Picture Library Friedrich-Fröbel-Museum Bad Blankenburg)

any interest in the kindergarten idea. Froebel still cared deeply about Keilhau, though. One can see the warm feelings in his letters – for example, his sadness when Keilhau didn't reply as quickly as he wished, or when he realized he wouldn't be there for Christmas.

It's interesting, too, how differently Froebel treated the families. If Christian is mentioned in letters, he is always shown respect. Middendorff's family was part of Froebel's life, Allwine is mentioned often, and Wilhelm Jr is also mentioned frequently. In contrast, Froebel was noticeably disinterested in Emilie's family. 'Barop's wife, Emilie, gave him a little boy named Reinhold in the month of May', he wrote to Muhme Schmidt in October 1847, 'so I think Barop now has eight children: – Johannes, Gertrud – Adelheid – Emil Thusnelda – Cäcilie – Maria – Reinhold. If I am not mistaken, he is so happy not to have lost any of them.'[95] He must have disliked his goddaughter Gertrud, a serious child who read a lot. Maybe that's why he wasn't close to her. Still, it's a strikingly cold statement about the children of his once favourite niece.

Froebel spent most of 1845 in Keilhau and only went to Dresden to attend Frankenberg's wedding in April. The Barops must have been away for a while, but there is no evidence that they were avoiding Froebel. While in Keilhau, he started another course for kindergartners, now focusing on women. The German teaching profession was traditionally male, but male teachers had rejected his pedagogy as sentimental and unscientific. Thus, Froebel now insisted that women possess a special gift for teaching young children, which he later referred to as 'spiritual motherhood'. Many women reacted enthusiastically to the new opportunity.[96]

Over the years that followed, he regularly gave such courses; among the first participants were Marie Christ and Amalie Krüger. However, the number of participants continually decreased. In the summer of 1847, only five female students and one male student participated, and in autumn, only Allwine and Luise Levin, who worked as a domestic helper in Keilhau, attended. Luise had grown up in Osterode and spent time in Christian's house as a child. She was immediately impressed by Froebel's personality, who, as she later said, 'often appeared at the table and for coffee as if from another world'.[97] However, she also witnessed Froebel's dark sides and violent behaviour. Had she known how much Froebel was suffering, she later explained, she would have understood him better, though. Nevertheless, in her eyes, Froebel was 'high above all other men' and 'high above herself'.[98] Soon, she had feelings for the man thirty-three years her senior. Henriette Breymann,[99] Froebel's grandniece and later one of the most influential people of the kindergarten movement, was another young woman who joined the circle. She also sensed Froebel's alienation when she stayed in Keilhau in 1848. Like Seele, she experienced the blind Christian and his wife as friendly, a 'venerable couple',[100] and Albertine as cheerful, utterly different to how she had initially thought. Especially Elise grew dear to her heart, a remarkable woman, according to Breymann. But what surprised her was that only Middendorff spoke kindly of Froebel while the others openly expressed their dislike of the 'impractical idealist'.[101] Especially the sisters didn't have much sympathy left for their 'domineering' uncle who had taken away their husbands and would have ruined Keilhau if he had had his way. 'I sense something like bitterness in them when they talk about their uncle',[102] was Henriette's succinct comment.

The problem, though, was that participation in the courses was decreasing. Once again, one of Froebel's grand ideas was in danger of failing.

Suddenly Politicized: The Revolution of 1848/49

In March 1848, Froebel – who had mainly developed his educational ideas in ignorance of and not as an answer to contemporary sociopolitical issues, maybe apart from his concept of national education – suddenly became political. When the March Revolution broke out, Froebel – who tended more towards the constitutional monarchy than the republican-democratic constitution due to his upbringing in Schwarzburg-Rudolstadt – expressed excitement, calling the revolution a 'surging storm, which, God grant it, thoroughly improved all conditions of life, and which came rushing over our little country and tore it down'.[103] Two days later, he ended the letter: 'Hail the German people, the free German people spring morning. With nature and sky spring began on the earth the German people and fatherland spring. Praised be God's eternal world government. Your rejuvenated cousin FrFr.'[104]

In a letter to Dr Karl Hagen, Froebel expressed similar enthusiasm about the dawn of a new era. Froebel had known Hagen since his first journey through the southern states of Germany, and their correspondence had always included political topics. While travelling and no longer only exposed to calm Thuringia, he had become a little more aware of sociopolitical issues. Hagen's insightful comments helped Froebel better understand these topics:

> But who could come to such a thing until now, when the conditions of life were pressing like the waves of the roaring sea? But just as after a violent thunderstorm, when the arch of peace showed itself in the sky in sunny splendour, the larks already rise in song to the blue sky, so also our dear little children and our vigorous youth come forth with their joyful hopes![105]

What Froebel wanted from Hagen was support for kindergarten. The moment seemed favourable; teacher associations in the duchies of Meiningen and Koburg as well as the kingdom of Saxony had already announced their support for kindergarten as part of German public education; and Froebel hoped that influential figures such as Hagen would follow. Suddenly, Froebel claimed that all his previous educational endeavours should be seen in such political contexts.

'Examine all my educational activities in their innermost core – I have been educating for an age for the republic and towards it, I educate and train for the practice of the republican virtues.'[106]

It was an opportunistic move. Froebel hoped that radical reforms of the educational system would give kindergarten more attention, maybe even with kindergarten as the first step of the public school system. 'All this now encourages, yes, I would like to say rejuvenates me as well.'[107]

For a while, Froebel's hopes seemed to come true. The second Saxon teachers' assembly listed kindergarten as educational institutions for the people that must exist in every community, and Frankfurt's national parliament adopted a resolution by the teacher association of Rudolstadt to name kindergarten as the first step in a consistent and unified educational system. Kindergarten would have been part of the public educational system if it had become a reality. But Froebel's hopes were short-lived, and with the reactionary forces regaining power by the end of 1848, things became worse. Froebel's name and kindergarten were now associated with the despised revolution. Kindergarten had been politicized and the state authorities were now suspicious of Froebel and his institution.

Froebel, though, continued to work relentlessly. Since he was friendly with many elementary teachers in Saxony and Thuringia, Froebel invited friends and students to Rudolstadt, where around three hundred people met from 17 to 19 August 1848 for a teacher and educator assembly.[108] Froebel had organized accommodation for them all. But all participants were supportive of kindergarten. Froebel was nervous, and when he gave a speech on 18 August, overwhelmed by working all through the previous weeks, he began to tremble. In the afternoon, he continued with an outdoor presentation of the gifts and games, but again it didn't go well. The listeners were confused and bored, and the crowd began asking for Middendorff. Froebel became even more nervous, seemingly forgetting where he was and what he was doing. The whole day was an embarrassment and disaster for the emerging kindergarten movement. However, the next day, when the assembly discussed the pros and cons with the agitated Froebel defending his idea, he was more convincing. In the end, the assembly drafted a petition to support kindergarten.

The Manager of the Kindergarten Network

Froebel's energy continued to be impressive for a man his age. From 28 to 30 September 1848, he attended another assembly of 'German people educators and teachers', this time in Eisenach. As a result of all his networking, Dresden invited him to give a training course during the winter of 1848/49. Froebel arrived in October and was pleased to learn that a big circle of forty to fifty male and female pupils – among them Henriette Breymann, the two Luise Frankenbergs, Emma Habicht, Wilhelmine Auguste Herz, Heinrich Hoffmann, Amalie Krüger, Bruno Marquart, or Johanna Küstner – were attending. It was a satisfying time, as the group was enthusiastic about the cause. It was a comprehensive programme, and Froebel's theoretical explanations were often challenging to follow because, as Henriette Breymann put it, he wasn't an eloquent speaker.[109] In addition, Froebel frequently gave lectures and was very social. Breymann lived in the same house, Liliengasse No. 19, on the third floor, and many of the participants met for lunch at Frankenberg's home. The highlights were the monthly Sunday parties at the upscale hotel 'Zur Stadt Wien', where course participants, friends, and patrons met in a tastefully decorated hall to listen to songs, speeches, poems, charades, and especially games performed by Froebel. Froebel described these evenings in detail to Elise.[110] To capture the spirit of the events as 'echoes of the celebration', one participant wrote a poem. It was a success, and Froebel worked so hard that the participants asked him to take a second day off because they were concerned about his health.[111]

From Dresden, Froebel wrote regular, often long letters to Luise, who was now working as the governess to chamberlain von Cossel's three children in Rendsburg, Holstein.[112] In these letters, Froebel gave an account of his life in Dresden and the progress of the course – and he also courted Luise. 'Therefore, my G ... [*Geliebte*, beloved] I thank you most sincerely for your friendly, feminine wish.'[113] The two had become closer, there was even a bit of romance, and Froebel enjoyed the much younger Luise's affection. 'How can a human being give so much joy to human beings ... . How can you, my heart, make me so intimately happy?'[114] Froebel's letters were mainly warm and caring. Sometimes, though, he had to calm Luise down and assure her of his feelings.[115] And from time to time, he couldn't help but lecture the young woman about life and everything else, for example, when he pointed out her grammatical mistakes.[116]

Soon it became clear that Froebel hoped Luise would live with him. Since Dresden had been such a success and Keilhau was no longer an option, efforts were made to persuade Froebel to stay in Dresden. But in the end, Froebel opted for Liebenstein in the dukedom of Meiningen. On 26 February 1849, he invited Allwine and Luise to join him in spring to help with the institute. Allwine was tentative, however, and so were her parents. 'Whether and when you now, dear Allwine, want to join our educational circle as an essential member and as an essential co-worker in our educational enterprises, will now still depend on your and your parents' approval.'[117] There were also issues with Wilhelm Jr, who appears to have suffered from depression:

> My situation is indeed a very sad one. What should I do? – I cannot and must not decide on anything firm because I see everywhere the probability that I will have to abandon my resolutions and plans without having achieved anything. This uncertainty in everything weighs heavily on me, it has a paralyzing effect on my whole being, on everything I do.[118]

Wilhelm also wanted to stay with his great uncle in Bad Liebenstein, and Froebel was open to the idea, though it never happened. It again shows how burdensome the situation in Keilhau must have been for Albertine and the families. Instead of Allwine, Henriette Breymann came to Bad Liebenstein in May, and Luise joined at the end of June.

Froebel had asked the duke about the little castle Marienthal as the location for the new institute, but still hadn't received a reply by May. Since the first pupils were arriving, he opened the *Anstalt für allseitige Lebenseinigung durch entwickelnd-erziehende Menschenbildung* (*Institute for All-Sided Life Unification through Developing-Educating Human Edification*) in the Kurhaus of the spa town Bad Liebenstein. Mrs Müller, the Kurhaus inspector, had offered him rooms. Eight students, young girls – or 'young ladies' (*Jungfrauen*) as they were called, participated in the course.[119] Shortly after Luise's arrival, Henriette left because there wasn't much to do for her, but mainly because of the ongoing disputes with her great uncle. Luise stayed, however – a very bold decision for an unmarried girl in those prudish times. Thanks to Luise, the relationship between the peculiar Froebel and the young women was mostly harmonious.

The courses and constant travels helped Froebel create a widespread kindergarten network. Many early kindergartners became friends and also stayed in touch with Froebel, and he stayed up late into the night responding to correspondence. The women often shared news about their kindergartens and reflected on their everyday practices, which helped Froebel keep track of the kindergarten movement. But he also used the correspondence as instruction and professional development.[120] The roles, however, were always clear with the 'Highly Esteemed Froebel', the 'Dear Professor' as the unquestioned dominant force. The only one who didn't seem to care as much was Christiane Erdmann, who called him 'Dear Good Little Froebel'.[121] However, she was also saddened when Froebel punished her with rage, hoping he would forgive her. 'If I could have cried, I would have done so, unfortunately, I could not … . I am deceived, very painfully deceived, to have been misjudged by you, and, as I see from your letter, to have been regarded as lost.'[122]

Undoubtedly, Froebel supported many kindergartners and helped them make a living as unmarried women, an unusual opportunity for the time. Many letters show a warm and caring Froebel, admired by his students. But Froebel also wanted to wield influence and could react harshly. When he felt a kindergartner wasn't supporting the cause as he wished, he used scathing criticism and silence to discipline them. Offers to former students to lead a kindergarten weren't only well-meaning opportunities; it was also what he felt best for the movement. If someone rejected such an offer, Froebel could withdraw his affection quickly. In a sense, Froebel became the manager of the kindergarten idea. He was no longer interested in the daily work, but wanted to organize and spread the kindergarten idea.

Today, it's almost impossible to reconstruct the various connections and correspondences that Froebel pursued during these last years, which also included supporters whom Froebel had met during his journeys. Recreating this network would be a different story, a different book. However, a few examples help illustrate Froebel's role and actions.

Ida Seele is one example, and Amalie Krüger another interesting one.[123] Born on 5 April 1816, Krüger probably spent a few weeks in Keilhau in spring 1846. Later, she accompanied Froebel on an extensive promotional trip before participating in another kindergartner course in Keilhau from November 1846 to May 1847. It was through Krüger that Froebel met the pastor Ludwig Hildenhagen in Quetz, who became a supporter and helped organize the children's festival in Quetz on 25 July 1847. At the festival, Froebel exhibited his play and activity materials with 150 children in front of around two thousand spectators; Krüger was at his side again. Later, she demonstrated Froebel's gifts at the teachers' and educators' meeting in Rudolstadt in August 1848. At the time she was working in Gotha as a kindergartner, Froebel had made her the offer. However, she had previously rejected Froebel's wish to take over a kindergarten in Nordhausen. In October 1848, Krüger left Gotha to participate in the course in Dresden. Finally, she took over the kindergarten of the Jewish couple Wilhelm and Jeannette Beit in Hamburg in February 1849. It was already the second kindergarten in Hamburg; the first one was run by Allwine Middendorff with whom Krüger had a warm friendship. Unhappy with the new task, she left Hamburg at the end of April 1849 for Zurich.[124]

Until this point, Froebel had thought highly of her: 'As I have already told you, Miss Krüger is one of the most independent kindergarten teachers in the world', he wrote to Dr Alexander Detmer, who was planning to open the first citizen kindergarten (*Bürgerkindergarten*) in Hamburg, 'her critical judgment about life and its phenomena is why her judgment is so important to me and her views on life are of value to me.'[125]

Suddenly, though, the relationship cooled. Krüger had promised Froebel's nephew, Karl Froebel, and his fiancée, Johanna Küster, that she would take over the kindergarten they opened in Zurich on 1 May 1849. Krüger and Karl Froebel had met in Quetz when Middendorff brought Karl Froebel to the festival.[126] Krüger and Küster had known each other since Rudolstadt and Dresden. Johanna had abandoned the course in Dresden due to her engagement with Karl, a decision that had angered Froebel. In his eyes, his nephew was stealing his students. While in Zurich, Krüger tried to reconcile Karl with his uncle, asking the latter not to reject Karl's 'hand of reconciliation'.[127] Froebel reacted rather coldly.

Shortly after, Krüger returned to Hamburg to work at Karl Froebel's *Hochschule für das weibliche Geschlecht* (*College for the Female Gender*). The college – innovative and independent of religious denominations – and the planned associated kindergarten were a thorn in Froebel's side. Froebel opposed the college's partisan political ventures and the employees' liberal lifestyles. Still, Krüger must have wanted Froebel to give lectures at the college, which he angrily refused. Instead, he wanted her to introduce kindergarten in Weimar, but she did neither that nor went to Halle.[128] It seems that she wanted to open a kindergarten in Hamburg instead. Still, Froebel wrote her a friendly letter at the end of August 1849 before he suddenly withdrew his affection and accused Krüger sharply: 'I was deeply hurt by your letter.'[129] Froebel was offended that Krüger didn't do as he had told her. Krüger tried to reconcile by giving up the idea of opening her kindergarten in Hamburg, but it was too late. The correspondence ended, and Froebel withdrew his affection. In November, he told Luise:

> Unexpectedly my hand was touched by a stranger; as if struck by lightning I looked up from the circle of my pupils surrounding me and who was standing in front of me? It was Amalie Krüger, smiling with a friendly look; this look and the whole appearance immediately had such an unpleasant effect on me that I quickly stepped out of the circle and left the room … she has only herself to blame for it because of her bold rashness and real audacity, for she knew how we stood together … . Now I hear she is weeping and lamenting.[130]

It was once again a case of whoever wasn't with him was against him.

Through Krüger, Froebel met the pastor Ludwig Hildenhagen, another example of how Froebel treated his supporters and friends.[131] Hildenhagen was married to Krüger's sister Luise. Froebel and Hildenhagen first met in 1846 and soon became friends; they even addressed each other with the informal you. Hildenhagen was part of the non-denominational movement and a supporter of the democratic movement, far more of a political person than Froebel. In August 1846, Hildenhagen opened a kindergarten in Quetz, which was run by Ida Weiler, who had been responsible for his children's education so far. Froebel was pleased by the development and considered Hildenhagen a capable and thoughtful supporter. In 1847, Hildenhagen developed a concept for training courses for kindergartners, and Froebel stayed in Quetz over the summer of 1847 for many weeks due to the children's festival.

The relationship cooled when Froebel sent Hildenhagen a draft of a plan for an educational institute for kindergartners, whereupon Hildenhagen replied with critical feedback and suggestions for improvement. 'The plan is simple and good in general, but it suffers from a flaw that you still need to change … . The idea itself must be expressed more directly, not so reflected, or even philosophically.'[132] Hildenhagen even offered to write a preface and epilogue. Froebel was enraged that Hildenhagen thought of himself as equal and had dared to criticize him and immediately broke off contact. He never answered Hildenhagen's follow-up letters or visited Quetz, even when he was nearby, as Ida Weiler criticized sharply.[133] Hildenhagen, however, continued to write. Because he had been involved in the revolution, Hildenhagen was prosecuted and lost both his position and income and even faced prison. Froebel never bothered to reply. Finally, the broken Hildenhagen addressed Froebel's silence, still perceiving him as a friend. 'I also can't refrain from … telling you that it was wrong to keep silent for so long … but I don't want to reproach you.' Froebel accused Hildenhagen of 'having given up kindergarten'.[134] Hildenhagen, who had sacrificed his life for the revolution and kindergarten, couldn't understand Froebel's reaction. Deeply hurt, he still stood by Froebel's ideas. 'Even under the storms of 1848, even during the jury trial in Berlin, even under the harassment of discipline, I thought of your system and your person … . I once will become the interpreter of your spirit rather than others.'[135] Froebel saw things differently. In his eyes, Hildenhagen had betrayed the kindergarten idea and was now not even worthy of a letter.

The Movement Expands

The kindergarten movement grew despite – or maybe because of – Froebel's peculiar personality. Liebenstein was helpful in this sense as he met influential supporters, the most important one being Bertha von Marenholtz-Bülow, who described their first meeting:

> At the end of May 1849, I arrived at Liebenstein in Thuringia … . She [the housekeeper] told me that for several weeks there had been a man on the estate (the name given to a small farm in the immediate vicinity of the bath) who played and danced with the village children and was therefore called the 'old fool'. A few days later, I met the man on a walk. A tall, gaunt man with long grey hair was leading a crowd of children from the village, mostly barefoot from three to eight years old, two and two paired, at a marching pace up a hill, where he lined them up to play and practiced the song that went with it.[136]

Later, the baroness approached Froebel: 'You seem to be devoted to popular education?' she asked. It was the prelude to many conversations. It was only on the way back that Marenholtz heard a young girl addressing the strange man as Mister Froebel.

Froebel, the 'Fool of Liebenstein', was quite infamous. Often, he abandoned people to run across country after young children, wipe their little noses, hop like a rabbit, make little men and long ears, or fly with his long arms like a bird. It was a behaviour that one didn't often see. Adolph Diesterweg, the famous pedagogue, who also stayed in Bad Liebenstein in summer 1849, heard the talk of an 'old fool' jumping around with young children in a meadow daily, too. Somewhat repulsed by Froebel's expressions, Diesterweg had avoided him so far. Now, Marenholtz-Bülow arranged a meeting, and soon after, Diesterweg was won over. 'The man really has something of a seer, he looks into the inner workings of the child's nature like no one else yet.'[137] Diesterweg became one of Froebel's warmest supporters.

Froebel's wish was to stay in Bad Liebenstein. To make it happen, he asked the ducal government in Meiningen for Marienthal castle close to Schweina. Thanks to the quick-witted nature of the baroness, it finally happened. When Froebel appeared at the duchess of Meiningen's house in a tailcoat that smelled of a cowshed, the duchess – assuming the smell was coming from outside – had the windows closed. When the odour intensified, Marenholtz-Bülow saved the embarrassing situation: 'Your Highness now sees how necessary it is for the institution to move to Marienthal.'[138] Shortly after, the count offered Froebel the small castle as his new residence. Froebel signed the contract for the castle's upper floor, a kitchen, and the cellar for 150 guilders per year, which was later reduced to only seventy guilders. In May 1850, Froebel moved into the castle.[139]

Before moving to Marienthal, the restless Froebel gave a half-year course from November 1849 to April 1850 in Hamburg. The woman association around Johanna Goldschmidt had asked him to come to Hamburg to give lectures, found kindergartens, and train kindergartners for a monthly salary of 100 thalers.[140] Once again, Middendorff had prepared Frobel's activities by giving a speech when he had visited his daughter Allwine in Hamburg in September. While in Hamburg, Froebel stayed at the home of Wilhelm Beit. Even if Johanna Froebel had invited him, Froebel refused to stay with her and Karl a second time.[141] But the course was successful; twenty pupils attended, and Froebel gave weekly lectures, which were often attended by one hundred people. He made new acquaintances such as Wichard Lange, Heinrich Hoffmann, and Doris Lütkens, and again worked to exhaustion – 'since I did not lie down until about 6 am due to overloaded business and got up again after 8 o'clock to prepare for my course which started at 9 o'clock.'[142]

While Hamburg was open to Froebel's ideas, his stay wasn't all pleasant. He didn't approve of Karl Froebel's college and associated kindergarten and disliked that his nephew had made kindergarten more political. Another issue was Frankenberg's claim that he, and not Froebel, had founded the first kindergarten in Dresden. This made Froebel furious.[143]

Froebel even began to publish again. From January 1850 on, *Friedrich Fröbels Wochenschrift. Ein Einigungsblatt für alle Freunde der Menschenerziehung* (*Friedrich Froebel's Weekly Journal. A Unifying Journal for All Friends of Human Education*) was published – for Froebel a continuation of the *Sonntagsblatt* (*Sunday Papers*). It was edited by Wichard Lange, who would marry Allwine and later edited Froebel's writings. The publication ceased after only one year and fifty-two issues, however. It was followed by six issues of *Zeitschrift für Friedrich Fröbels Bestrebungen zur Durchführung entwickelnd-erziehender Menschenbildung in allseitiger Lebensvereinigung* (*Journal of Friedrich Froebel's Endeavours for the Realization of Developing-Educating Human Education in All-Round Life Unification*) (1851/52), edited by Dr Bruno Marquart. Around this time, Froebel started to think about the connection between kindergarten and school, a kind of mediation class (*Vermittlungsklasse*).

There were also new kindergartens, for example, in Göttingen, Nürnberg, Schmalkalden, Quetz, Sonneberg, Berlin, Baden-Baden, and Nordhausen. Froebel tirelessly advocated the kindergarten idea, giving lectures and writing letters until late at night. He was relentless, and his vitality and productivity were remarkable for a man of his age.

One Last Love: The Marriage to Luise

Around the beginning of 1850, Froebel started to think about making the relationship with Luise official. While she already ran his household, she wasn't fully respected by the other women who saw her as one of them. And because they weren't married, Luise couldn't physically nurse the elderly Froebel as a wife would have. In addition, there was romantic affection.

Froebel wrote to Luise regularly from Hamburg to update her on daily life, but also to assure her of their relationship. 'So, calm down; I certainly have only one, only one thought now: to give our life also external rounding, firmness and security.'[144] Luise must have blamed him, but mainly accused herself of making mistakes which Froebel found childish. 'You are quite a child, to cause yourself such childish pain for no reason at all. – Don't do it again! – Become strong!'[145] Froebel's fatherly attitude sums up the relationship quite well.

Finally, Froebel went to Keilhau to settle his affairs. There were still unresolved questions regarding the estate Froebel had given to his brother as a bond. The institute was still in debt, which Barop had to pay off after Froebel's death.[146] The institute's intellectual rights belonged to Barop, however, who wanted to buy a big estate in Keilhau from David Sössing as the new place for the institute. Froebel wanted to be paid off and informed Keilhau of the planned marriage with Luise – who was thirty-three years his junior – to safeguard her future after his death, probably the assertion that Keilhau would support Luise. Once again, everyone in Keilhau was irritated, and Christian insisted 'that several things should be clearly agreed in writing.'[147] Ultimately, Froebel's demands were met with 'vivid resistance'[148] as Keilhau was suspicious of the unusual relationship. They thought it was ridiculous that the old man was marrying again. Keilhau's cold refusal hurt Froebel once more.

Notwithstanding, the marriage took place in Marienthal on 9 June 1851. Neither Luise's family nor previous friends attended, even though Froebel had asked her mother for her blessing. They all disapproved of the marriage.[149] Keilhau was piqued too. Only Middendorff attended the wedding, accompanying Luise to the altar, while Marenholtz-Bülow did the same for Froebel, and the new friend Julie Traberth presented the bridal crown. At least the celebration ended pleasantly, with Middendorff and Froebel dancing like young men.[150]

It wasn't a love match, though. Rather, the relationship was characterized by childlike worship and caring. Luise later wrote:

Figure 7.4 Luise Levin.
Bildarchiv Friedrich-Fröbel-Museum Bad Blankenburg (Picture Library Friedrich-Fröbel-Museum Bad Blankenburg)

In the initially childlike adoration with which I was attached to Froebel, I had always striven to come closer to him spiritually, and his infinite kindness, which he always showed to the weak, had awakened and nurtured my self-confidence. I dared to stand by the man whom I always saw high above me, but to whom I could be a support in other ways … . Froebel's age did not disturb me, in my eyes he stood high above all other men, and I only felt how insignificant I stood next to him.[151]

The marriage made Froebel happy. For the last months of his life, he again had someone loyal at his side who supported him in everything he did.

It wasn't the only marriage of the time, though. Elise, already thirty-six years old, had married Siegfried Schaffner, a teacher, on 27 December 1850. Schaffner was fifteen years younger than Elise – this was rare at the time. The couple had invited Froebel, though he again refused to attend the wedding of one of his nieces. While he declined the invitation in friendly terms,[152] his words to Middendorff were colder. 'Elise takes a man therefore I cannot come; and the Christmas takes me, therefore I cannot come. There are other high times to celebrate now than a wedding. There are other lights to burn than wax lights.'[153] It's again an astonishing remark about his niece, who had once been so dear to his heart.

We don't know if Froebel ever saw Keilhau again. 'To all those who are dear to my greeting in the circle of your surroundings I ask to say the same,'[154] he ended his last letter to Elise. Besides Middendorff and Barop, Keilhau had enough of the community's founder. Elise also left Keilhau, but the rest stayed. Christian and Caroline died in Keilhau, and Albertine only joined Allwina and Wichard Lange in Hamburg at the end of her life, passing away there in 1880. Emilie died in 1860 after having brought eight children into the world; she was survived by her husband, who would live until 1878.

After the marriage, Froebel became calmer, even if he still couldn't tolerate violating his principles. For example, he demanded his pupils memorize the kindergarten songs by heart and pass them on by word of mouth. Thanks to the ever-mediating Luise, a secret 'cheat sheet' was shared, which made it easier to practise the songs and that Froebel allegedly never learned of.

Luise also unobtrusively took care of the practical administration of the enterprise, as Froebel still couldn't handle money. Renner, Luise's nephew, who had been in charge of selling Froebel's writings and materials since autumn 1849, was in despair that Froebel gave away his writings to strangers but never took anything in return. Some things would never change.

Still, despite all his peculiarities, Froebel exerted a 'captivating attraction' even in his old age, as Diesterweg put it.[155] Listeners were fascinated when he spoke, despite his tiring, long-windedness. Notwithstanding the justified criticism, old friends ultimately stood by him, and new supporters who devoted themselves to his cause joined his circle.

Still, there was no happy end for him.

The Destruction of Froebel's Life Work: The Kindergarten Ban

7 August 1851 marked a caesura: the Ministry of Spiritual, Instructional, and Medicinal Affairs and the Ministry of the Interior signed an order prohibiting the few kindergartens that existed in Prussia. The latter's involvement suggests that there weren't only educational but also political reasons for this decision. Froebel learned of the ban on a Sunday afternoon. He was among his usual circle when a spa patient shared the news. Froebel took it calmly and wasn't too concerned. Officially, kindergarten was banned because, as allegedly seen in the pamphlet *Hochschule für Mädchen und Kindergärten als Glieder einer vollständigen Bildungsanstalt* (*College for Girls and Kindergartens as Links of a Complete Educational Institution*) by Karl Froebel, it is part of the Froebelian socialistic system with the goal of raising children to atheism. Karl was indeed close to socialist ideas; the aforementioned brochure was an almost eighty-page document he had published with Johanna in 1849. In Zurich, many persecuted revolutionists had stayed with the Froebels, which made them suspicious. In addition, many of their circle wanted to achieve the revolution through education, including kindergarten. The situation in Hamburg was similar; the college was an 'informal meeting and networking point for opposition members'.[156]

The name 'Froebel' was moreover suspicious because kindergarten was associated with the detested revolution. Diesterweg was a well-known democrat, and Julius Froebel had been a left-wing member of the Frankfurt National Assembly. He and Robert Blum had been arrested during the October Revolution of 1848 in Vienna, and while Blum was executed, Julius was pardoned and emigrated to America. The name 'Froebel' was thus obviously well known in Prussia in 1851 and reason enough for the ban.

It also made sense in the political climate of the time, known as the reactionary era.[157] For the next ten years, the German states tried to restore the German Confederation and oppress all progressive and revolutionary movements. Constitutional revisions, police surveillance and persecution, the establishment of a police and military system, a reactionary constitutional practice, increased censorship and control of the press and book market, massive electoral interference, and the triumph of the conservative-bureaucratic state of law and order altogether shaped the time.

However, why was only kindergarten, and not the other contemporary early childhood institutions, banned? 'In my opinion', Secretary von Raumer wrote in a private note, 'Friedrich Froebel differs from Karl Froebel only in that the latter says clearly and consistently what he wants, whereas Friedrich Froebel expresses himself in a very confused and mysterious way and probably does not quite know what he wants ... there is no reason to judge Friedrich Froebel substantially differently from Karl Froebel.'[158]

Only kindergarten was considered a danger to the existing order; this had to do with a kindergarten in Nordhausen that the local *Freie Gemeinde* (Free Community) had established. The Free Community consisted of members of the Friends of the Light, which was an interdenominational and democratic-liberal movement. The group renounced any denomination, pushed for a rational interpretation of the Bible, and questioned the ecclesiastical authorities. Furthermore, they demanded the states' and churches' democratization and propagated equal rights for all parishioners. Due to the secular-rational orientation, the Friends of the Light were more political than religious. One protagonist was Eduard Baltzer (1814–1887), a Protestant theologian and democrat who had been involved in establishing the kindergarten. Baltzer and Froebel had corresponded,[159] and Froebel had trained Ernestine Storch and Emmi Wolfgang, who were also members of the Friends of the Light and now worked in the kindergarten in Nordhausen. Unlike Froebel, Baltzer saw kindergartens as explicitly 'partisan' institutions, meaning free religious and political institutions. In contrast, Froebel opposed the political instrumentalization of kindergarten.

For the authorities, it didn't matter that Froebel disagreed with Baltzer. In their eyes, kindergarten was related to the Friends of the Light and thus a threat to the existing order. Consequently, the district government in Erfurt had closed the kindergarten in Nordhausen on 14 June 1851, two months before the kindergarten ban. Emmi Wolfgang had informed Friedrich Froebel about the closure on 28 June 1851, but thought it was only a formal mistake.[160]

Froebel was therefore aware of the problematic connection with the Friends of the Light. Notwithstanding, he insisted that the ban was nothing but a misunderstanding. To calm his friends and supporters, he published a clarification in the Hildburghausen village newspaper, emphasizing that the ban was based on a 'name-, person-, matter, and aspiration confusion.'[161] Froebel would stick to this argument until the end. Two days later, he wrote to the Prussian Ministry of Spiritual, Instructional, and Medical Affairs to draw attention to the confusion and submitted writings to show the difference between him and his nephew. He never received a reply. Von Raumer, as his response to the Prussian king shows, saw no reason to lift the 'carefully considered ban.'[162] On 31 October 1851, Froebel even wrote to King Friedrich Wilhelm of Prussia himself to clarify that he opposed the kindergarten's political instrumentalization and that 'the cause of childhood cannot belong to any party'.[163] Again, he never received an answer. Instead, the Prussian Ministry of Spiritual, Instructional, and Medical Affairs underlined its demands with another public letter addressed primarily to educators to confirm the ban and emphasize the connection to the 'Free Community'. Other German governments followed suit, and kindergarten fell into disrepute in more places.

Froebel's Final Months

The destruction of his life work deeply wounded Froebel. In a certain way, he never recovered, even if he came up with new ideas, among them the 'mediation class' mentioned previously. Froebel was tired and once more thinking about emigrating to America.

There were a few last highlights, though. In September 1851, an assembly of pedagogues took place in Liebenstein where they signed a public explanation supporting Froebel and the kindergarten idea. In addition, the assembly expressed hope that Froebel would publish a coherent overview of his system and the materials.[164] It never happened because Froebel continued to write the weekly magazine, often until complete fatigue, and also worked on a public defence of kindergarten, which he finished on 31 October as *Zweite und weitere öffentliche Erklärung in der Friedrich Fröbelschen Angelegenheit und in der Sache der Kindergärten* (*Second and Further Public Statement in the Friedrich Froebel Matter and in the Matter of Kindergartens*). Froebel had hoped that Middendorff would help with the piece, but Middendorff had stayed in Keilhau.[165] It was another disappointment. Without Middendorff, Froebel didn't feel comfortable writing a systematic book on his pedagogy of kindergarten and play.

What hurt the deeply religious Froebel – who had always wanted humanity to live in unification with God – the most was the accusation that his idea, the 'as deeply religious in itself, as it is truly Christian'[166] kindergarten, was accused of promoting atheism. To defend himself and clarify his position, he published *Ueber das Prinzip, das Wesen der Erziehung überhaupt, über das christliche Prinzip und besonders über das christliche Prinzip und Wesen der Kindergärten* (*About the Principle, the Essence of Education in General, about the Christian Principle and Especially about the Christian Principle and Essence of Kindergartens*) in the November and December volumes of his last journal.[167] This didn't help to get the ban lifted either, though.

Figure 7.5 Friedrich Froebel, lithography by Emil Fröhlich.
Bildarchiv Friedrich-Fröbel-Museum Bad Blankenburg (Picture Library Friedrich-Fröbel-Museum Bad Blankenburg)

The kindergarten ban wasn't the only devastating news in Froebel's last few months. Christian had died in Keilhau on 10 January 1851.[168] Froebel was again astonishingly silent about the passing of a loved one. While he hadn't been as close to Christian as he had been to Christoph, his brother had saved his institute thirty years ago with his money and supported the community tirelessly ever since. Still, he didn't mourn – at least not in his correspondence.

Even more devastating was Ferdinand Froebel's death. In January 1852, Ferdinand died in Burgdorf after taking care of a child suffering from typhoid. Froebel was 'almost petrified'.[169] The loss of his beloved nephew – who had first been his pupil and then his associate, whom he had welcomed 'twice in Willisau and Burgdorf as heir and continuator of two of my founded efficacies'[170] – might have been the final blow. That Ferdinand's wife, Friederike, hadn't deemed it necessary to inform him personally, as he complained bitterly to her, hurt even more.[171]

Froebel grew increasingly weak and now often needed Luise's support. On 21 April 1852, they celebrated his seventieth birthday. Middendorff had prepared the celebration and many came.[172] In the morning, Froebel was woken with a song composed for the purpose and performed by students and friends. He was touched. Later, 'young ladies' dressed in white and decorated with ribbons in the colours of the rainbow and green wreaths brought an orange tree as a joint gift. In the afternoon, crowds of children came from Salzungen and Liebenstein. Innumerable letters and gifts arrived from all parts of Germany. In the evening, after an ovation by teachers, Froebel was garlanded with a wreath of ivy, myrtle, and evergreen to an accompaniment of more singing. At the end of the emotional day, Froebel said calmly and cheerfully that the celebration had been of one cast and one thought, a true unification of life.

Nevertheless, Froebel's strength was dwindling. Shortly thereafter, during a kindergarten visit in Salzungen, Froebel needed to sit down, something that had never happened before. He wasn't feeling well, and the doctor recommended bed rest. 'Froebel's body and mind suffered in the same way through that drastic change', Luise later described the last weeks, 'with effort of all forces he worked on the refutation in which he wanted to explain everything clearly once more .... But soon it became apparent that the illness went deeper, and that Froebel's strong willpower could no longer control it.'[173] Now, Froebel was often quiet; if outside, he felt cold. Still, he enjoyed walks or rides to the surrounding mountains and cherished those moments of quiet happiness, particularly when he visited his favourite places.

The final highlight was the teachers' assembly in Gotha on 3 June and the respect shown to him there. On the way back from Gotha, Froebel was surprisingly cheerful and chatty, and when they passed the *Glöckner*, Froebel dismounted and walked, leaning on Luise, to one of his favourite places, a granite rock. There, he talked to a forester. 'I want my name to be here when I am no longer.'[174] It was Froebel's final trip.

Three days later, his condition worsened. From then on, Froebel mainly rested in bed. He must have been kind and mild and pleased by the sight of flowers or trees through the open window. On 17 June, Middendorff came from Hamburg, and Barop from Keilhau. Christian Friedrich Clemens was around, too. With Barop and Middendorff, Froebel discussed his will, and then Middendorff read his godmother's letter. 'My creed! My creed!' Froebel allegedly interrupted the reading, especially when Middendorff read: 'From now on, this our Saviour will trust with you in justice, grace and mercy.'[175]

In his final days, Froebel was kind and quiet, urging everyone to unity, harmony, and creating a model family in Keilhau. 'Unity, unification, unison', he allegedly said, 'one family – one united pursuit (*Streben*).'[176] He also once again expressed his hope that Keilhau would welcome Luise. On 20 June, both Barop and Clemens had to leave, and only Middendorff stayed. 'I remain there', Middendorff told Froebel, whereupon he replied: 'Nice, that's right, good.'[177] It was clear that the end was near. 'How heavy, how painfully my heart feels the approaching separation', Luise wrote. 'At the deathbed of my dear husband, I vow to You, my God and Father, to continue to work with love on the work he has begun under Your protection.'[178]

During the afternoon of 21 June, Froebel broke out in a sweat, and his eyes glazed over but remained open. Luise and Middendorff were at Froebel's side when he drew his last breath at 6:30 p.m. When he was buried three days later in the cemetery in Schweina fifteen minutes from Marienthal, friends and family, children, and strangers joined the funeral procession. When the coffin, covered with flowers, was lowered into the ground, the clouds parted and Middendorff approached the grave to bid a final farewell to his 'master': 'Thus heaven reveals your thoughts and now, as on a scattered seed, looks down on it with warm sunbeams to let it germinate and arise for blessing on earth, while He Himself leads you over to the freer work in the higher community, which you were striving to create here independently.'[179]

Froebel's death broke the heart of his most loyal friend; Middendorff passed away in Keilhau just 1½ years later.

Kindergarten, however, lived on.

Notes

Introduction

1 For the teachers' assembly, see Heerwart 1902: 60f.
2 Weston 1998: 1.
3 März 1998: 473.
4 Krone 2016: 18.
5 See Krone 2016; Heiland 2017; Sauerbrey and Winkler 2018.
6 Until today, Halfter's biography from 1931 is the most comprehensive one. Despite the contemporary nationalist tone and being source-uncritical, it is still worth reading. Other valuable biographies are Boldt and Eichler 1982; Heiland 1982, 2002; Krone 2016; Kuntze 1952; Osann 1952. Biographical remarks can also be found in the authors' previous works (Sauerbrey and Winkler 2018; Wasmuth 2020). For English biographies, see Brosterman [1997] 2014; Downs 1978; Hanschmann 1897; Liebschner 1992; Michaelis and Moore 1889; Snider 1900. Most of the biographies are outdated and often inaccurate.
7 See Bruce 2020 and our analyses: Sauerbrey and Winkler 2018; Wasmuth 2020.
8 Oelkers 1998: 12.
9 Seele 1888: 85.
10 See Krone 2016: 48.
11 Translations, if not otherwise indicated, are all done by the authors.

1 An Unfortunate Childhood

1 See Nipperdey 2014; Smith 2011.
2 Nipperdey 2014: 1.
3 The correct German term is *Fürst* and not *Prinz*.
4 As written by Johann Jakob Froebel in the church register. See Halfter 1931: 4.
5 Froebel talks about his childhood in length in two letters (Fröbel 1827, 1832a). A very detailed description of the early years can be found in Halfter 1931.
6 Fröbel 1827: 32.
7 Fröbel 1832a: 2.
8 Biographies sometimes mention that the new church was still being built during Friedrich's childhood. This is incorrect.

9 Fröbel 1831h: 2R.

10 Fröbel 1828: 35.

11 Ibid., 32/33.

12 Nipperdey 2014; Smith 2011.

13 Halfter 1931: 11.

14 As an example, see Downs 1978: 12.

15 See Kuntze 1952.

16 Fröbel 1801a: 2.

17 See Fröbel 1831h: 33.

18 Froebel emphasizes this in Fröbel 1827.

19 Fröbel 1827: 42.

20 Ibid.

21 Heiland and Gebel 2004: 48.

22 Ibid., 49.

23 Fröbel 1832a: 2.

24 As an example, see Fröbel 1827: 34.

25 For premonition as the appropriate translation of *Ahnung*, see Wasmuth 2020: 55.

26 Fröbel 1827: 38.

27 Fröbel 1828: 4, 4R.

28 As cited in Heiland 1982: 8/9.

29 Fröbel 1807a: 5.

30 Fröbel 1832: 1R.

31 Ibid., 3.

32 Fröbel 1827: 35.

33 Fröbel 1808: 1R.

34 For this discussion, see Krone 2016.

35 As cited in Halfter 1931: 28/29.

36 Ibid., 31.

37 Ibid.

38 Fröbel 1827: 43. See also Fröbel 1831: 4R.

39 Fröbel 1832: 4R.

40 Fröbel 1827: 45.

41 See Fröbel 1827, 1831h.

42 Fröbel 1827: 45R.

43 Fröbel 1831h: 5.

44 Halfter 1931: 33.

45 Fröbel 1827: 46.

46 Fröbel 1846: 113R.

47 Fröbel 1832a: 5R.

48 Ibid., 6.

49 Fröbel 1831h: 5R.

50 See Fröbel 1810f.

51 As cited in Halfter 1931: 41.

52 Ibid., 42.

53 Fröbel 1807a: 16.

54 Ibid., 23.

55 According to Karl Froebel, the apprenticeship occurred in Scheibe, close to Neuhaus am Rennsteig, only four hours away from Oberweißbach. Froebel himself changed the location because the forester was still alive. See Osann 1956: 13.

56 Fröbel 1827: 52.

57 Fröbel 1807a: 30/31.

58 Cited as in Boldt and Eichler 1982: 16.

59 Fröbel 1799: 1R.

60 For Jena, see Beiser 2002; Fesser 2008; Rush 2015.

61 Halfter 1931: 58.

62 As cited in Kuntze 1952: 18.

63 See Halfter 1931: 63.

64 Fröbel 1810: 3R.

65 As cited in Halfter 1931: 72.

66 Fröbel 1801: 1R.

67 Fröbel 1801b: 5.

68 Fröbel 1827: 5.

69 As cited in Heiland 1982: 10/11.

70 Little is known about this time. Halfter's detailed summary isn't source-critical. Source-critical historical research assures itself of the origin and authenticity of a historical source.

71 As cited in Halfter 1931: 111.

72 See Bollnow 1952.

73 Fröbel 1831h: 15R.

74 As cited in Halfter 1931: 130.

2 Suddenly, an Educator

1 As an example of this discussion, see Heiland 2017: 190.

2 Fröbel 1828: 10.

3 For example, see Fröbel 1831h: 12.

4 For Gruner, see Halfter 1931: 138; Kuntze 1952: 22f.; Stadler 1993: 178ff.

5 As cited in Halfter 1931: 141.

6 Fröbel 1805: 533.

7 Halfter 1931; Sauerbrey and Winkler 2018.

8 For Caroline von Holzhausen, see Halfter 1931; Heiland 2017; Hoffmann and Wächter 1982; Krone 2011; Kuntze 1952. Initially, the relationship was described as a very positive and spiritual one. Halfter (1931) and Kuntze (1930/1951) were the first to emphasize the personal, enthusiastic-respectful aspects of the relationship.

9 Fröbel 1831h: 20.

10 These letters are lost.

11 Fröbel 1827: 11R.

12 As cited in Halfter 1931: 156.

13 Fröbel 1827: 11R.

14 See Fröbel 1831: 20.

15 See especially Krone 2016.

16 Fröbel 1828: 9R.

17 Fröbel 1808a: 8R.

18 Fröbel 1808c: 4R.

19 Fröbel 1827: 15R.

20 Gruner became director of the new teacher seminary in Idstein in the Duchy of Nassau and was one of the leading pedagogues of the small duchy. See Halfter 1931: 172.

21 For example, see Fröbel 1831h. The idea of a born and masterful teacher can be found in many biographies.

22 See Krone 2016: 48.

23 Fröbel 1807: 2.

24 This correspondence has been lost. Traugott, so it seems, never replied to him.

25 Fröbel 1808b: 1R.

26 See Halfter 1931: 192f.; Heiland 2017.

27 See Kuntze 1952: 30f.

28 For the von Holzhausen family, see Lerner 1953; Heiland 2017: 191.

29 Fröbel 1807a: 48.

30 See Heiland 2017: 192.

31 Halfter 1931: 194, and especially Lerner 1953.

32 The *Gedankenbuch* is sometimes described as a diary. It consists of excerpts and thoughts but doesn't necessarily reflect Caroline's life situation at a particular time.

33 As cited in Halfter 1931: 177.

34 See Fröbel 1807: 1; Halfter 1931: 178.

35 Heiland 2017: 190.

36 Fröbel 1807: 2.

37 Ibid.

38 Froebel, 1807a, 2.

39 Frobel 1807: 2.

40 Ibid.

41 As examples, see Fröbel 1806, 1807.

42 Fröbel 1807: 1.

43 Fröbel 1806: 6R.

44 Ibid., 9R.

45 Ibid., 10.

46 Ibid., 13R.

47 Ibid., 14R

48 Ibid., 15.

49 See Heiland 2017.

50 Liebschner 1992: 5.

51 For the extensive readings at this time, see Halfter 1931.

52 Halfter 1931: 181.

53 Ibid., 183.

54 See Fröbel 1807a: 72ff.

55 Ibid., 77.

56 Fröbel 1807b: 3R.

57 Fröbel 1808a: 13/13R.

58 Halfter has described these months in detail. See 1931: 202f.

59 Fröbel 1831h: 22.

60 See the official documents on ancestry.com. Other sources give 8 February 1807 as her date of birth, which also seems incorrect.

61 For this discussion, see Halfter 1931: 192; Heiland 2017; Kuntze 1952. Interestingly, English biographies often mention that Froebel could be the father of the youngest von Holzhausen child, born in 1812.

62 Hoffmann and Wächter 1986: 340.

63 Fröbel 1831h: 22R.

64 Ibid.

65 Lerner 1953: 204.

66 Fröbel 1807b.

67 See Halfter 1931: 213.

68 Fröbel 1807b: 4.

69 Fröbel 1808b: 1R.

70 Ibid.

71 See Halfter 1931: 228.

72 See Lerner 1953: 206.

73 See Fröbel 1808c.

74 Fröbel 1808d: 9R.

75 Fröbel 1808f: 5R.

76 See Adelman 2000: 105; Stadler 1993: 282.

77 For Pestalozzi's method, see Grell and Sauerbrey 2016: 15; Sauerbrey and Winkler 2018.

78 Fröbel 1808f: 1R.

79 Ibid., 5.

80 Giel 1979: 255.

81 Adelman 2000: 103.

82 Fröbel 1808f: 1R.

83 Fröbel 1809a: 3R.

84 Fröbel 1809: 1.

85 Ibid., 132R.

86 For this discussion, see Grell and Sauerbrey 2016: 16; Heiland 1982: 30.

87 Fröbel 1810: 2.

88 Fröbel 1827: 25.

89 Ibid., 25R.

90 Fröbel 1809b: 7.

91 See Halfter 1931: 273.

92 Fröbel 1809b: 7.

93 Ibid., 7R.

94 See Halfter 1931: 293.

95 Fröbel 1809b: 6R/7.

96 For Schmid's influence on Froebel, see Friedman and Alvis 2021.

97 See Halfter 1931: 286f.

98 Fröbel 1810d: 66.

99 Fröbel 1810g: 2.

100 Fröbel 1810a: 56.

101 Ibid., 59.

102 Fröbel 1810d: 63.

103 Fröbel 1810e: 69R–70.

104 Ibid., 70.

105 Fröbel 1810d: 66R.

106 Fröbel 1810b: 1.

107 Fröbel 1810e: 71.

108 Fröbel 1810c: 3.

109 Ibid., 3R.

110 Fröbel 1810f: 53.

111 Ibid., 51–51R.

112 Fröbel 1810g: 2.

113 Fröbel 1831: 23.

114 As an example, see Heiland 1982: 37f.

115 As quoted in Halfter 1931: 307.

116 See Lerner 1953: 206.

117 As quoted in Halfter 1931: 308.

118 As cited in Heiland 2017: 212.

119 Such an assumption can be found in Heiland 2017; Kuntze 1952: 41.

120 See Heiland 2017: 229.

121 Dated 2 August 1811, 5 August 1811, 9 December 1812, 28 May 1815, 26 December 1816.

122 Hoffmann and Wächter 1986: 340.

123 Ibid., 381.

124 See Heiland 2017: 210.

125 Fröbel 1831h: 24.

126 See Lerner 1953: 202/203; Heiland 2017.

127 See Halfter 1931: 325.

128 See Allen 2017a.

129 Fröbel 1811: 7R.

130 Hoffmann and Wächter 1986: 339ff.

3 From Studies to War Then Back to Education

1 Frbel 1811a: 2.

2 Fröbel 1827: 30.

3 Halfter 1931: 341.

4 Hoffmann and Wächter 1986: 379.

5 Ibid., 345/346.

6 See ibid., 309ff.

7 See ibid., 355f., 377f.

8 Heiland 1982: 41.

9 See Halfter 1931: 333.

10 Fröbel 1812: 1R.

11 For family relationships, see Halfter 1931: 326f.

12 https://gedbas.genealogy.net/person/show/1117815856.

13 See Fröbel 1827: 29R.

14 As cited in Halfter 1931: 343.

15 Fröbel 1827: 30.

16 See Stadler 1993: 181/182.

17 For the war and Froebel's nationalism, see Boldt and Eichler 1982: 55.

18 Fröbel 1831h: 27R.

19 Fröbel 1827: 31R.

20 Halfter 1931: 346.

21 For the war, see in more detail Halfter 1931.

22 Fröbel 1828: 16.

23 For Middendorff's life, see Höltershinken 2010.

24 Lange and Diesteweg 1855: 24.

25 See Fröbel 1813.

26 Halfter 1931: 362f.

27 Fröbel 1813a: 1.

28 Fröbel 1814: 66R.

29 Fröbel 1814a: 109.

30 Fröbel 1831h: 29.

31 Ibid., 31R.

32 Ibid.

33 See Halfter 1931: 441.

34 As cited in ibid., 418.

35 Fröbel 1827: 34 R.

36 See Hoffmann and Wächter 1986.

37 See ibid.

38 Ibid., 68.

39 As cited in Osann 1956: 75.

40 Hoffmann and Wächter 1986: 118/119.

41 It is not clear why both Langethal and Middendorff spoke of 3 August as Froebel's birthday, or why Froebel would have deceived his friends. Hoffmann speculates that the deeper friendship was seen as a birthday. See Hoffmann and Wächter 1986: 111f.

42 Hoffmann and Wächter 1986: 122.

43 Heiland 2017: 233.

44 Fröbel 1815: 33.

45 Ibid., 33R/34.

46 Heiland 2017: 233/234.

47 Hoffmann and Wächter 1986: 103.

48 Ibid., 105.

49 As cited in Heiland 2017: 211.

50 Hoffmann and Wächter 1986: 381.

51 Ibid., 384.

52 Fröbel 1831h: 23R.

53 At Schleiermacher's lecture, Froebel probably met his later wife, Wilhelmine Henriette Klöpper, for the first time.

54 For this time, see Fröbel 1831h: 37ff.

55 See Halfter 1931: 470.

56 See Fröbel 1828: 11R.

57 Ibid.

58 As cited in Halfter 1931: 459.

59 See Heiland and Gebel 2004: 8.

60 It's possible that the compilation of the sentences took place only in the years 1822 and 1823.

61 Boldt, Knechtel and König 1982i: 269.

62 It is interesting that Froebel still wanted to use the pseudonym under which he had intended to publish his work *SPHAIRA, das einzige Gesetz im All, in der physischen wie in der moralischen Welt* (*SPHAIRA, the Only Law in the Universe, in the Physical as Well as in the Moral World*) namely 'Manthanoh'.

63 Boldt, Knechtel and König 1982i: 269.

64 Ibid., 80/81.

65 Ibid., 136.

66 As cited in Kuntze 1952: 53.

67 Halfter 1931: 472/473.

68 See Fröbel 1843b: 18.

4 Keilhau's Rise and the Development of 'Developing-educating Humane Edification'

1 Heiland 2017: 37.

2 Osann 1956: 78.

3 Fröbel 1890: 9.

4 Ibid., 5/6.

5 Ibid., 7.

6 Ibid., 11.

7 Ibid., 14.

8 Osann 1956: 80.

9 Langethal 1867: 11.

10 Fröbel 1890: 15.

11 As cited in Halfter 1931: 592.

12 As cited in Osann 1956: 80.

13 Lange and Diesterweg 1855: 24.

14 Langethal 1867: 9; 1910: 6.

15 Langethal 1867: 9.

16 Ibid., 13.

17 Ibid., 15.

18 See Osann 1956: 81.

19 Fröbel 1817: 1.

20 Langethal 1910: 101.

21 Fröbel 1890: 18.

22 For the first months in Keilhau, see Langethal 1867. Julius Froebel has also shared his memories; see Fröbel 1890. Osann (1956) has described this time vividly.

23 For Keilhau at this time, see Langetha 1910: 87f., 103f.

24 As a result of the volcanic eruption, Europe experienced the lowest temperatures in the summer of 1816 since records began in 1766. For the impact of the eruption on Europe, see Behringer 2017.

25 Boldt, Knechtel, and König, 1982: 146.

26 Osann 1956: 83.

27 Langethal 1867: 17.

28 Ibid., 18.

29 Ibid., 24.

30 Heerwart 1905: 2.

31 Fröbel 1890: 17.

32 Langethal 1867: 11.

33 Fröbel 1890: 27.

34 Ibid., 16.

35 See Osann 1956: 84.

36 See Langethal 1867: 32.

37 Osann 1956: 86.

38 As cited in Halfter 1931: 496.

39 See Langethal 1867: 35.

40 See Halfter 1931: 496.

41 Langethal 1867: 37.

42 Ibid., 36.

43 See Osann 1956: 89.

44 See Langethal 1867: 37/38.

45 Fröbel 1890: 27.

46 Langethal 1867: 51.

47 Ibid., 58.

48 Ibid., 57.

49 Ibid., 63.

50 Fröbel 1817: 1R.

51 Heerwart 1905: 2.

52 Fröbel 1831h: 45R.

53 Fröbel 1818: 27R.

54 For Christiane's departure, see Halfter 1931: 499; Osann 1956: 91.

55 Fröbel 1831h: 45R.

56 Halfter 1931: 499.

57 Fröbel 1831h: 46–46R.

58 Ibid., 45R.

59 For Wilhelmine's life, see Heerwart 1905.

60 Heerwart mentions it.

61 See Heerwart 1905: 17.

62 Fröbel 1831h: 41R.

63 Halfter 1931: 515.

64 See Halfter 1931: 515f.; Krone 2011: 39; Osann 1956: 75/76.

65 See Halfter 1931: 500.

66 See ibid., 508.

67 Fröbel 1817c.

68 Halfter 1931: 517.

69 See ibid., 528.

70 See Langethal 1867: 67.

71 Ibid., 68.

72 Ibid., 69.

73 Ibid., 70.

74 Ibid., 71.

75 See Boldt and Eichler 1982: 60.

76 Halfter 1931: 532.

77 Osann 1956: 95.

78 Langethal 1867: 77.

79 Halfter 1931: 534, 546.

80 Heerwart 1902: 27.

81 Langethal 1867: 81.

82 See Halfter 1931: 551.

83 Lange and Diesterweg 1855: 16.

84 Langethal 1867: 65/66.

85 See Halfter 1931: 558.

86 See Langethal 1867: 81.

87 Langethal 1867: 82.

88 Halfter 1931: 554.

89 Langethal 1867: 84/85.

90 Ibid., 82.

91 As cited in Prüfer 1927: 36/37.

92 Edification is used when the term refers to the German concept of *Bildung*.

93 See Heiland and Gebel 2004: 9.

94 For the daily papers and the trinity philosophy, see Heiland and Gebel 2004; Rinke 1935.

95 Heiland and Gebel 2004: 16.

96 Heiland 1982: 71/72. See also *Die Feier des Christfestes der Erziehungsanstalt in Keilhau* (*The Christmas celebration of the educational institution in Keilhau*).

97 Heiland and Gebel 2004: 98/99.

98 Ibid., 59/60.

99 As examples see Heiland and Gebel 2004: 21, 55, 66 or 87.

100 Ibid., 50.

101 Ibid., 62.

102 Ibid., 63.

103 Ibid., 87/88.

104 Ibid., 15.

105 See Boldt and Eichler 1982: 64.

106 The following remarks are short. For a more detailed discussion of Froebel's law of the sphere, see Heiland 2002; Sauerbrey and Winkler 2018; Wasmuth 2020.

107 Heiland 2008: 233.

108 'Panentheism' is a constructed word composed of the English equivalents of the Greek terms 'pān' (pan) meaning all, 'εν' (en) meaning in, and 'θεός' (theós) meaning God.

109 Krause 1828/1981: 256.

110 Fröbel 1826/1968: 7.

111 See Heiland and Gebel 2004: 9; Osann 1956: 100.

112 Heiland 1982: 73.

113 Ibid., 78.

114 See Prüfer 1927: 37/38.

115 Boldt and Eichler 1982: 61f.; Halfter 1931: 624.

116 Halfter 1931: 600, 607.

117 Osann 1956: 100.

118 Langethal 1867, 1910; Fröbel 1890.

119 As cited in Bold and Eichler 1982: 61.

120 Langethal 1867: 42.

121 Ibid., 44.

122 Fröbel 1890: 29.

123 Langethal 1867: 14.

124 Ibid., 46.

125 Ibid., 47.

126 Boldt and Eichler 1982: 61f.

127 Langethal 1867: 49.

128 Ibid., 44.

129 Ibid., 49.

130 Halfter 1931: 497.

131 Langethal 1867: 47.

132 Ibid., 49.

133 Fröbel 1829.

134 Langethal 1867: 49.

135 Ibid.

5 Keilhau's Decline and Froebel's Departure

1 Langethal 1867: 13.

2 Langethal 1910: 110.

3 Halfter 1931: 588; Osann 1956: 94.

4 Langethal 1867: 45.

5 Lange 1862: 28/29.

6 See Halfter 1931: 634.

7 Lange 1862: 22–4.

8 Fröbel 1890: 29.

9 See Langethal 1867: 89.

10 See Höltershinken 2010: 26. English literature sometimes mentions that in 1827, the Prussian government decreed that children had to be educated in their own state (Liebschner 1992: 17). It seems to be incorrect.

11 Fröbel 1828.

12 As cited in Osann 1956: 100.

13 Fröbel 1817a: 7.

14 Langethal 1867: 47.

15 Fröbel 1890: 17.

16 Ibid., 31.

17 See Halfter 1931: 629; Heerwart 1905: 56.

18 Osann 1956: 90.

19 See Halfter 1931: 589ff.

20 Fröbel 1839c: 243.

21 Fröbel 1890: 34.

22 Ibid., 34.

23 As cited in Liebschner 1992: 14. Liebschner does not cite the source, which is Julius Froebel's memoirs.

24 Fröbel 1890: 36.

25 Ibid., 35.

26 Ibid., 38.

27 Ibid.

28 Ibid.

29 Fröbel 1838: 7R.

30 Osann 1956: 101.

31 Gumlich 1835: XII.

32 Fröbel 1831h: 49R.

33 Ibid., 49.

34 Ibid., 52/53.

35 Ibid., 53.

36 See Halfter 1931: 552.

37 Fröbel 1829.

38 Ibid.

39 The other letter from December 1844 is a fragment.

40 Fröbel 1807b: 1.

41 Fröbel 1831e: 1.

42 Gumlich 1835: XI.

43 Fröbel 1825a: 4R.

44 Ibid., 5R.

45 As cited in Halfter 1931: 618.

46 See ibid., 618ff.

47 Ibid., 620.

48 As cited in ibid., 632.

49 Fröbel 1831e: 1.

50 See Heiland and Gebel 2004: 9/10.

51 Halfter 1931: 630.

52 Langethal 1910: 111.

53 As cited in Halfter 1931: 651.

6 The Swiss Years

1 See Hoffmann and Wächter 1986: 225, 259.

2 Fröbel 1831a: 1R/2.

3 Fröbel 1831b: 4.

4 Fröbel 1831: 5.

5 See Fröbel 1834i: 1R.

6 See Hoffmann and Wächter 1986: 265.

7 Fröbel 1831k: 3.

8 See Fröbel 1831b: 4.

9 Fröbel 1831c: 3R.

10 Fröbel 1831d: 3.

11 Hoffmann and Wächter 1986: 290.

12 Fröbel 1831d.

13 Fröbel 1831e: 2.

14 Fröbel 1831f: 1.

15 Fröbel 1831g: 1R.

16 As cited in Halfter 1931: 660.

17 Fröbel 1831i: 1.

18 See Osann 1956: 104f.

19 See Heiland 1982: 82/83.

20 Heiland and Gebel 2004: 113.

21 Fröbel 1831j: 2.

22 Ibid., 9/9R.

23 See Heiland and Gebel 2004: 7f.

24 On 4 November, Froebel informed the Keilhau community that he still hadn't started teaching (Fröbel 1831j: 4).

25 Fröbel 1831j: 1.

26 Nohl 1931: 388.

27 Fröbel 1832b: 1; see also Fröbel 1832e.

28 Fröbel 1832b.

29 Nohl 1931: 394.

30 Fröbel 1832d.

31 Fröbel 1832b.

32 Fröbel 1832c: 1R.

33 Fröbel 1832d: 8.

34 Fröbel 1832c: 2.

35 Fröbel 1832b.

36 See Krone 2011: 67.

37 See Fröbel 1832d.

38 Fröbel 1832f: 7.

39 Ibid., 9/9R.

40 Ibid., 13.

41 Fröbel 1832g: 7.

42 Fröbel 1832h: 4, 5.

43 Fröbel 1832j: 1.

44 Fröbel 1832i: 1R.

45 Fröbel 1832k: 2.

46 Fröbel 1832l: 3R.

47 Fröbel 1832k: 4R.

48 Ibid.

49 Fröbel 1832m: 1.

50 Ibid., 1R.

51 Fröbel 1832n: 2.

52 Ibid., 3R.

53 Ibid.

54 According to Heerwart, Wilhelmine's letter to Froebel was dated 9 September 1832. However, that seems incorrect as the letter clearly replies to Froebel's accusations.

55 As cited in Heerwart 1905: 73.

56 Barop in Lange 1862: 7.

57 See Fröbel 1832o, 1833.

58 See Halfter 1931: 672.

59 Fröbel 1832o: 1R.

60 Fröbel 1833: 2R/3.

61 Fröbel 1833a, 1833b.

62 Fröbel 1833a: 3.

63 See Hoffmann 1982: 207.

64 Fröbel 1833c: 2R.

65 See Heerwart 1905: 86f., 90f.

66 Fröbel 1833c.

67 See Nipperdey 2014.

68 Barop in Lange 1862: 8/9.

69 As cited in Lange 1862: 9/10.

70 See Fröbel 1833e, 1833f.

71 Fröbel 1833g: 1R.

72 As cited in Heerwart 1905: 84.

73 As cited in ibid., 80.

74 Fröbel 1833h: 7/7R.

75 See Fröbel 1839f.

76 As an example, see Fröbel 1834b.

77 Fröbel 1834: 4

78 See www.myheritage.com/research/record-40001-666725334/heinrich-langethal-in-familysearch-family-tree?s=809823011.

79 See Fröbel 1834. Wilhelm and Albertine had seven children of whom four survived.

80 Fröbel 1834a: 1R.

81 Halfter 1931: 695.

82 Fröbel 1834c: 5R.

83 Ibid.

84 Fröbel 1834e: 2.

85 Fröbel 1834h: 2.

86 See Halfter 1931: 704.

87 Fröbel 1834f: 1.

88 Ibid., 1R.

89 Ibid.

90 Fröbel 1834g: 1.

91 Ibid., 1R.

92 See Fröbel 1834j.

93 As an example, see Fröbel 1834k.

94 See Fröbel 1834o, 1834p.

95 As cited in Halfter 1931: 716.

96 Fröbel 1834q: 1.

97 Ibid., 4.

98 As cited in Halfter 1931: 708.

99 As cited in ibid., 707.

100 Fröbel 1834r.

101 As cited in Boldt and Eichler 1982: 76.

102 Halfter 1931: 706.

103 See Heeerwart 1905: 103f.

104 Fröbel 1834l: 1.

105 Fröbel 1834t.

106 Fröbel 1834w.

107 See Heerwart 1905: 127f.

108 Fröbel 1835h: 1.

109 Fröbel 1834k: 2.

110 As examples see Fröbel 1834q: 1R; 1834s.

111 Fröbel 1834q: 2.

112 Fröbel 1834s.

113 Fröbel 1834t: 1R.

114 Ibid.

115 Ibid., 2.

116 Ibid., 3.

117 Fröbel 1834k: 2. See also the letter to Emilie from September 1834: Fröbel 1834n.

118 Fröbel 1834l: 1R.

119 Fröbel 1834k: 2.

120 As examples see Fröbel 1835c: 8; 1835f: 1R.

121 Fröbel 1834m: 1R.

122 As examples see Fröbel 1834p, 1834t, 1834u.

123 Fröbel 1834i: 1.

124 Ibid., 2.

125 Ibid., 5.

126 Ibid., 5R.

127 Ibid.

128 Fröbel 1834n: 1.

129 Ibid., 1R.

130 Fröbel 1834y.

131 Fröbel 1834q: 2R.

132 Fröbel 1834t: 2R.

133 Fröbel 1835: 1.

134 Fröbel 1834s: 2R.

135 Fröbel 1834v: 2.

136 Fröbel 1835c: 4.

137 Fröbel 1835f: 1.

138 As an example, see Fröbel 1835c: 5R.

139 Fröbel 1835f: 2R.

140 As examples Fröbel 1835j, 1835l.

141 Fröbel 1835m: 1. The dozen people were Wilhelm Middendorff, Elise Fröbel, Ferdinand Fröbel, Alex Roda, Luise Frankenberg, Adolf Frankenberg, Georges Audemars, Ernestine and Heinrich Langethal, Titus Pfeiffer, Friedrich and Wilhelmine Fröbel.

142 Fröbel 1835m: 1.

143 www.ancestry.de/family-tree/person/tree/88073400/person/30562849328/ facts?_phsrc=HZj27&_phstart=successSource. Retrieved 25 March 2022. See also www.myheritage.com/research/record-40001-380647860/friedrike-martha-gert rud-barop-in-familysearch-family-tree. Retrieved 25 March 2022.

144 Fröbel 1835b.

145 See Hoffmann 1982: 208.

146 Fröbel 1835c: 8.

147 Fröbel 1835e: 1.

148 www.ancestry.de/family-tree/person/tree/88073400/person/30562849328/ facts?_phsrc=HZj27&_phstart=successSource. Retrieved 25 March 2022. See also www.myheritage.com/research/record-40001-380647860/friedrike-martha-gert rud-barop-in-familysearch-family-tree. Retrieved 25 March 2022.

149 See Hoffmann 1982: 208.

150 As cited in Heerwart 1905: 130.

151 Fröbel 1835s.

152 Froebel wrote to her to remind her that she would bring his old letters, his written 'soul messages', with her.

153 Fröbel 1836f: 1.

154 Besides Gertrud, the daughters were Albertine Henriette Elise Adelheid Barop (*1836), Caroline Wilhelmine Hermine Amalie (*1840), Emilie Julie Charlotte Cacelia (*1842), and Mathilde Marie (*1844). Altogether, the Barops had eight children; the youngest one was Johann Lebrecht Reinhold, born in 1847.

155 Fröbel 1835n: 1R.
156 See Nohl 1931.
157 Ibid., 386.
158 Heiland 1982: 92.
159 Nohl 1931: 393.
160 Fröbel 1835g: 1.
161 The letters are lost.
162 Fröbel 1835o: 1.
163 Fröbel 1835p: 1.
164 Fröbel 1835q: 401.
165 Ibid., 402.
166 Ibid.
167 See Heiland 1982; Krone 2011: 69.
168 See Heerwart 1905: 139.
169 Fröbel 1834q: 3.
170 Fröbel 1834x. See also Fröbel 1835b.
171 Fröbel 1835d.
172 Fröbel 1836a: 5.
173 Fröbel 1834x: 4.
174 See Fröbel 1836a: 2.
175 Fröbel 1835a: 1.
176 Fröbel 1836: 2.
177 Fröbel 1835a: 4.
178 Fröbel 1834s: 4. For similar thoughts, see Fröbel 1834u, 1835k.
179 Fröbel 1835f: 3.
180 Fröbel 1835i: 1.
181 Ibid.
182 Krone 2011: 68.
183 Fröbel 1836a.
184 Ibid., 7–8.
185 Fröbel 1835r: 1R/2.
186 Fröbel 1835t: 266. Similar statements can be found in many letters; examples include Fröbel 1836, 1836a.
187 See Heiland 1982: 92/93; Osann 1956: 110–13.
188 Fröbel 1836a, 1836d.
189 Fröbel 1836d: 1R.
190 Fröbel 1836: 2R.
191 See Fröbel 1836b.
192 See Fröbel 1836c; Halfter 1931: 738.
193 Fröbel 1836e: 1.

7 The Kindergarten Years

1 See Heerwart 1905: 163/164, 181.

2 Lange and Diesterwegm 1855: 17.

3 Heerwart 1905: 173.

4 See Sauerbrey and Friedrich Fröbel Museum Bad Blankenburg 2013.

5 See Heerwart 1905: 192.

6 Due to the ambiguity of Froebel's motto, countless different interpretations – and therefore also translations – are possible.

7 See Boldt and Eichler 1982.

8 Heerwart 1905: 183.

9 Fröbel 1839: 240.

10 Fröbel 1838b: 165.

11 See Fröbel 1838a.

12 Fröbel 1839a: 244.

13 See Osann 1956: 119f.

14 Fröbel 1839d: 4.

15 Fröbel 1839e: 250R.

16 As cited in Heerwart 1905: 311.

17 Fröbel 1839b: 326/327.

18 Seele 1887: 68–9.

19 Ibid., 69.

20 As cited in Heerwart 1905: 328.

21 Fröbel 1848c: 50/50R.

22 Erning and Gebel 1999: 98f.

23 For the history of early childhood education in Germany, see Wasmuth 2011; Wasmuth 2020.

24 Fröbel 1840.

25 Insightful examples are Fröbel 1841, 1842.

26 See Fröbel 1840: 121.

27 Kuntze 1952: 109.

28 Osann 1956: 124.

29 Seele 1887: 22.

30 Fröbel 1839g: 248.

31 Fröbel 1840c: 304.

32 Fröbel 1842: 370R.

33 See Fröbel 1840d.

34 See Fröbel 1840a, 1840b, 1840c.

35 See Fröbel 1840e; Fröbel, Middendorff, and Barop 1840.

36 Fröbel 1840e: 323R.

37 Fröbel 1840f: 325.

38 See Halfter 1931: 755.

39 Fröbel 1841: 348.

40 Fröbel 1851a: 48.

41 Fröbel 1850a: 2.

42 See Fröbel 1841a, 1842a, 1842b, 1842c; the correspondence with Muhme Schmidt, Fröbel 1846b, 1851c. For analyses, see Bruce 2021 and the authors' works.

43 Fröbel 1851c: 727.

44 Ibid., 195.

45 For more extensive analyses, see Sauerbrey and Winkler 2018; Heiland 2003. For English literature, see Brosterman 2014.

46 Fröbel 1842c: 92.

47 Fröbel 1842a.

48 For this period, see Seele 1886, 1887.

49 Fröbel 1842a: 7R.

50 Seele 1886: 71.

51 Fröbel 1842a: 7.

52 Seele 1886: 71.

53 See ibid., 168.

54 Osann 1956: 126.

55 Fröbel 1843.

56 Fröbel 1843a: 109. Seele means soul in German.

57 Seele 1886: 21.

58 Ibid., 120.

59 See ibid., 39.

60 See Seele 1887: 4, 169.

61 Seele 1886: 39.

62 Ibid., 73, 100f.

63 Ibid., 55.

64 Ibid., 56.

65 Ibid., 84f.

66 Seele 1887: 119.

67 Seele 1886: 68.

68 Fröbel 1840g: 1R.

69 Fröbel 1840h: 1.

70 Seele 1886: 37.

71 See Heiland 2010; Kuntze 1952.

72 See Seele 1887: 84; Fröbel 1844.

73 For the time in Darmstadt, see Seele 1887, 1888.

74 Seele 1887: 166.

75 Seele 1888: 72.

76 König 1990: 77.

77 Fröbel 1850, 1850c.

78 Seele 1888: 73.

79 Ibid., 85.

80 See Osann 1956.

81 Seele 1886: 70.

82 As cited in Osann 1956: 128.

83 Seele 1886: 123.

84 As cited in Osann 1956: 120.

85 See ibid., 127/128.

86 See Lange and Diesterweg 1855: 18f.

87 See Fröbel 1844c.

88 Fröbel 1844d: 1R.

89 Fröbel 1844a: 1R/2.

90 As examples, see Fröbel 1844b, 1844e.

91 Fröbel 1844f: 1R.

92 See Prüfer 1927.

93 Fröbel 1844f: 2.

94 See Lange and Diesterweg 1855: 19, 25f.

95 Fröbel 1847: 210R.

96 See Allen 2017.

97 As cited in Osann 1956: 131.

98 As cited in ibid.

99 For Breymann, see Wasmuth 2020.

100 Lyschinska 1922: 55.

101 Ibid., 61.

102 Ibid.

103 Fröbel 1848: 219.

104 Ibid., 220R.

105 Fröbel 1848a: 88.

106 Ibid., 93/94.

107 Ibid., 89.

108 See Prüfer 1927: 111f.

109 See Münchow 2000: 121.

110 Fröbel 1849b.

111 König 1990: 103/104.

112 Fröbel 1848d.

113 Fröbel 1848c: 51.

114 Fröbel 1848b: 39.

115 Fröbel 1849e: 21.

116 See Fröbel 1849.

117 Fröbel 1849c: 1R.

118 Ibid., 3.

119 See Heerwart 1902: 2f.

120 See Föllner 2008; Sauerbrey 2020.

121 König 1990: 100.

122 Ibid., 285.

123 For her life, see Münchow 2000.

124 See Fröbel 1849a: 128.

125 Fröbel 1849f: 15–17.

126 See Heiland 2000: 93.

127 König 1990: 123.

128 See Fröbel 1849f.

129 As cited in Münchow 2000: 126.

130 Fröbel 1849e: 22R.

131 For Hildenhagen and Quetz, see Heiland 2000; Krone 2020; Münchow 2000.

132 As cited in Heiland 2000: 86/87.

133 See ibid., 89.

134 As cited in ibid., 91.

135 As cited in ibid., 93.

136 See Halfter 1931: 754/755; Osann 1956: 134f.

137 As cited in Osann 1956.

138 Ibid., 134.

139 For Froebel's last two years of life, see Heerwart 1902.

140 See Lange and Diesterweg 1855: 3f.

141 See König 1990: 107, 134f., 366.

142 Fröbel 1850a: 1.

143 Ibid.

144 Fröbel 1850b: 77R.

145 Ibid.

146 See Langethal 1910: 117/118.

147 Fröbel 1850d: 154.

148 Halfter 1931: 756.

149 See Fröbel 1851b.

150 See Boldt and Eichler 1982: 118/119.

151 As cited in Prüfer 1927: 124.

152 Fröbel 1850.

153 Fröbel 1850e: 1.

154 Fröbel, 1850f: 483.

155 See Osann 1956: 133.

156 Palatschek, as cited in Münchow 2002: 128.

157 For the reactionary era, see Siemann 1990: 37ff.

158 As cited in Sauerbrey and Winkler 2018: 148.

159 The correspondence is lost. Froebel also mentioned Baltzer four times in his letters between the beginning of November 1850 and March 1852.

160 König 1990: 272.

161 As cited in Prüfer 1927: 126.

162 As cited in Sauerbrey and Winkler 2018: 148.

163 Fröbel 1851c: 380R.

164 See Heerwart 1902: 19ff.

165 See ibid., 23, 34/35.

166 As cited in Prüfer 1927: 127.

167 See Heerwart 1902: 31f.

168 See Fröbel 1851.

169 Fröbel 1852: 1.

170 Fröbel 1852a: 1.

171 See ibid.

172 Middendorff gave an account of Froebel's last birthday celebration in detail. See Heerwart 1902: 33f.

173 As cited in Heerwart 1902: 58.

174 As cited in ibid., 62.

175 See Halfter 1931: 760; Heerwart 1902: 67.

176 See Heerwart 1902: 69.

177 Ibid., 71.

178 As cited in ibid., 72.

179 As cited in ibid., 90.

References

Adelman, C. (2000). Over two years, what did Froebel say to Pestalozzi? *History of Education*, 29(2), pp. 103–14.

Allen, A. T. (2017). *The Transatlantic Kindergarten: Education and Women's Movements in Germany and the United States*. New York: Oxford University Press.

Behringer, W. (2017). *Tambora und das Jahr ohne Sommer*. Munich: C. H. Beck.

Beiser, F. C. (2002). *German Idealism: The Struggle against Subjectivism, 1781–1801*. Cambridge, MA: Harvard University Press.

Boldt, R. and Eichler, W. (1982). *Friedrich Wilhelm August Fröbel*. Leipzig: Urania.

Boldt, R., Knechtel, E. and König, H. (eds) (1982). *Kommt, lasst uns unsern Kindern leben!*, vol. 1. Berlin: Volk und Wissen.

Bollnow, O. F. (1952). *Die Pädagogik der deutschen Romantik. Von Arndt bis Fröbel*. Stuttgart: Kohlhammer.

Downs, R. B. (1978). *Friedrich Froebel*. Boston, MA: Twayne.

Erning, G. and Gebel, M. (1999). 'Kindergarten' – nicht von Fröbel? Zur Wortgeschichte des 'Kindergartens'. In H. Heiland (ed.), *Friedrich Fröbel. Aspekte international vergleichender Historiographie* (pp. 83–101). Weinheim: Deutscher Studien-Verlag.

Fesser, G. (2008). Jenas goldene Jahre. *Die Zeit*, 4, 17.

Föllner, U. (2008). 'Teuerster Lehrer und Freund!' – Briefe von Frauen an den Begründer des Kindergartens Friedrich Fröbel. In G. Brandt (ed.), *Bausteine zu einer Geschichte des weiblichen Sprachgebrauchs. Vol. VIII: sprachliches Agieren von Frauen in approbierten Textsorten* (pp. 85–92). Stuttgart: Heinz.

Friedman, M. and Alvis, J. M. (2012). Haüy, Weiß, Fröbel: The influence of nineteenth century crystallography on the mathematics of Friedrich Fröbel's kindergarten. Part 2: New evidence from unpublished notes. *Paedagogica Historica*, pp. 212–32 doi: 10.1080/00309230.2021.1876744.

Fröbel, F. (1799). Letter to Johann Jakob Fröbel in Oberweißbach, 12.8./14.8.1799 (Jena). KN 9, 2, pp. 1–3.

Fröbel, F. (1801). Letter to Christoph Fröbel in Eyba, 29.4.1801 (Jena). BN 435, pp. 1–2.

Frbel, F. (1801a). Letter to Johann Jakob Fröbel in Oberweißbach, 29.4.1801 (Jena). KN 9, 5, pp. 1–2.

Fröbel, F. (1801b). Letter to Christoph Fröbel in Eyba, 3.9.1801 (Weitersroda). KN 9, 8, pp. 1–6.

Fröbel, F. ([1805] 1862). Letter to Christoph Fröbel in Griesheim, 24.8.–26.8.1805 (Frankfurt/M.). In W. Lange (ed.), *Friedrich Fröbel's gesammelte pädagogische Schriften. Erste Abteilung: Friedrich Fröbel in seiner Erziehung als Mensch und*

Pädagoge. Vol. 1: Aus Fröbels Leben und erstem Streben. Autobiographie und kleinere Schriften (pp. 532–3). Berlin: Enslin.

Fröbel, F. (1806). Letter to Georg von Holzhausen in Frankfurt/M., End of 1806 (Frankfurt/M.). BN 494, pp. 2–35.

Fröbel, F. (1807). Letter to Christoph Fröbel in Griesheim, 16.2./21.2.1807 (Frankfurt/M.). KN 10, 1, pp. 1–7.

Fröbel, F. (1807a). Letter to Christoph Fröbel in Griesheim, 26.3./3.4.1807 (Frankfurt/M.). KN 10, 2, pp. 1–87.

Fröbel, F. (1807b). Letter to Christoph Fröbel in Griesheim, 3.5.1807 (Frankfurt/M.). BN 435, pp. 3–4.

Fröbel, F. (1808). Letter to Christoph Fröbel in Griesheim, 8.3./13.3./21.3.1808 (Frankfurt/M.). KN 11, 1, pp. 1–14.

Fröbel, F. (1808a). Letter to Christoph Fröbel in Griesheim, 8.3./13.3./21.3.1808 (Frankfurt/M.). KN 11, 1, pp. 1–14.

Fröbel, F. (1808b). Letter to Christoph Fröbel in Griesheim, 5.6.1808 (Frankfurt/M.). KN 11, 2, pp. 1–2.

Fröbel, F. (1808c). Letter to Christoph Fröbel in Griesheim, beginning of July/11.7./13.7./14.7./15.7./16.7.1808 (Frankfurt/M.). KN 11, 3, pp. 1–6.

Fröbel, F. (1808d). Letter to Johann Heinrich Pestalozzi in Yverdon, 10.7.1808 (Frankfurt/M.). BN 588, pp. 1–8, 9–14.

Fröbel, F. (1808e). Letter to Georg von Holzhausen in Frankfurt/M., between November and 15.12.1808 (Yverdon). BN 494, pp. 39–46.

Fröbel, F. (1808f). Letter to Christoph Fröbel in Griesheim, 16.12./20.12.1808 (Yverdon). KN 11, 9, pp. 1–6.

Fröbel, F. (1809). Letter to Karoline-Luise Fürstin von Schwarzburg-Rudolstadt, 1.5.1809 (Yverdon). ThStA Rudolstadt, Geheimes Ratskollegium, E IX 2h Nr.1, pp. 130–5.

Fröbel, F. (1809a). Letter to Christoph Fröbel in Griesheim, 15.5.1809 (Yverdun). KN 12, 3, pp. 1–6.

Fröbel, F. (1809b). Letter to Christoph Fröbel in Griesheim, 21.5./23.5.1809 (Yverdon). KN 12, 4, pp. 1–8.

Fröbel, F. (1810). Letter to Caroline von Holzhausen in Frankfurt/M. (Yverdon), 17.1.1810. KN 13, 1, pp. 1–2.

Fröbel, F. (1810a). Letter to Georg von Holzhausen in Frankfurt/M., 1.5.1810 (Yverdon). BN 494, pp. 50–61.

Fröbel, F. (1810b). Letter to Johann Heinrich Pestalozzi in Yverdon, 20.5.1810 (Yverdon). BlM, II, 4/F 900, p. 1.

Fröbel, F. (1810c). Letter to Caroline von Holzhausen in Frankfurt/M., 5.6.1810 (Yverdon). BN 492, pp. 3–4.

Fröbel, F. (1810d). Letter to Georg von Holzhausen in Frankfurt/M., 11.6.1810 (Yverdon). BN 494, pp. 63–7.

Fröbel, F. (1810e). Letter to Georg von Holzhausen in Frankfurt/M., 15.6.1810 (Yverdon). BN 494, pp. 68–72.

Fröbel, F. (1810f). Letter to Karoline-Luise Fürstin von Schwarzburg-Rudolstadt in Rudolstadt, 13.6.1810 (Yverdon). ThStA Rudolstadt, Geheimes Ratskollegium, E IX 2h Nr.1, pp. 44–59.

Fröbel, F. (1810g). Letter to Christoph Fröbel in Griesheim, 26.6.1810 (Yverdon). KN 13, 7, pp. 1–3.

Fröbel, F. (1811). Letter to Christoph Fröbel in Griesheim, 21.5./24.5.1811 (Frankfurt/M.). BN 435, pp. 7–9.

Fröbel, F. (1811a). Letter to Christoph Fröbel in Griesheim, 25.6.1811 (Göttingen). KN 14, 4, pp. 1–3.

Fröbel, F. (1812). Letter to Christoph Fröbel in Griesheim, 5.4.1812 (Osterode). KN 14, 12, p. 1.

Fröbel, F. (1813). Letter to Christian Samuel Weiß in Berlin, 2.10.1813 (Dannenberg). GNM, p. 49.

Fröbel, F. (1813a). Letter to Christian Samuel Weiß in Berlin, 8.12.1813 (Lütgensee). GNM, pp. 62–4.

Fröbel, F. (1814). Letter to Christian Samuel Weiß in Berlin, 12.4.1814 (Ham). BlM II, 12, pp. 66–7.

Fröbel, F. (1814a). Letter to Christian Samuel Weiß in Berlin, 22.6.1814 (Frankfurt/Main). BlM II, 24, pp. 109–10.

Fröbel, F. (1815). Letter to Caroline von Holzhausen in Frankfurt/M., 28.5.1815 (Berlin). BN 492, pp. 33–4.

Fröbel, F. (1817). Letter to Heinrich Langethal in Berlin, 1.7.1817 (Keilhau). KN 19, 3, pp. 1–2.

Fröbel, F. (1817a). Letter to Heinrich Langethal in Berlin, 27.1./29.1./30.1.1817 (Griesheim). KN 19, 1, pp. 1–15.

Fröbel, F. (1817b). Letter to Emilie Fröbel in Osterode, 30.4.1817 (Griesheim). KN 19, 2, pp. 1–3.

Fröbel, F. (1818). Letter to Henriette Wilhelmine Klöpper in Berlin, 19.1.– 30.1.1818 (Keilhau). BN 444, pp. 24–32.

Fröbel, F. (1825). Letter to Henriette Wilhelmine Fröbel in Berlin, 10.4.1825 (Keilhau). BN 445, pp. 32–3.

Fröbel, F. (1825a). Letter to Emilie Fröbel in Keilhau, 23.4.1825 (Berlin). KN 21, 7, pp. 1–5.

Fröbel, F. (1827). Letter to Bernhard II. Erich Freund Herzog von Sachsen-Meiningen in Meiningen, <before> 6. / 25.7.1827 (Keilhau). KN 108; 4 (Mappe I) LI, 1, 32-116, pp. 1–36.

Fröbel, F. (1828). Letter to Karl Christian Friedrich Krause in Göttingen, 24.5./2.6./17.6.1828 (Keilhau). KN 23, 5, pp. 1–25.

Fröbel, F. (1829). Letter to Johannes Arnold Barop in Berlin, 8.2.1829 (Keilhau). KN 24, 3, pp. 1–5.

Fröbel, F. (1831). Letter to Henriette Wilhelmine Fröbel in Keilhau, 17.5.1831 (Frankfurt/M.). KN 27, 7, pp. 1–5.

Fröbel, F. (1831a). Letter to Henriette Wilhelmine Fröbel in Keilhau, 25.5.1831 (Frankfurt/M.). KN 27, 8, pp. 1–4.

Fröbel, F. (1831b). Letter to Henriette Wilhelmine Fröbel in Keilhau, 9.6.1831 (Auf der Öde bei Frankfurt/M.). KN 27, 10, pp. 1–4.

Fröbel, F. (1831c). Letter to Henriette Wilhelmine Fröbel in Keilhau, 17.6./20.6.1831 (Frankfurt/M.). KN 27, 11, pp. 1–11.

Fröbel, F. (1831d). Letter to Henriette Wilhelmine Fröbel in Keilhau, 3.7.1831 (Frankfurt/M.). KN 28, 2, pp. 1–3.

Fröbel, F. (1831e). Letter to Emilie Fröbel in Keilhau, 11.7.1831 (Frankfurt/M.). KN 28, 4, pp. 1–2.

Fröbel, F. (1831f). Letter to Johannes Arnold Barop in Keilhau, 11.7.1831 (Frankfurt/M.). KN 28, 5, p. 1.

Fröbel, F. (1831g). Letter to the >Keilhau Community<, 11.7.1831 (Frankfurt/M.). KN 28, 3, p. 1.

Fröbel, F. (1831h). Letter to the Women in Keilhau, 18.8./<before> 21.9.1831 (Wartensee). BN 724, pp. 4–72.

Fröbel, F. (1831i). Letter to Henriette Wilhelmine Fröbel in Keilhau, 16.9.1831 (Wartensee). BlM VII, 1, p. 1.

Fröbel, F. (1831j). Letter to the >Keilhau Community<, 4.11.1831 (Wartensee). KN 31, 1, pp. 1–11.

Fröbel, F. (1831k). Letter to the >Keilhau Community<, 28./30.5.1831 (Frankfurt/M.). KN 27, 9, pp. 1–15.

Fröbel, F. (1832). Letter to the >Keilhau Community<, 15.3./16.3./18.3./21.3./23.3.1832 (Wartensee). KN 37, 1, pp. 1–8.

Fröbel, F. (1832a). Felix Minerow, Karl Clemens, Adolph Schepß, August Busse in Keilhau, 6.4.1832 (Wartensee). KN 37, 2, pp. 1–10.

Fröbel, F. (1832b). Letter to the >Keilhau Community<, 3./5./7./9./10./11.6.1832 (Wartensee). KN 38, 4, pp. 1–15.

Fröbel, F. (1832c). Letter to the >Keilhau Community<, 2.7.1832 (Wartensee). KN 39, 1, pp. 1–5.

Fröbel, F. (1832d). Letter to the >Keilhau Community<, 4.7./6.7./7.7./8.7.1832 (Wartensee). KN 39, 2, pp. 1–20.

Fröbel, F. (1832e). Letter to the >Keilhau Community</Henriette Wilhelmine Fröbel, 20.7.1832 (Wartensee). KN 40, 3, pp. 1–6.

Fröbel, F. (1832f). Letter to the >Keilhau Community<, 25.7./27.7./28.7.1832 (Wartensee). KN 40, 4, pp. 1–14.

Fröbel, F. (1832g). Letter to the >Keilhau Community<, 29.7./2.8./4.8.1832 (Wartensee). KN 40, 5, pp. 1–19.

Fröbel, F. (1832h). Letter to the >Keilhau Community<, 10.8.1832 (Wartensee). KN 41, 2, pp. 1–8.

Fröbel, F. (1832i). Letter to Henriette Wilhelmine Fröbel in Keilhau, 10.8.1832 (Wartensee). KN 41, 4, pp. 1–2.

Fröbel, F. (1832j). Letter to Johannes Arnold Barop in Keilhau, 10.8.1832 (Wartensee). KN 41, 3, p. 1.

Fröbel, F. (1832k). Letter to the >Keilhau Community<, 2.9.1832 (Wartensee). KN 42, 3, pp. 1–2.

Fröbel, F. (1832l). Letter to the >Keilhau Community<, 3.9.1832 (Wartensee). KN 42, 4, pp. 1–6.

Fröbel, F. (1832m). Letter to Henriette Wilhelmine Fröbel in Keilhau, 16.10.1832 (Wartensee). KN 43, 2, pp. 1–2.

Fröbel, F. (1832n). Letter to the >Keilhau Community<, 19./21.10.1832 (Wartensee). KN 43, 3, pp. 1–3.

Fröbel, F. (1832o). Letter to Johannes Arnold Barop in Wartensee, 14.12.1832 (Keilhau). KN 43, 5, p. 1.

Fröbel, F. (1833). Letter to Johannes Arnold Barop in Wartensee, 9.1.1833 (Keilhau). KN 43, 6, pp. 1–8.

Fröbel, F. (1833a). Letter to Johannes Arnold Barop in Wartensee, 2.2.1833 (Keilhau). KN 44, 1, pp. 1–4.

Fröbel, F. (1833b). Letter to Johannes Arnold Barop in Wartensee, 11.2./12.2./14.2.1833 (Keilhau). KN 44, 4; 44, 9, p. 1.

Fröbel, F. (1833c). Letter to Emilie Barop in Keilhau, 24.2.1833 (Berlin). KN 44, 6, pp. 1–2.

Fröbel, F. (1833d). Letter to Johann Arnold Barop and the >Keilhau Community<, 1.5.1833 (Willisau). KN 45, 8, pp. 1–2.

Fröbel, F. (1833e). Letter to the >Keilhau Community<, 15.5.1833 (Willisau). KN 45, 10, pp. 1–2.

Fröbel, F. (1833f). Letter to the >Keilhau Community<, 18.5./20.5./22.5.1833 (Willisau). KN 45, 11, pp. 1–2.

Fröbel, F. (1833g). Letter to the >Keilhau Community<, 4.8.1833 (Willisau). KN 45, 13, pp. 1–2.

Fröbel, F. (1833h). Letter to the >Keilhau Community<, 29.12./30.12./31.12.1833/2.1.1834 (Willisau). KN 46, 11, pp. 1–8.

Fröbel, F. (1834). Letter to Heinrich Langethal in Keilhau, 25.1.1834 (Willisau). UBB 2, pp. 3–4.

Fröbel, F. (1834a). Letter to Wilhelm Middendorff and Johannes Arnold Barop in Keilhau, 27.1./7.2.1834 (Willisau). KN 46, 15; 46, 19, pp. 1–2.

Fröbel, F. (1834b). Letter to Johannes Arnold Barop in Keilhau, 15.2.1834 (Willisau). KN 46, 22, p. 1.

Fröbel, F. (1834c). Letter to Heinrich Langethal in Keilhau, 25.2./26.2.1834 (Willisau). UBB 3, pp. 5–6.

Fröbel, F. (1834d). Letter to the >Keilhau Community<, 28.3./29.3.1834 (Willisau). KN 47, 3, pp. 1–2.

Fröbel, F. (1834e). Letter to Johannes Arnold Barop in Keilhau, 13.4./16.4./19.4.1834 (Willisau). KN 47, 5, pp. 1–2.

Fröbel, F. (1834f). Letter to the >Keilhau Community<, 25.4./26.4.1834 (Willisau). KN 47, 7, pp. 1–2.

Fröbel, F. (1834g). Letter to the >Keilhau Community<, 17.5.1834 (Willisau). KN 47, 10, p. 1.

Fröbel, F. (1834h). Letter to the >Keilhau Community<, 24.5.1834 (Willisau). KN 47, 12, pp. 1–3.

Fröbel, F. (1834i). Letter to Emilie Barop in Keilhau, 20.6./28.6./29.6./30.6./10.7.1834 (Burgdorf). KN 47,16, pp. 1–5.

Fröbel, F. (1834j). Letter to Henriette Wilhelmine Fröbel in Willisau, 21.6.1834 (Burgdorf). BN 445, pp. 55–6.

Fröbel, F. (1834k). Letter to the >Keilhau Community<, 16.7./17.7./18.7./19.7.1834 (Burgdorf). KN 48, 2, pp. 1–2.

Fröbel, F. (1834l). Letter to the >Keilhau Community<, 21.7.1834 (Burgdorf). KN 48, 3, pp. 1–2.

Fröbel, F. (1834m). Letter to Wilhelm Middendorff in Keilhau, 30.7.1834 (Burgdorf). KN 48, 5, p. 1.

Fröbel, F. (1834n). Letter to Emilie Barop in Keilhau, 3.9.1834 (Burgdorf). KN 48, 6, pp. 1–2.

Fröbel, F. (1834o). Letter to Heinrich Langethal in Willisau, 4.9.1834 (Burgdorf). KN 48, 8, pp. 72–3.

Fröbel, F. (1834p). Letter to the >Keilhau Community<, 4.9.1834 (Burgdorf). KN 48, 9, p. 1.

Fröbel, F. (1834q). Letter to the >Keilhau Community<, 17.9./18.9./20.9.1834 (Willisau). KN 48, 10, pp. 1–4.

Fröbel, F. (1834r). Letter to the >Keilhau Community<, 26.9./27.9.1834 (Willisau). KN 48, 11, pp. 1–4.

Fröbel, F. (1834s). Letter to Wilhelm Middendorff and Johann Arnold Barop in Keilhau, 30.10./8.11.1834 (Willisau). KN 48, 15, pp. 1–5.

Fröbel, F. (1834t). Letter to the >Keilhau Community<, 6.11./8.11.1834 (Willisau). KN 49, 2, pp. 1–3.

Fröbel, F. (1834u). Letter to the >Keilhau Community<, 12./14./15.11.1834 (Willisau). KN 49, 4, pp. 1–2.

Fröbel, F. (1834v). Letter to the >Keilhau Community<, 16.11.1834 (Willisau). KN 49, 6, pp. 1–2.

Fröbel, F. (1834w). Letter to the >Keilhau Community<, 6.12.1834 (Willisau). KN 49, 9, pp. 1–2.

Fröbel, F. (1834x). Letter to the >Keilhau Community<, 20.11./8.12.1834 (Willisau). KN 49, 7, pp. 1–4.

Fröbel, F. (1834y). Letter to Emilie Barop in Keilhau, 27.12.1834 (Willisau). KN 49, 11, pp. 1–2.

Fröbel, F. (1835). Letter to the >Keilhau Community<, 3.1.1835 (Willisau). KN 50, 3, pp. 1–2.

Fröbel, F. (1835a). Letter to Johannes Arnold Barop in Keilhau, 14.1. /17.1./18.1./19.1./2 1.1./24.1.1835 (Willisau). KN 50, 5; 50, 6; 50, 7, pp. 1–2.

Fröbel, F. (1835b). Letter to Johann Arnold Barop in Keilhau, 25.1./27.1./31.1.1835 (Willisau). KN 50, 10; 50,11, pp. 1–4.

Fröbel, F. (1835c). Letter to Johann Arnold Barop in Keilhau, 7./9.2.1835 (Willisau). KN 51, 1, pp. 1–8.

Fröbel, F. (1835d). Letter to Johann Arnold Barop and the >Keilhau Community<, 12./13./14.2.1835 (Willisau). BlM F 588; Mappe VI/7, pp. 1–4; KN 51, 2, pp. 1–5.

Fröbel, F. (1835e). Letter to Emilie Barop in Keilhau, 28.2.1835 (Willisau). KN 51, 8, p. 1.

Fröbel, F. (1835f). Letter to the >Keilhau Community<, 15.3.1835 (Willisau). KN 51, 10, pp. 1–3.

Fröbel, F. (1835g). Letter to Elise Fröbel in Keilhau, 28.3.1835 (Willisau). In H. Nohl (1931/2). Friedrich Fröbels Briefe an Elise. *Die Erziehung*, 7, ppp. 395–6.

Fröbel, F. (1835h). Letter to the >Keilhau Community<, 21.4.1835 (Burgdorf). KN 51, 14, pp. 1–2.

Fröbel, F. (1835i). Letter to Heinrich Langethal in Burgdorf, 29.4.1835 (Willisau). UBB 6, pp. 11–14.

Fröbel, F. (1835j). Letter to Johannes Arnold Barop in Keilhau, 30.4./1.5./2.5.1835 (Willisau). KN 51, 18, pp. 1–2.

Fröbel, F. (1835k). Letter to Heinrich Langethal in Burgdorf, 16.5.1835 (Willisau). UBB 8, pp. 16–17.

Fröbel, F. (1835l). Letter to >Keilhau Community<, 16.5.1835 (Willisau). KN 52, 2, pp. 1–2.

Fröbel, F. (1835m). Letter to the >Keilhau Community<, 7.6.1835 (Burgdorf). KN 52, 5, p. 1.

Fröbel, F. (1835n). Letter to Johannes Arnold Barop in Keilhau, 15.6.1835 (Burgdorf). KN 52, 6, p. 1.

Fröbel, F. (1835o). Letter to Elise Fröbel in Willisau, 8.7.1835 (Burgdorf). In H. Nohl (1931/2). Friedrich Fröbels Briefe an Elise. *Die Erziehung*, 7, pp. 396–7.

Fröbel, F. (1835p). Letter to Elise Fröbel in Willisau, 12.7.1835 (Burgdorf). In H. Nohl (1931/2). Friedrich Fröbels Briefe an Elise. *Die Erziehung*, 7, 398.

Fröbel, F. (1835q). Letter to Elise Fröbel in Willisau, 18.10.1835 (Burgdorf). In H. Nohl (1931/2). Friedrich Fröbels Briefe an Elise. *Die Erziehung*, 7, pp. 400–2.

Fröbel, F. (1835r). *Letter to Johannes Arnold Barop in Keilhau, 18.11./19.11.1835 (Burgdorf).* KN 52, 12, pp. 1–2; KN 52, 13, p. 1.

Fröbel, F. (1835s). Letter to the >Keilhau Community<, 15.12.1835 (Burgdorf). BN 565, pp. 4–6; 565, pp. 7–10.

Fröbel, F. (1835t/1874). Letter to Adolph Frankenberg in Willisau, 31.12.1835 (Burgdorf). In A. B. Hanschmann (ed.), *Friedrich Fröbel. Die Entwickelung seiner Erziehungsidee in seinem Leben; nach authentischen Quellen* (pp. 262–8). Eisenach: Bacmeister.

Fröbel, F. (1836). Letter to Johannes Arnold Barop in Keilhau, 22.2.1836 (Burgdorf). KN 52, 22, pp. 1–2.

Fröbel, F. (1836a). Letter to Johannes Arnold Barop in Keilhau, 29.2./1.3./2.3.1836 (Burgdorf). KN 52, 23, pp. 1–8.

Fröbel, F. (1836b). Letter to Johannes Arnold Barop in Keilhau, 14.3.1836 (Burgdorf). KN 52, 26, pp. 1–2.

Fröbel, F. (1836c). Letter to Johannes Arnold Barop in Keilhau, 15.3.1836 (Burgdorf). KN 52, 27, pp. 1–2.

Fröbel, F. (1836d). Letter to Johannes Arnold Barop in Keilhau, 21.3.1836 (Burgdorf). KN 52, 28, pp. 1–2.

Fröbel, F. (1836e). Letter to Johannes Arnold Barop in Keilhau, 3.6.1836 (Kehl). KN 52, 32, p. 1.

Fröbel, F. (1836f). Letter to Heinrich und Ernestine Langethal in Burgdorf, 1.12./2.12.1836 (Keilhau). UBB 18, pp. 33–6.

Fröbel, F. (1838). Letter to Julius Fröbel / Karl Fröbel / Theodor Fröbel, 27.1.1838 (Blankenburg). BN 438, pp. 1–13.

Fröbel, F. (1838a). Letter to Henriette Wilhelmine F. in Blankenburg, 12.12.1838 (Dresden). Rheinische Blätter 1878, pp. 147–52.

Fröbel, F. (1838b). Letter to Henriette Wilhelmine F. in Blankenburg, 23./25.12.1838 (Dresden). Rheinische Blätter 1878, pp. 159–71.

Fröbel, F. (1839). Letter to Henriette Wilhelmine F. in Blankenburg, 3.1.1839 (Dresden). Rheinische Blätter 1878, pp. 239–42.

Fröbel, F. (1839a). Letter to Henriette Wilhelmine F. in Blankenburg, 9.1.1839 (Dresden). Rheinische Blätter 1878, pp. 242–6.

Fröbel, F. (1839b). Letter to Henriette Wilhelmine F. in Blankenburg, 4.2.1839 (Dresden). Rheinische Blätter 1878, pp. 322–7.

Fröbel, F. (1839c). Letter to Heinrich Langethal in Burgdorf, 23.4./25.4./26.4./27.4.1839 (Blankenburg). UBB 71, pp. 238–46.

Fröbel, F. (1839d). Letter to Johannes Arnold Barop in Keilhau, 4.5.1839 (Blankenburg). KN 55, 21, p. 1.

Fröbel, F. (1839e). Letter to Heinrich Langethal in Burgdorf, 7.5.1839 (Blankenburg). UBB 72, pp. 247–50.

Fröbel, F. (1839f). Letter to Heinrich Langethal in Burgdorf, 24.9.1839 (Blankenburg). UBB 80, pp. 273.

Fröbel, F. (1839g). Letter to Heinrich Langethal in Burgdorf, 7.12.1839 (Blankenburg). UBB 85, pp. 282–3.

Fröbel, F. ([1840] 1951). Entwurf eines Planes zur Begründung und Ausführung eins Kinder-Gartens, einer allgemeinen Anstalt zur Verbreitung allseitiger Beachtung des Lebens der Kinder, besonders durch Pflege ihres Tätigkeitstriebes. Den Deutschen

Frauen und Jungfrauen als ein Werk zu würdiger Mitfeier des vierhundertjährigen Jubelfestes der Erfindung der Buchdruckerkunst zur Prüfung und Mitwirkung vorgelegt. In E. Hoffmann (ed.), *Friedrich Fröbel. Ausgewählte Schriften. Erster Band: Kleine Schriften und Briefe von 1809-1851* (pp. 114-25). Godesberg: Küpper.

Fröbel, F. (1840a). Letter to Heinrich Langethal in Burgdorf, 13.1./14.1.1840 (Blankenburg). UBB 91, pp. 291-4.

Fröbel, F. (1840b). Letter to Heinrich Langethal in Burgdorf, 27.1.1840 (Blankenburg). UBB 95, pp. 302-3.

Fröbel, F. (1840c). Letter to Heinrich Langethal in Burgdorf, 19.2./20.2.1840 (Blankenburg). UBB 96, pp. 304-6.

Fröbel, F. (1840d). Letter to Heinrich Langethal in Burgdorf, 9.3.1840 (Keilhau). UBB 98, pp. 308-11.

Fröbel, F. (1840e). Letter to Heinrich Langethal in Burgdorf, 21.4./22.4.1840 (Blankenburg). UBB 103, pp. 322-3.

Fröbel, F. (1840f). Letter to Heinrich Langethal in Burgdorf, 23.4./24.4.1840 (Blankenburg). UBB 104, pp. 324-9.

Fröbel, F. (1840g). Letter to Wilhelm Middendorff in Keilhau, 30.8.1840 (Blankenburg). KN 56, 2, pp. 1-2.

Fröbel, F. (1840h). Letter to Wilhelm Middendorff in Keilhau, <Summer 1840> (Blankenburg). KN 56, 3, p. 1.

Fröbel, F. (1841). Letter to Heinrich Langethal in Burgdorf, 1.2.1841 (Blankenburg). UBB 115, pp. 347-9.

Fröbel, F. (1841a/1982). Die Kindergärten als um- und erfassende Pflege- und Erziehungsanstalten der Kindheit, der Kinder bis zum schulfähigen Alter und der deutsche Kindergarten als eine Musteranstalt dafür insbesondere. In E. Hoffmann (ed.), *Friedrich Fröbel. Ausgewählte Schriften. Vierter Band. Die Spielgaben* (pp. 149-78). Stuttgart: Klett-Cotta.

Fröbel, F. (1842). Letter to Heinrich Langethal in Bern, 3.1./8.1.1842 (Blankenburg). UBB 120, pp. 364-73.

Fröbel, F. (1842a). Letter to Amalie Müller in Döllstedt, 8.8.1842 (Blankenburg). BN 576, pp. 7-12.

Fröbel, F. (1842b/1982). Über die Bedeutung und das Wesen des Kindergartens über-haupt und das Wesen und die Bedeutung des deutschen Kindergartens insbesondere. In E. Hoffmann (ed.), *Friedrich Fröbel. Ausgewählte Schriften. Vierter Band. Die Spielgaben* (pp. 203-35). Stuttgart: Klett-Cotta.

Fröbel, F. (1843). Letter to Ida Seele in Nordhausen, 17.2.1843 (Keilhau). BN 651, pp. 4-5.

Fröbel, F. (1843a/1929). Letter to Friederike Schmidt in Gera, 21.3.1843 (Keilhau). In C. Lück (ed.), *Friedrich Fröbel und die Muhme Schmidt. Ein Briefwechsel aus der Mitte des vorigen Jahrhunderts* (pp. 108-12). Leipzig: Quelle & Meyer.

Fröbel, F. (1843b). Letter to Christian Samuel Weiß in Berlin, 20.8.1843 (Blankenburg). BN 687, pp. 14-15, 17-19.

Fröbel, F. (1844). Letter to Johannes Arnold Barop in Keilhau, 25.6.1844 (Frankfurt/M.). KN 56, 23, pp. 1–4.

Fröbel, F. (1844a). Letter to Johannes Arnold Barop in Keilhau, 9.8.1844 (Darmstadt). KN 56, 26, pp. 1–2.

Fröbel, F. (1844b). Letter to Wilhelm Middendorff and Johannes Arnold Barop in Keilhau, 18.11.1844 (Frankfurt/M.). KN 56, 29, pp. 1–6.

Fröbel, F. (1844c). Letter to Johannes Arnold Barop in Keilhau, 19.11.1844 (Frankfurt/M.). KN 56, 30, pp. 1–7.

Fröbel, F. (1844d). Letter to Johannes Arnold Barop in Keilhau, 20.11.1844 (Frankfurt/M.). KN 56, 31, pp. 1–2.

Fröbel, F. (1844e). Letter to Wilhelm Middendorff and Johannes Arnold Barop in Keilhau, 11.12.1844 (Frankfurt/M.). KN 56, 36, pp. 1–2.

Fröbel, F. (1844f). Letter to Johannes Arnold Barop and Wilhelm Middendorff in Keilhau, 19.12.1844 (Frankfurt/M.). KN 56, 39, pp. 1–4.

Fröbel, F. (1846). Letter to H. Windorf in Stadtilm, 8.4.1846 (Keilhau). BlM XV, 3, pp. 113–14.

Fröbel, F. (1847). Letter to Friederike Schmidt in Gera, 14.10.1847 (Keilhau). BlM XIV, 61, pp. 207–10.

Fröbel, F. (1848). Letter to Friederike Schmidt in Gera, 20.3./21.3./22.3.1848 (Keilhau). BlM XIV, 65, pp. 219–21.

Fröbel, F. (1848a/1948). Letter to Karl Hagen in Heidelberg, 17.7.1848 (Keilhau). In E. Hoffmann (ed.), *Friedrich Fröbel und Karl Hagen. Ein Briefwechsel aus den Jahren 1844–1848* (pp. 87–94). Weimar: Verlag Werden und Wirken.

Fröbel, F. (1848b). Letter to Luise Levin in Rendsburg, 21.10./22.10.1848 (Dresden). BlM XXIII, 15, pp. 39–42.

Fröbel, F. (1848c). Letter to Luise Levin in Rendsburg, 11.11./14.11.1848 (Dresden). BlM XXIII, 17, pp. 49–58.

Fröbel, F. (1848d). Letter to Ida Seele in Darmstadt, 14.12.1848 (Dresden). BN 651, pp. 43–4.

Fröbel, F. (1849). Letter to Luise Levin in Rendsburg, 3.1./4.1.1849 (Dresden). BlM XXIII, 27, pp. 95–8.

Fröbel, F. (1849a). Letter to Luise Levin in Rendsburg, 2.2./3.2./5.2./6.2.1849 (Dresden). BlM XXIII, 32, pp. 123–8.

Fröbel, F. (1849b). Letter to Elise Fröbel in Keilhau, 14./15.2.1849 (Dresden). In H. Nohl (1931/2). Friedrich Fröbels Briefe an Elise. *Die Erziehung*, 7, pp. 475–81.

Fröbel, F. (1849c). Letter to Allwine Middendorff in Hamburg, 15.4.1849 (Dresden). BN 530, pp. 1–4.

Fröbel, F. (1849d). Letter to Luise Levin in Bad Liebenstein, 2.11.1849 (Hamburg). BlM XXIV, 3, pp. 7–8.

Fröbel, F. (1849e). Letter to Luise Levin in Bad Liebenstein, 18.11./19.11.1849 (Hamburg). BlM XXIV, 6, pp. 20–3.

Fröbel, F. (1849f). Letter to Dr. Alexander Detmer in Hamburg (Dresden). In I.
Schamberger and K. Stern (eds), *Beiträge zu 180 Jahre Bildungsort Kindergarten* (pp.
15–17). Rudolstadt: Thüringer Landesmuseum Heidecksburg.

Fröbel, F. (1850). Letter to Ida Seele in Darmstadt, 21.1.1850 (Hamburg). BN 651, p. 57.

Fröbel, F. (1850a). Letter to Wilhelm Middendorff in Keilhau, 24.1.1850 (Hamburg).
KN 57, 8, pp. 1–2.

Fröbel, F. (1850b). Letter to Luise Levin in Bad Liebenstein, 7.2.1850 (Hamburg). BlM
XXIV, 30, pp. 77–8.

Fröbel, F. (1850c). Letter to Ida Seele in Darmstadt, 15.2.1850 (Hamburg). BN 651,
pp. 60–1.

Fröbel, F. (1850d). Letter to Luise Levin in Marienthal, 23.5.1850 (Keilhau). BlM XXIV,
61, pp. 154–5.

Fröbel, F. (1850e). Letter to Wilhelm Middendorff in Keilhau, 15.12.1850 (Marienthal).
BlM XX, 1, pp. 20–1.

Fröbel, F. (1850f). Letter to Elise Fröbel in Keilhau, 23.12.1850 (Marienthal). In H. Nohl
(1931/2). Friedrich Fröbels Briefe an Elise. *Die Erziehung*, 7, pp. 482–3.

Fröbel, F. (1851). Letter to Luise Frankenberg in Dresden, 18.1.1851 (Marienthal). BlM
XXI, 2, pp. 1, 25–6.

Fröbel, F. (1851a). Letter to Wilhelm Middendorff in Keilhau, 7.4.1851 (Marienthal).
BN 566, pp. 47–8.

Fröbel, F. (1851b). Letter to Doris Levin in Osterode, 18.5.1851 (Marienthal). BlM XXI,
2, pp. 28–9.

Fröbel, F. (1851c). Letter to King Friedrich Wilhelm IV of Prussia in Berlin, 31.10.1851
(Marienthal). BN 600, pp. 1–2; BlM XXI, 70, pp. 376–7; BlM XXI, 70, pp. 379–81.

Fröbel, F. (1852). Letter to Johannes Arnold Barop in Keilhau, 3.1.1852 (Marienthal).
KN 57, 16, p. 1.

Fröbel, F. (1852a). Letter to Friederike Fröbel in Burgdorf, 16.3.1852 (Marienthal). BN
437, pp. 1–4.

Fröbel, J. (1890). *Ein Lebenslauf*, vol. 1. Stuttgart: Cotta'sche Buchhandlung.

Fröbel, F., Middendorff, W. and Barop, J. A. (1840). Letter to Karoline-Luise Fürstin von
Schwarzburg-Rudolstadt in Rudolstadt, 7.5.1840 (Blankenburg und Keilhau). ThStA
Rudolstadt, Schloßarchiv D Nr. 9, pp. 27–8.

Giel, K. (1979). Friedrich Fröbel (1782–1852). In H. Scheuerl (ed.), *Klassiker der
Pädagogik. Vol. 1: Von Erasmus von Rotterdam bis Herbert Spencer* (pp. 249–73).
München: Beck.

Grell, F. and Sauerbrey, U. (2016). Das 'ABC der Kunst'. Ästhetische Elementarbildung
bei Friedrich Fröbel. In R. Staege (ed.), *Ästhetische Bildung in der frühen Kindheit*
(pp. 14–40). Weinheim: Beltz Juventa.

Gumlich, B. (ed.) (1935). *Brief an die Frauen in Keilhau. Friedrich Fröbel*.
Weimar: Böhlau.

Halfter, F. (1931). *Friedrich Fröbel. Der Werdegang eines Menschenerziehers*.
Halle: Verlag Max Niemeyer.

Hanschmann, A. B. (1874). *Friedrich Fröbel. Die Entwickelung seiner Erziehungsidee in seinem Leben; nach authentischen Quellen.* Eisenach: Bacmeister.

Heerwart, E. (1902). *Fröbel's letztes Lebensjahr. Tod und Beerdigung. Nach den im Fröbel-Museum befindlichen Quellenschriften.* Eisenach: Hofbuchdruckerei, pp. 2–3.

Heerwart, E. (1905). *Wilhelmine Fröbel, Friedrich Fröbels erste Gattin. Mit einem Portrait von Wilhelmine Fröbel und zwei Ansichten von Keilhau.* Eisenach: Kahle.

Heiland, H. (1982). *Friedrich Fröbel in Selbstzeugnissen und Bilddokumenten.* Reinbek: Rowohlt.

Heiland, H. (2000). Friedrich Fröbels Beziehungen zu Quetz. In Friedrich-Fröbel-Museum (ed.) *Anfänge des Kindergartens*, vol. 2 (pp. 53–106). Bad Blankenburg: Friedrich-Fröbel-Museum.

Heiland, H. (2002). *Basiswissen Pädagogik. Vol. 5: Friedrich Wilhelm August Fröbel (1782–1852).* Baltmannsweiler: Schneider-Verlag Hohengehren.

Heiland, H. (2008). *Friedrich Fröbel in seinen Briefen.* Würzburg: Königshausen & Neumann.

Heiland, H. (2012). *Fröbelforschung aktuell. Aufsätze 2001–2010.* Würzburg: Königshausen & Neumann.

Heiland, H. (2017). *Neue Beiträge zur Fröbelforschung.* Würzburg: Königshausen & Neumann.

Heiland, H. and Gebel, M. (Hrsg.). *Friedrich Fröbel: 'Das Streben der Menschen'. Autobiographische, anthropologische und spielpädagogische Texte.* Würzburg: Königshausen & Neumann.

Hoffmann, E. (ed.) (1982). *Friedrich Fröbel. Ausgewählte Schriften. Vol. 1: Kleine Schriften und Briefe von 1809–1851.* Stuttgart: Klett-Cotta.

Hoffmann, E. and Wächter, R. (eds) (1986). *Friedrich Fröbel. Ausgewählte Schriften. Vol. 5. Briefe und Dokumente über Keilhau. Erster Versuch der Sphärischen Erziehung.* Stuttgart: Klett-Cotta.

Höltershinken, D. (2010). *Wilhelm Middendorff–ein vergessener Pädagoge.* Bochum: projekt verlag.

König, H. (1990). *Mein lieber Herr Fröbel! Briefe von Frauen und Jungfrauen an den Kinder- und Menschenfreund.* Berlin: Volk und Wissen.

Krause, K. D. F. ([1828] 1981). *Vorlesungen über das System der Philosophie.* Breitenfurt: Pflegerl.

Krone, D. (2011). *Der Pädagoge F. Fröbel und die Frauen. Beziehungsbedürfnisse aus den Anfangstagen des Kindergartens.* Frankfurt/M.: Peter Lang.

Krone, D. (2016). *Biografische Studie zur Person und zum Werk Friedrich Fröbels.* Frankfurt/M.: Peter Lang.

Kuntze, M. A. ([1930] 1951). *Friedrich Fröbel. Ein Lebensbild nach seinen Schriften und Briefen.* Frankfurt/M.: Diesterweg.

Kuntze, M. A. (1952). *Friedrich Fröbel. Sein Weg und sein Werk*, 2nd edn. Heidelberg: Quelle & Meyer.

Lange, W. (1862). *Friedrich Fröbel's gesammelte pädagogische Schriften. Erste Abteilung: Friedrich Fröbel in seiner Erziehung als Mensch und Pädagoge. Vol. 1: Aus Fröbels Leben und erstem Streben. Autobiographie und kleinere Schriften.* Berlin: Enslin.

Lange, W. and Diesterweg, A. (1855). Wilhelm Middendorff. In *Jahrbuch für Lehrer und Schulfreunde* (pp. 1–79). Berlin: n,p.

Langethal, C. E. (1867). *Keilhau in seinen Anfängen. Erinnerungen des ältesten Zöglings der Anstalt.* Jena: Frommann.

Langethal, C. E. (1910). *Die Geschichte Keilhaus in der Landesgeschichte.* Leipzig: Bund ehemaliger Keilhauer.

Lerner, F. (1953). *Gestalten aus der Geschichte des Frankfurter Patrizier-Geschlechtes von Holzhausen.* Frankfurt/M.: Kramer.

Liebschner, J. (1992). *A Child's Work: Freedom and Guidance in Froebel's Educational Theory and Practice.* Cambridge: Lutterworth Press.

Lyschinska, M. (1922). *Henriette Schrader-Breymann. Ihr Leben aus Briefen und Tagebüchern,* vol. 1. Berlin: de Gruyter.

März, F. (1998). *Personengeschichte der Pädagogik.* Bad Heilbrunn: Klinkhardt.

Münchow, K. (2000). Amalie Krüger – eine der ersten Kindergärtnerinnen. In Friedrich-Fröbel-Museum (ed.) *Anfänge des Kindergartens,* vol. 2 (pp. 107–36). Bad Blankenburg: Friedrich-Fröbel-Museum.

Nipperdey, T. (2014*). Germany from Napoleon to Bismarck.* Translated by Daniel Nolan. Princeton, NJ: Princeton University Press.

Nohl, H. (1831). Friedrich Fröbels Briefe an Elise. *Die Erziehung. Monatsschrift für den Zusammenhang von Kultur und Erziehung in Wissenschaft und Leben,* 7(7), pp, 385–405.

Osann, C. (1956). *Friedrich Fröbel. Lebensbild eines Menschenerziehers.* Düsseldorf: Progress.

Prüfer, J. (1927). *Friedrich Fröbel. Sein Leben und Schaffen.* Leipzig: Teubner.

Rinke, A. J. (1935). *Friedrich Fröbels philosophische Entwicklung unter dem Einfluß der Romantik.* Langensalza: Beyer.

Rush, F. (2015). Romanticism. In M. N. Forster and K. Gjesdal (eds), *The Oxford Handbook of German Philosophy in the Nineteenth Century.* doi: 10.1093/oxfor dhb/9780199696543.013.0013.

Sauerbrey, U. (2020). Kindergärtnerinnen-Briefe als Dokumente historischer kindheitspädagogischer Forschung. *Fallarchiv Kindheitspädagogische Forschung,* 1(3), pp. 3–25. doi: 10.18442/091.

Sauerbrey, U. and Friedrich Fröbel Museum Bad Blankenburg (eds) (2013). *Friedrich Fröbel – Die Entstehung des Kindergartens und der Spielpädagogik im Spiegel von Briefen.* Leipzig: Evangelische Verlagsanstalt.

Sauerbrey, U. and Winkler, M. (2018). *Friedrich Fröbel und seine Spielpädagogik.* Paderborn: Schöningh.

Seele, I. (1886). Meine Erinnerungen an Friedrich Fröbel. *Kindergarten,* 27, pp. 20–181.

Seele, I. (1887). Meine Erinnerungen an Friedrich Fröbel. *Kindergarten*, 28, pp. 4–180.

Seele, I. (1888). Meine Erinnerungen an Friedrich Fröbel. *Kindergarten*, 29, pp. 5–186.

Siemann, W. (1990). *Gesellschaft im Aufbruch. Deutschland 1849–1871*. Frankfurt/M.: Suhrkamp.

Smith, H. W. (2011). Introduction. In H. W. Smith (ed.), *Modern German History* (pp. 1–28). Oxford: Oxford University Press.

Stadler, P. (1993). *Pestalozzi. Geschichtliche Biographie. Vol. 2: Von der Umwälzung zur Restauration: Ruhm und Rückschläge (1798–1827)*. Zürich: Verlag NZZ.

Wasmuth, H. (2011). *Kindertageseinrichtungen als Bildungseinrichtungen: zur Bedeutung von Bildung und Erziehung in der Geschichte der öffentlichen Kleinkindererziehung in Deutschland bis 1945*. Bad Heilbrunn: Klinkhardt.

Wasmuth, H. (2020). *Fröbel's Pedagogy of Kindergarten and Play. Modifications in Germany and the United States*. New York: Routledge.

Index

Index of Persons

We have not included Friedrich Froebel, Wilhelm Middendorff, and Heinrich Langethal as they are mentioned throughout the book frequently